Casario

HTML5 Solutions: Essential Techniques for HTML5 Developers

Marco Casario, Peter Elst, Charles Brown, Nathalie Wormser, and Cyril Hanquez

friendsof

DESIGNER TO DESIGNER™

an Apress® company

HTML5 SOLUTIONS: ESSENTIAL TECHNIQUES FOR HTML5 DEVELOPERS

Credits

President and Publisher:
Paul Manning

Lead Editor:
Ben Renow-Clarke

Technical Reviewer:
Jason Nadon

Editorial Board:
Steve Anglin, Mark Beckner,
Ewan Buckingham, Gary Cornell,
Jonathan Gennick, Jonathan Hassell,
Michelle Lowman, James Markham, Matthew Moodie,
Jeff Olson, Jeffrey Pepper,
Frank Pohlmann, Douglas Pundick,
Ben Renow-Clarke, Dominic Shakeshaft,
Matt Wade, Tom Welsh

Coordinating Editor:
Jennifer L. Blackwell

Copy Editor:
Seth Kline

Compositor:
Mary Sudul

Indexer:
Toma Mulligan

Artist:
April Milne

Cover Artist:
Anna Ishchenko

Cover Designer:
Corné van Dooren

To the memory of my grandmother Maria

—Marco Casario

In loving memory of those who continue to inspire me

—Peter Elst

To S.P.

—Nathalie Wormser

To my wife for her love and support and my lovely children for their patience

—Cyril Hanquez

Contents at a Glance

About the Authors ix

About the Technical Reviewer xi

About the Cover Image Artist xii

Acknowledgments xiii

Introduction xiv

Chapter 1: HTML5 Page Structures 1

Chapter 2: HTML5 Markup 19

Chapter 3: HTML5 Structural and Semantic Elements 31

Chapter 4: HTML5 Forms 63

Chapter 5: HTML5 Media Elements: Audio and Video 97

Chapter 6: HTML5 Drawing APIs 137

Chapter 7: HTML5 Canvas 175

Chapter 8: HTML5 Communication APIs 215

Chapter 9: HTML5 WebSocket 241

Chapter 10: HTML5 Geolocation API 263

Chapter 11: HTML5 Local Storage 281

Chapter 12: HTML5 Accessibility 305

Index 331

Contents

About the Author ix

About the Technical Reviewer..xi

About the Cover Image Artist xii

Acknowledgments xiii

Introduction xiv

Chapter 1: HTML5 Page Structures 1

Solution 1-1: Creating a DOCTYPE in HTML5 1

Solution 1-2: Creating a character encoding declaration in HTML5 3

Solution 1-3: Dividing a document into sections 3

Solution 1-4: Making parts of the document distributable............................4

Solution 1-5: Creating an aside 5

Solution 1-6: Creating a header..7

Solution 1-7: Grouping <h1> to <h6> elements..8

Solution 1-8: Creating a footer..9

Solution 1-9: Creating navigation in an HTML5 document 11

Solution 1-10: Inserting figures 13

Solution 1-11: Browser compatibility...15

Summary 18

Chapter 2: HTML5 Markup 19

Solution 2-1: Using the <hr> tag in HTML5 19

Solution 2-2: Using the <iFrame> tag 21

Solution 2-3: Embedding media into a page...23

Solution 2-4: Using the <area> tag 25

Summary 29

Chapter 3: HTML5 Structural and Semantic Elements..............................31

Understanding microdata..31

Solution 3-1: Using the itemprop and itemscope attributes 34

Solution 3-2: Creating a custom vocabulary 40

Solution 3-3: Understanding link types and relations...................................45

Solution 3-4: The header and hgroup elements 48

Solution 3-5: Connecting images with their captions 52

Solution 3-6: Adding tangent content.. 56

Summary 61

Chapter 4: HTML5 Forms **63**

Understanding the new input types 64

Solution 4-1: Using the e-mail input type 65

Solution 4-2: Using the URL input type.. 69

Solution 4-3: Using a spinner control for numbers.. 71

Solution 4-4: Adding a slider to your form with the range input type 75

Solution 4-5: Sending multiple files... 79

Solution 4-6: Creating a suggest-like autocomplete with the data list
                    component 81

Solution 4-7: Validating form controls 84

Solution 4-8: Creating custom input types using regular expressions 88

Solution 4-9: Setting placeholder text in an input field.. 91

Solution 4-10: Creating date and time controls.. 92

Summary 96

Chapter 5: HTML5 Media Elements: Audio and Video **97**

Solution 5-1: Embedding a video in a web page 99

Solution 5-2: Detecting video support across browsers... 102

Solution 5-3: Creating a custom video controller 106

Solution 5-4: Preloading a video... 115

Solution 5-5: Creating a custom seek bar for a video... 117

Solution 5-6: Using multiple source video elements 125

Solution 5-7: Opening a video in full screen 127

Solution 5-8: Applying a mask to a video.. 131

Solution 5-9: Using the audio element.. 134

Summary 136

Chapter 6: HTML5 Drawing APIs... **137**

Solution 6-1: How to draw with HTML5 using the canvas element's
                    drawing API 138

Solution 6-2: Using paths and coordinates 141

Solution 6-3: Drawing shapes: rectangles and circles 150
Solution 6-4: Filling shapes with solid colors 154
Solution 6-5: Using gradients to fill shapes..158
Solution 6-6: Drawing texts in a canvas...163
Solution 6-7: Working with relative font sizes to draw text on a canvas 167
Solution 6-8: Saving a shape as a PNG file..169
Summary 174

Chapter 7: HTML5 Canvas **175**

Solution 7-1: Understanding the canvas APIs 176
Solution 7-2: Detecting the canvas and canvas text support..................................184
Solution 7-3: Understanding the standard screen-based coordinate system
                    and canvas transformations...190
Solution 7-4: Pixel manipulations...195
Solution 7-5: Applying shadows and blurring..201
Solution 7-6: Animating canvas 207
Summary 214

Chapter 8: HTML5 Communication APIs..**215**

Understanding the postMessage API 216
Securing the postMessage communication 217
Solution 8-1: Checking for postMessage API browser support 218
Cross-documents messaging and CORS 220
Solution 8-2: Sending messages between windows and iframes.............................221
Solution 8-3: Using Server-Event technologies to write real-time web
                    applications..226
Solution 8-4: Running code in different browsing contexts using message
                    channels 231
Solution 8-5: Uploading files using the XMLHttpRequest Level 2 232
Solution 8-6: Checking for XMLHttpRequest level 2 cross-origin browser support 237
Summary 240

Chapter 9: HTML5 WebSocket..**241**

Solution 9-1: Checking for WebSocket browser support 241
Solution 9-2: Establishing a WebSocket connection 244
Solution 9-3: Handling WebSocket events 247

Solution 9-4: Using a WebSocket server with the WebSocket API 250
Summary 261

Chapter 10: HTML5 Geolocation API 263

Understanding the Geolocation API 264
Solution 10-1: Using the navigator object 264
Solution 10-2: Getting the current position 266
Solution 10-3: Using the position object 270
Solution 10-4: Handling position errors..273
Solution 10-5: Tracking the user's position..275
Solution 10-6: Using the geo.js open source library 278
Summary 280

Chapter 11: HTML5 Local Storage 281

Solution 11-1: Understanding Occasionally-Connected Applications.................282
Solution 11-2: Checking for HTML5 storage support...284
Solution 11-3: Declaring a manifest for your page..291
Solution 11-4: Using the ApplicationCache object..294
Solution 11-5: The ApplicationCache events..296
Solution 11-6: Deleting the local cache 299
Summary 303

Chapter 12: HTML5 Accessibility 305

The four principles of accessibility 305
The purpose of the WCAG 306
Solution 12-1: Creating skip links with the nav element 308
Solution 12-2: Creating accessible tabular data 312
Solution 12-3: Creating accessible forms 316
Solution 12-4: Captioning and annotations using video elements 319
Solution 12-5: Using the ARIA project 323
Summary 330

Index 331

About the Authors

Marco Casario has been passionate about informatics since he was little more than a child and used to program games in BASIC for the Commodore 64 before dedicating himself, while still very young, to innovative projects for the Web using HTML, JavaScript, Flash, and Director.

In 2001, he began to collaborate with Macromedia. Since that year, he has produced and headed a long series of presentations, conferences, and articles, which you can find listed in detail in his blog (casario.blogs.com).

In 2005, Marco has founded Comtaste (www.comtaste.com), a company dedicated to exploring new frontiers in Rich Internet and Mobile Applications and the convergence between the Web and the world of mobile devices. Now his focus is on User Experience (UX) aspects in order to provide users with a valuable experience. He also is a proponent of cloud computing with Google Apps APIs and the Google App Engine.

Marco is founder of the biggest worldwide Flash Lite UG and of www.augitaly.com, a reference point for the Italian community of Adobe users in which he serves in the role of Channel Manager for the section dedicated to Flex (www.augitaly.com/flexgala.). Recently, he became Community Manager for the Google Technology User Group (www.gtug.it) in Milan.

Marco is an Adobe Certified Instructor for Flex 4, LCDS 3, and AIR (ACI), and an Adobe Certified Expert for the Livecycle Platform, Flash, and Dreamweaver. He is also a SCRUM Master.

Marco is author of several books including HTML5 Solutions (Apress); Flex 4 Cookbook (O'Reilly); Professional Flash Catalyst (Wrox); AIR Cookbook (O'Reilly); and Flex 4 Solutions (FriendsOfED), Advanced AIR Applications (FriendsOfED), The Essential Guide to AIR with Flash CS4 (FriendsOfED), and Flex Solutions: Essential Techniques for Flex 3 developers (FriendsOfED).

Some of his speaking engagements include international conferences such as FlashOnTheBeach, AJAXWorld Conference, O'Reilly Web 2.0 Summit, FITC, Adobe MAX, FATC New York, FlexCamp, 360Flex, TAC Singapore, MultiMania Belgium, Adobe CEM, and many others.

Peter Elst is a Belgian freelance IT consultant and Founding Partner of Project Cocoon based in Pondicherry, South India. As a respected member of the online community, Peter has spoken at various international industry events and has had his work published in leading journals.

Charles Brown is one of the most noted authors, consultants, and trainers in the IT industry today. His books on Flex have received strong critical acclaim and are used worldwide as a teaching tool.

In addition to his work in the IT industry, Charles is also a noted concert pianist, organist, and guitarist appearing in major concert centers worldwide. He began his musical studies at age 4, and he went on to study with famed pianist Vladimir Horowitz. At age 14, he made his debut with Leonard Bernstein and went on to study at the famed Juilliard School. Eventually he went to Paris to study with the 20th century legend, Igor Stravinsky. While working with Stravinsky, Charles developed a close friendship with one of the most powerful artistic forces of the 20th century: Pablo Picasso. What he learned about creativity from Picasso he uses today in his writings and training work.

Charles is a certified Adobe trainer who is in heavy demand worldwide. He frequently speaks at major conferences such as MAX and NAB. His website can be found at www.charlesebrown.net. You can find Charles on Facebook.

Nathalie Wormser is a freelance web developer who is passionate about emerging multimedia technologies and games. She is the co-founder of Project Cocoon Multimedia, a development and web design company based in Pondicherry, South India.

Cyril Hanquez is a consultant focusing on ColdFusion, Rich Internet and Mobile Applications. He has worked in the IT industry for about 15 years, mainly on European Union institutions projects in Belgium. He is the co-manager of the local ColdFusion User Group where he speaks frequently. Happily married and a proud father of two, Cyril is blogging at cyrilhanquez.com/blog/. When he is not working, you can find Cyril playing games or wandering around some popular social networks as "Fitzchev."."....

About the Technical Reviewer

Jason Nadon has over ten years' experience working with complex web applications. From content delivery, architecting, optimizing and marketing down to coding in a mix of PHP, Java, ASP.NET, and CFML. Jason holds several industry certifications and is currently employed at a global information company as an IT Infrastructure Manager. In his spare time, Jason enjoys reading and keeping up with technology trends, photography, and songwriting. You can check him out at: www.thinknadon.com

About the Cover Image Artist

Corné van Dooren designed the front cover image for this book. After taking a brief hiatus from friends of ED to create a new design for the Foundation series, Corné worked at combining technological and organic forms with the results now appearing on this and other book covers.

Corné spent his childhood drawing on everything at hand, and then he began exploring the infinite world of multimedia—His journey of discovery hasn't stopped since! His mantra has always been, "The only limit to multimedia is the imagination," a saying that keeps him constantly moving forward.

Corné works for many international clients, writes features for multimedia magazines, reviews and tests software, authors multimedia studies, and works on many other friends of ED books. You can see more of his work and contact him through his website at: www.cornevandooren.com.

Acknowledgments

It happens all the time. During the writing of a book, I often have the feeling that I will never reach the end. It is only with the help and support of many people who tirelessly work behind the scenes that the book is ready on time and in good form.

Here I want to thank them all:

I would like to thank for their hard work of my coauthors: Charles, Peter, Nathalie, and Cyril. I want to thank Ben Renow-Clarke, Jennifer Blackwell, Matthew Moodie Dominic Shakeshaft, and all the Friends of ED team for giving me the opportunity and the support to write and improve this book. Their guidance and input throughout the development of this book was essential. It's awesome and incredible how their work in coordinating the editing effort with authors across different continents and time zones made collaboration so easy.

Also, special thanks are due to my technical editor, Jason Nadon, and my developmental editor, Gary Schwartz, who contributed to making the content and the examples easy to understand and follow.

And, of course, thank you to my Mom for having always pushed me to improve myself and to see beyond the surface of things.

To my brother Alessio for understanding why sometimes I did not have enough time for him.

To Katia for her patience with all the weekend and night hours spent working on this book in the past several months.

This book is significantly better because of these great people.

Introduction

The development of Hypertext Markup Language stopped in 1999 with its final version, n.4, made by the World Wide Web Consortium (W3C). Technology, however, has not stood still in the meantime: the W3C also worked on interesting projects such as the generic Standard Generalized Markup Language (SGML) to XML, as well as on new markup languages such as Scalable Vector Graphics (SVG), XForms, and MathML.

Web browser vendors, on the other hand, preferred to concentrate on new functions for their programs, whereas web developers started to learn CSS and the JavaScript language to build their applications on frameworks that use Asynchronous JavaScript + XML (AJAX).

However, things have changed, and recently HTML has been brought back to life thanks to the work of the companies such as Apple, Google, Opera Software, and the Mozilla Foundation, who collaborated (under the name of WhatWG, the Web Hypertext Application Technology Working Group) on the development of an updated and enhanced version of the old HTML.

Following this major interest, the W3C began to work on a new version of HTML, called HTML5, taking on the official name of Web Applications 1.0 and introducing new structural elements to HTML that have not been seen before.

The new elements introduced by HTML5 tend to bridge the gap between structure, defined by the markup; rendering characteristics, defined by styling directives; and the content of a web page, defined by the text itself. Furthermore, HTML5 introduced a native open standard to deliver multimedia content such as audio and video, collaboration APIs, local storage, geolocation APIs, and much more.

In this practically-oriented book, we wanted to provide a series of solutions to common problems faced by people approaching the new language. You will therefore find a lot of ready-to-use code that you can build on in your web applications.

Who is this book for?

No matters if you're a designer or a developer, this book is aimed at anybody who wants to start using HTML5 right now.

HTML5 Solutions is, in fact, intended for readers who want to take their knowledge further with quick-fire solutions to common problems and best practice techniques to improve their HTML5 skills. The book is full of solutions with real world examples and code to support you as you enter the world of HTML5 development.

Conventions used in this book

This book uses several of conventions that are worth noting. The following terms are used throughout this book:

- *HTML* refers to both the HTML and XHTML languages.

- Unless otherwise stated, *CSS* relates to the CSS 2.1 specification.

- *Modern browsers* are considered to be the latest versions of Firefox, Safari, Chrome, and Opera, along with IE 7 and above.

It is assumed that all the HTML examples in this book are nested within the <body> of a valid document, while the CSS is contained in an external style sheet. Occasionally, HTML and CSS have been placed in the same code example for brevity.

Sometimes code won't fit on a single line in a book. Where this happens, I've used an arrow to break the line.

With these formalities out of the way, let's get started.

What you need

To follow and create the examples shown in this book you'll need a simple text editor. TextMate, UltraEdit, and Notepad++ are just some examples of powerful text editors with code support.

My advice is to use one of the following tools that will allow you to improve the productivity of your coding activities:

Google Web Toolkit Incubator project supports some features of HTML5 through classes like GWTCanvas. It's completely free and it can be downloaded from this uhttp://code.google.com/p/google-web-toolkit-incubator/

The HTML5 pack extension for Dreamweaver CS 5. It enhances Dreamweaver CS5 adding complete support to HTML5. You can download a free trial from the Adobe website http://www.adobe.com/support/dreamweaver/

Questions and Contacts

Please direct any technical questions or comments about the book to m.casario@comtaste.com.

For more information about other HTML5 and CSS books, see our website: www.friendsofed.com.

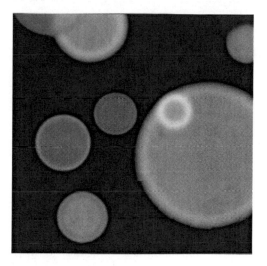

Chapter 1

HTML5 Page Structures

In 2004, a group of developers from Apple, Opera, and Mozilla were unhappy with the direction that HTML and XHTML were heading. In response, they formed a group called the Web Hypertext Application Technology Working Group (WHATWG). They published their first proposals in 2005 under the name Web Applications 1.0. In 2006, the World Wide Web Consortium (W3C) decided to support WHATWG officially rather than to continue developing XHTML. In 2007, the new specification was republished by the W3C under the name HTML5.

While it was thought that the final specifications would not be published until 2022, that timeline is now being reconsidered. In 2009–2010, there was an explosion of interest in HTML5 and, as a result, an increasing number of browsers and devices were introduced that support it.

This first chapter will introduce many of the new structures within the HTML5 specification. In addition, it will examine those devices that will support the new HTML5 structures.

Solution 1-1: Creating a DOCTYPE in HTML5

Because there are several versions of HTML, a browser requires a DOCTYPE type to tell it what version is in use and how to render it properly.

In this solution, you will learn to form a DOCTYPE for HTML5 properly.

What's involved

In a traditional HTML or XHTML document, the DOCTYPE tag might look as follows:

```
<!DOCTYPE html PUBLIC "-//W3C//DTD XHTML 1.0 Transitional//EN"
"http://www.w3.org/TR/xhtml1/DTD/xhtml1-transitional.dtd">
```

There are many variations of the DOCTYPE.

HTML5 simplifies the DOCTYPE to:

```
<!DOCTYPE html>
```

How to build it

1. Open the HTML or text editor of your choice. For the examples shown in this chapter, we use Dreamweaver CS5. Do not use a word processor because that could embed extra characters not recognized by HTML.

2. If necessary, start a new HTML document and give it the name and location of your choice.

If you use an HTML editor like Dreamweaver, you might get code that looks as follows:

```
<!DOCTYPE html PUBLIC "-//W3C//DTD XHTML 1.0 Transitional//EN"↵
 "http://www.w3.org/TR/xhtml1/DTD/xhtml1-transitional.dtd">
<html xmlns="http://www.w3.org/1999/xhtml">
    <head>
        <meta http-equiv="Content-Type" content="text/html; charset=UTF-8" />
        <title>Untitled Document</title>
    </head>
     <body>
     </body>
</html>
```

If your code looks a little different from the above, do not worry about that for now.

3. Change the DOCTYPE tag as follows:

```
<!DOCTYPE html>
```

Expert tips

Do not leave any spaces before the DOCTYPE tag. A space could cause errors in browser rendering of the HTML5 code.

Solution 1-2: Creating a character encoding declaration in HTML5

Different languages use different character sets, or charsets. This tag declares which character set is to be used. The most common charset used by most languages is UTF-8.

In this solution, you will learn how to format the charset in HTML5 properly.

What's involved

In most HTML documents, you see the following tag at the beginning:

```
<meta http-equiv="Content-Type" content="text/html; charset=UTF-8" />
```

HTML5 has now simplified this tag to:

```
<meta charset="UTF-8" />
```

How to build it

Under the `<IDOCTYPE html>` tag shown in Solution 1-1, type the following:

```
<meta charset = "UTF-8" />
```

Expert tips

While UTF-8 will work in most instances, a lot of developers have found that using ISO-8859-1 as the charset gives even more flexibility. Another charset, UTF-16, sometimes results in wrong characters and, in some cases, applications operating improperly.

Solution 1-3: Dividing a document into sections

In HTML, the only real way to subdivide a document into distinct sections is to use the `<div>` tag. HTML5 presents some new options.

In this solution, you will learn how to use the new HTML5 tags to create distinct document sections. In the subsequent solutions, we will discuss other structural division elements.

What's involved

The HTML `<div>` tag successfully divides the document into sections. But the word `<div>` has very little meaning in identifying the parts of a document. HTML5 provides several new structural elements that will divide the document into meaningful sections.

The first of these elements is the `<section></section>` tag. This element represents any logical division of the document. This could mean product descriptions, chapters, discussions, and so forth. While its functionality is similar to the <div> tag, it provides a more descriptive and content-sensitive way of dividing the document.

When creating a section in HTML5, as when you used the <div> tag in HTML, you can use either the id or class attributes. Since both of these attributes can be applied to any HTML5 element, they are referred to as global attributes. Each id must be unique, as in HTML, and class can be used multiple times to call predefined scripting or formatting.

All HTML5 elements have three types of attributes: global, which is common to all elements; element-specific, which applies only to this element, and event handler content attributes, which will be triggered depending on content within the document. Many of these will be discussed as you progress throughout this book.

How to build it

Let's say you were creating a document about making cheesecakes. The following represents a typical use for the <section></section> elements.

```
<section id="mixing">
    <h2>The proper way to mix ingredients</h2>
    <p>When using a stand-mixer, it is important that you do not over-mix the
ingredients<.../p>
</section>
<section id="baking">
    <h2>Proper baking techniques</h2>
    <p> It is important that you bake your cheesecake using a lot of moisture in the
oven...</p>
</section>
```

Expert tips

The purpose of the <section></section> element and the subsequent structural elements shown in this chapter is not to replace the HTML <div> tag. If you are dividing your document into logical document sections, use the <section></section> element or one of the structural elements. However, if you are dividing the document only for purposes of formatting, then the <div> tag is appropriate to use.

Solution 1-4: Making parts of the document distributable

Increasingly, it is important to make all or part of the contents of a page distributable. For instance, forum discussion, blogs, reader comments, and so on could all be candidates for distribution or syndication.

In this solution, we will discuss the new HTML5 element, <article></article>, which makes accomplishing this much easier than with traditional HTML.

What's involved

The purpose of this structural tag is not to serve as another way to divide your document into sections. Rather, it is used to identify the portions of the document that you want to be independent and distributable from the rest of the document.

Since the `<article></article>` element is independent, it can have its own sections and subdivisions.

You can make any element distributable by surrounding it with the `<article></article>` element.

How to build it

Using the example shown in Solution 1-3, you can make the cheesecake instructions distributable as follows.

```
<article>
    <section id="mixing">
        <h2>The proper way to mix ingredients</h2>
        <p>When using a stand-mixer, it is important that you do not over mix the
ingredients…</p>
    </section>
    <section id="baking">
        <h2>Proper baking techniques</h2>
        <p> It is important that you bake your cheesecake using a lot of moisture in the
oven…</p>
    </section>
</article>
```

Expert tips

Treat the `<article></article>` element as an independent document and not as part of a larger document. That way, when it is distributed, it will be fully readable and understandable.

Solution 1-5: Creating an aside

If want to create a side discussion in traditional HTML, you use `<div>` tags and correct use of Cascading Style Sheets (CSS) for proper positioning. HTML5 makes the process easier by providing a new structural element, `<aside></aside>`. Like the `<section>` element, it provides a more descriptive way of sectioning the document.

In this solution, you will learn how to use the `<aside></aside>` element.

What's involved

Often, you might want to create what is commonly called a sidebar discussion. Figure 1-1 shows an example of accomplishing this with the `<aside></aside>` tag.

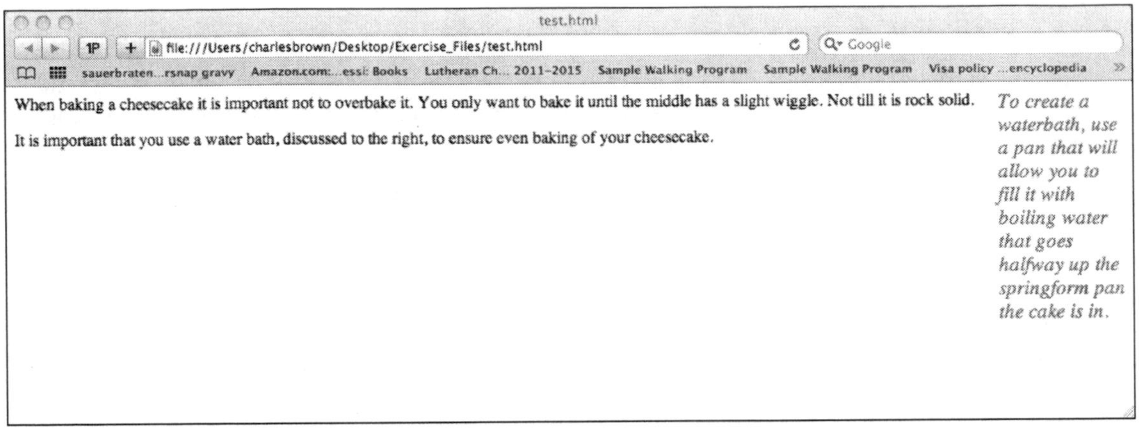

Figure 1-1. Using the `<aside></aside>` element

Of course, it could have been accomplished with the use of the `<div>` element. The use of the `<aside></aside>` element, however, provides for a much more meaningful structural description.

How to build it

the example shown in the previous section was built was accomplished with the following code:

```
<aside style="font-size:larger;font-style:italic;color:blue;float:right;width:120px;">
    To create a water bath, use a pan that will allow you to fill it with boiling water that
goes halfway up the springform pan in which the cake is placed.
</aside>
<p>
    When baking a cheesecake, it is important not to over bake it. You only want to bake it
until the middle has a slight wiggle, not until it is rock solid.
</p>
<p>
    It is important that you use a water bath, discussed at the right, to ensure even baking
of your cheesecake.
</p>
```

Expert tips

Placement of the `<aside></aside>` element is critical. In the above example, it is placed as part of the main document. However, if you want the sidebar to be specific to a certain section, then you must place it within that section. This is especially important if you are using the `<article></article>` element so that the sidebar publishes with the rest of the related material.

Solution 1-6: Creating a header

Use the structural `<header></header>` element to create a document or section header. It can also contain `<h1>` to `<h6>`; although, as you will see later in this chapter, they are better served by the `<hgroup></hgroup>` element. You can also use it to help place logos and a section's table of contents.

In this solution, you will see an example of using the `<header></header>` element.

What's involved

The `<header></header>` element is an easy way to create introductions to both the document and to sections. Figure 1-2 shows the `<header></header>` element added to our example.

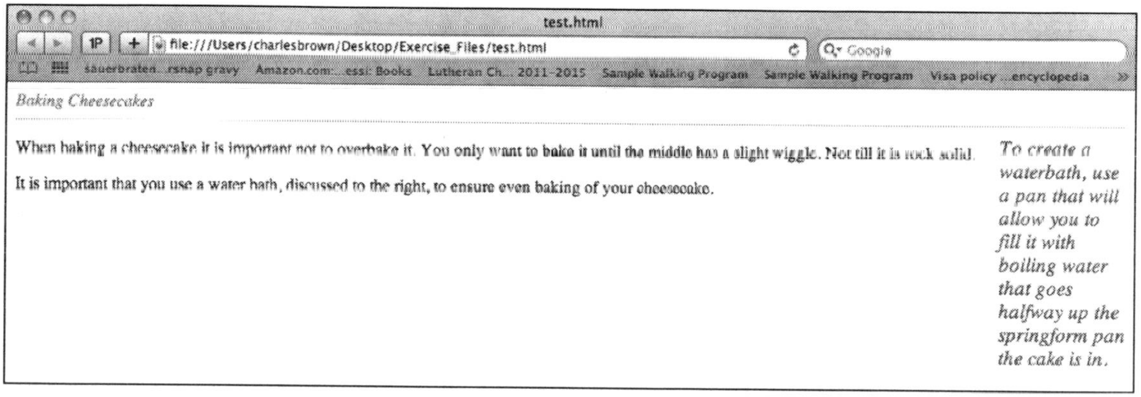

Figure 1-2. Using the `<header></header>` element

Notice that in this example, the `<hr>` element is used to draw the horizontal line. This is not a requirement of any kind.

How to build it

the following code is used to create the document shown in Figure 1-2.

```html
<header>
    <span style="color:red;font-style:italic;">
        Baking Cheesecakes</span>
    <hr>
</header>
<aside style="font-size:larger;font-style:italic;color:blue;float:right;width:120px;">
    To create a water bath, use a pan that will allow you to fill it with boiling water that
goes halfway up the spring form pan in which the cake is placed.
</aside>
<p>
    When baking a cheesecake, it is important not to over bake it. You only want to bake it
until the middle has a slight wiggle, not until it is rock solid.
</p>
```

```
<p>
     It is important that you use a water bath, discussed at the right, to ensure even baking
of your cheesecake.
</p>
```

You can use the <header></header> structural element as an introduction to most of the other structural elements in the document.

Expert tips

You cannot use the <header></header> element within the <footer>, <address>, or other <header> elements. If you do, the result will be improper rendering.

Solution 1-7: Grouping <h1> to <h6> elements

In some cases, you might want to group the <h1> to <h6> elements together. As an example, you may want to create a section title that uses an <h1> element. Then, right under that, place a subtitle that uses the <h2> element. In HTML5, you can group the <h1> and <h2> elements in a new structural element called <hgroup>.

In this solution, you will see an example of using the <hgroup></hgroup> element.

What's involved

The structural <hgroup></hgroup> gives you the ability to show that you are grouping headings (<h1> to <h6>) together for needs such as alternative titles and subheadings.

Adding to the example from Solution 1-6, an <hgroup> would appear as shown in Figure 1-3.

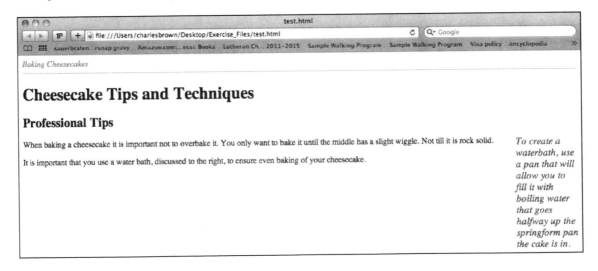

Figure 1-3. Using the <hgroup> </hgroup> element

In this case, `<h1>` and `<h2>` headings were used within the `<hgroup>`.

How to build it

In the example shown in Figure 1-3, the following code is used.:

```
<header>
      <span style="color:red;font-style:italic;">
          Baking Cheesecakes
      </span>
      <hr>
</header>
<hgroup draggable="true">
      <h1>Cheesecake Tips and Techniques</h1>
      <h2>Professional Tips</h2>
</hgroup>
<aside style="font-size:larger;font-style:italic;color:blue;float:right;width:120px;">
      To create a water bath, use a pan that will allow you to fill it with boiling water that
goes halfway up the spring form pan in which the cake is placed.
</aside>
<p>
      When baking a cheesecake, it is important not to over bake it. You only want to bake it
until the middle has a slight wiggle, not until it is rock solid.
</p>
<p>It is important that you use a water bath, discussed at the right, to ensure even baking of
your cheesecake.</p>
```

Notice that we placed the `<hgroup>` element below the `<header></header>` element. While this is not required, it is a good practice. You can use the `<hgroup>` element in any section of the HTML5 document.

Expert tips

In a well-built HTML5 document, the `<hgroup></hgroup>` element is a great way to tie together various headings and subheadings. This is especially true if you are using the `<article></article>` element. You are assured then that any headings and their connected subheadings will move as a group.

Solution 1-8: Creating a footer

As the name suggests, the `<footer></footer>` element will create a footer for the HTML5 document—a structural division of that document. The footer can contain copyright information, author information, citations, privacy policy, and so on.

In this solution, you will examine how the `<footer></footer>` element works.

What's involved

You can use the structural `<footer></footer>` element to create footers for an HTML5 document or any divisions within that document.

Building on Solution 1-3, the results of the `<footer>` element are shown in Figure 1-4.

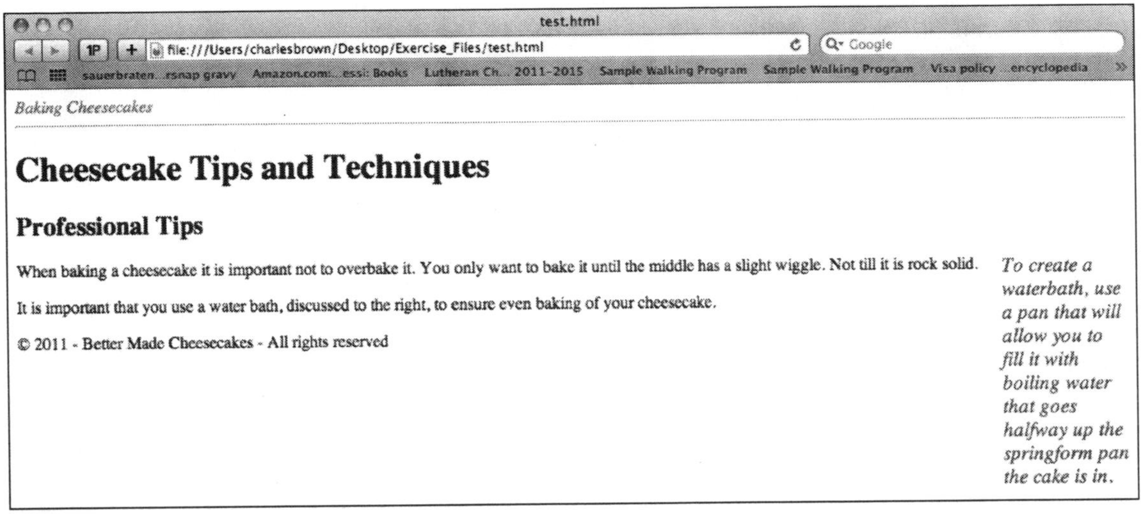

Figure 1-4. Using the `<footer></footer>` element

The copyright symbol, "&copy," and any text regarding rights and ownership are placed within the footer.

How to build it

In Figure 1-4, the following code is used:

```
<header>
      <span style="color:red;font-style:italic;">
          Baking Cheesecakes
      </span>
      <hr>
</header>
<hgroup draggable="true">
      <h1>Cheesecake Tips and Techniques</h1>
      <h2>Professional Tips</h2>
</hgroup>
<aside style="font-size:larger;font-style:italic;color:blue;float:right;width:120px;">
      To create a water bath, use a pan that will allow you to fill it with boiling water that
goes halfway up the spring form pan in which the cake is placed.
</aside>
<p>
      When baking a cheesecake, it is important not to over bake it. You only want to bake it
until the middle has a slight wiggle, not until it is rock solid.
</p>
<p>It is important that you use a water bath, discussed at the right, to ensure even baking of
your cheesecake.</p>
<footer> &copy; 2011 - Better Made Cheesecakes - All rights reserved </footer>
```

The `<footer></footer>` element can be used either for the whole HTML5 document, as it is here, or for a structural division within the document.

Expert tips

The `<footer>` element cannot be used within the `<header>` element or within another `<footer>` element. This would result in improper rendering.

Solution 1-9: Creating navigation in an HTML5 document

Most websites have navigational links. The links, whether they are hyperlinks or buttons of some sort, are usually separated from the rest of the document through the use of a `<div>` element. Again, other than it being a division, it does not identify the section as being specifically used for navigation. In HTML5, you can now identify the section for navigational aids in the markup.

In this section, you will learn about the new structural HTML5 element: `<nav></nav>`.

What's involved

Structural element `<nav></nav>` can be used to create a container to hold navigational elements within the entire HTML5 document or in any divisions within the document.

The result is shown in Figure 1-5.

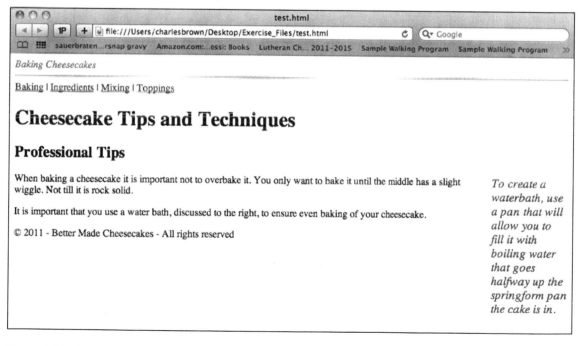

Figure 1-5. Using the `<nav></nav>` element

This gives the navigation section its own markup, which makes it easier to identify.

How to build it

The following code is used for Figure 1-5. The navigational links shown are for illustrative purposes only and are non-functional.

```
<header>
      <span style="color:red;font-style:italic;">
          Baking Cheesecakes
      </span>
      <hr>
</header>
<nav>
      <a href="/Baking/" target="_blank">Baking</a> |
      <a href="/ingredients/" target="_blank">Ingredients</a> |
      <a href="/mixing/" target="_blank">Mixing</a> |
      <a href="/toppings/" target="_blank">Toppings</a>
</nav>
<hgroup draggable="true">
      <h1>Cheesecake Tips and Techniques</h1>
      <h2>Professional Tips</h2>
</hgroup>
<aside style="font-size:larger;font-style:italic;color:blue;float:right;width:120px;">
      To create a water bath, use a pan that will allow you to fill it with boiling water that
goes halfway up the spring form pan in which the cake is placed.
</aside>
<p>
      When baking a cheesecake, it is important not to over bake it. You only want to bake it
until the middle has a slight wiggle, not until it is rock solid.
</p>
<p>It is important that you use a water bath, discussed at the right, to ensure even baking of
your cheesecake.</p>
<footer> &copy; 2011 - Better Made Cheesecakes - All rights reserved </footer>
```

As you can see, the navigational elements of your document now have their own easily identifiable markup. They can be placed either for the whole HTML5 document, as shown here, or for any subdivision of the document.

Expert tips

You are not limited to hyperlinks as shown in Figure 1-5. Within the <nav></nav> container element, you can put any navigational aids that you wish.

A second tip is to not use a <nav></nav> container within the <footer> element. While not strictly forbidden, it could result in improper rendering.

Solution 1-10: Inserting figures

It is fairly common to insert photos, illustrations, diagrams, and so on into a web page. Up to now, a developer could just insert an `<img>` element wherever it was needed. Now you can use markup to designate where the figures should be placed using the new `<figure></figure>` element in HTML5.

In this solution, you will see an example of using the `<figure></figure>` element.

What's involved

The structural element `<figure></figure>` can be used to create a container to hold illustrative elements within the HTML5 document or in any divisions within the document.

The result is shown in Figure 1-6.

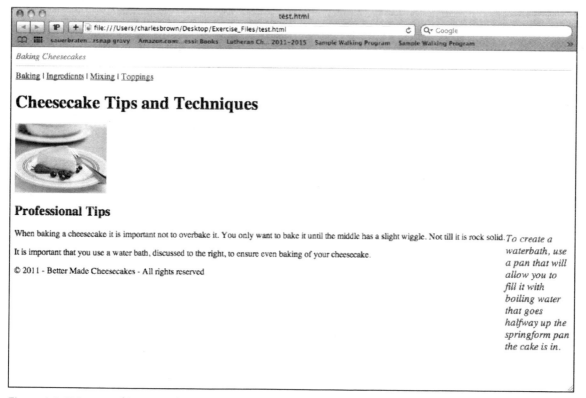

Figure 1-6. Using the `<figure></figure>` element

The illustrative elements of your document now have their own easily identifiable markup. It can be used in any subdivision of the document.

How to build it

The following code is used for Figure 1-6. The navigational links shown are for illustrative purposes only and are non-functional.

```
<header>
     <span style="color:red;font-style:italic;">
          Baking Cheesecakes
     </span>
     <hr>
</header>
<nav>
     <a href="/Baking/" target="_blank">Baking</a> |
     <a href="/ingredients/" target="_blank">Ingredients</a> |
     <a href="/mixing/" target="_blank">Mixing</a> |
     <a href="/toppings/" target="_blank">Toppings</a>
</nav>
<hgroup draggable="true">
     <h1>Cheesecake Tips and Techniques</h1>
     <figure>
          <img src="cheescake.jpg" width="170" height="128" />
     </figure>
     <h2>Professional Tips</h2>
</hgroup>
<aside style="font-size:larger;font-style:italic;color:blue;float:right;width:120px;">
     To create a water bath, use a pan that will allow you to fill it with boiling water that
goes halfway up the spring form pan in which the cake is placed.
</aside>
<p>
     When baking a cheesecake, it is important not to over bake it. You only want to bake it
until the middle has a slight wiggle, not until it is rock solid.
</p>
<p>It is important that you use a water bath, discussed at the right, to ensure even baking of
your cheesecake.</p>
<footer> &copy; 2011 - Better Made Cheesecakes - All rights reserved </footer>
```

It is easy to identify where the photo is located because it now has its own container markup using the `<figure></figure>` element.

Expert tips

Along with the new `<figure>` element comes another new HTML5 element called `<figcaption>` `</figcaption>`. You place this within the `<figure>` element as follows:

```
<figure>
     <img src="cheescake.jpg" width="170" height="128" />
     <figcaption>One of our many cheesecakes</figcaption>
</figure>
```

If you place the `<figcaption>` element below the picture, as shown in the example above, it will appear to the right. If you place it above, it will appear to the left.

Solution 1-11: Browser compatibility

The figures shown in this chapter were captured from Safari version 5.0.3 and Mozilla Firefox version 3.6.13. While it works with all popular browsers, HTML5 compatibility is neither consistent nor universal.

In this solution, we discuss how to test for browser compatibility and, if not compatible, how to correct the incompatibilities.

What's involved

While the current versions of most popular browsers handle the latest HTML5 specifications well, this is not the case for older browsers. Of particular concern are versions of Internet Explorer before version 9.

How to build it

A favorite website is: www.findmebyip.com.

As shown in Figure 1-7, this site will test your browser for HTML5 compatibility.

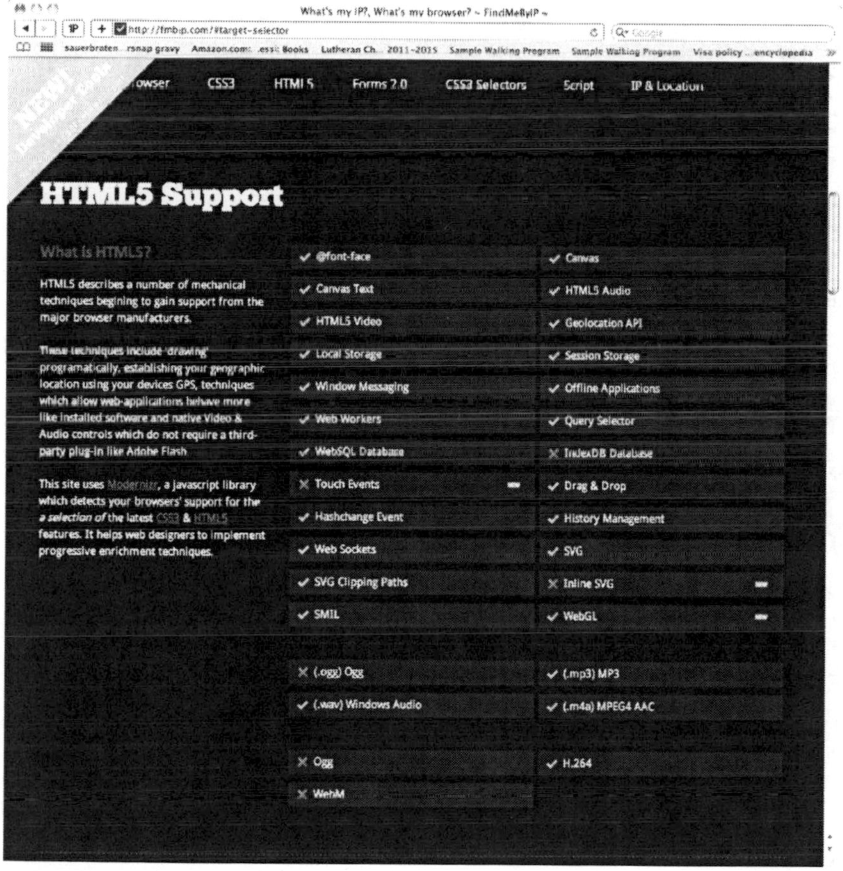

Figure 1-7. An example of www.findmebyip.com

As you can see, most of the features of HTML5 work fine on this browser. Depending on your browser, or browser version, you may get different results.

Another site, www.caniuse.com, presents a comprehensive group of tables that discuss the compatibility of various browsers with HTML5. This site is shown in Figure 1-8.

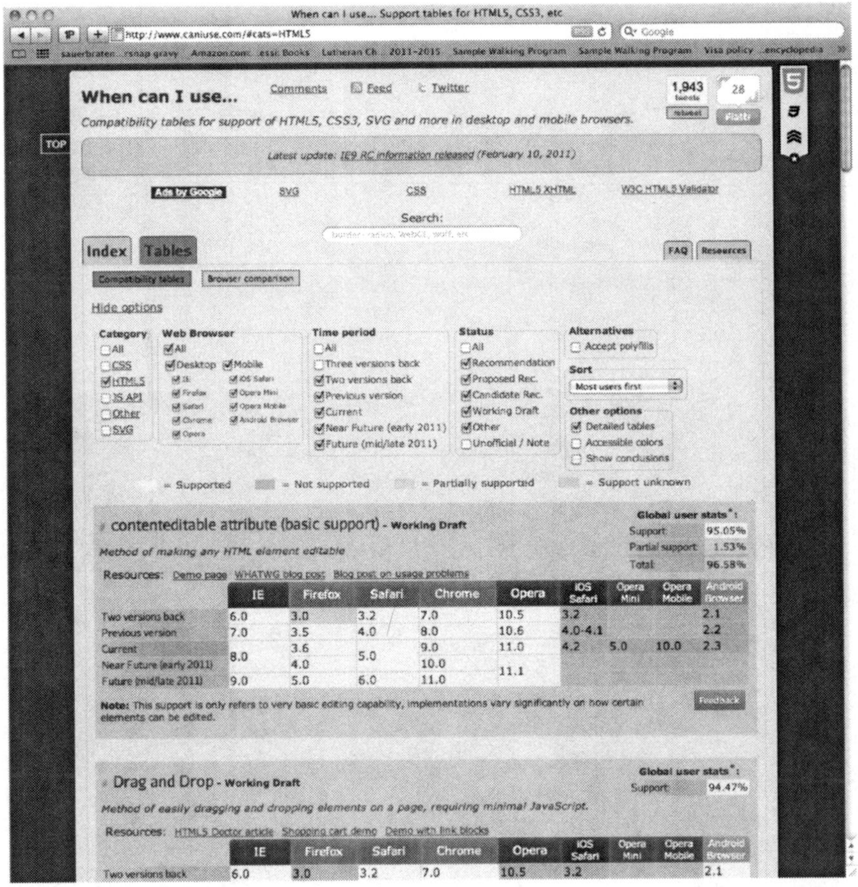

Figure 1-8. HTML5 compatibilities listed on www.caniuse.com

One of the great features of www.caniuse.com is the ability to filter information and focus in on the elements you are concerned about. There are also numerous discussions and tutorials associated with this website.

One of the most widely used HTML5/CSS resource sites is www.modernizr.com. This site is shown in Figure 1-9.

Figure 1-9. The home page of www.modernizr.com

This site offers a powerful downloadable JavaScript library that will adjust HTML5 and CSS3 code in order to target specific browsers. This project is open-source, and is therefore entirely free. Most developers using HTML5 are using this library as a means of checking and adjusting code.

Expert tips

Because HTML5 standards are evolving, we strongly recommend that you do not revise existing sites entirely. Instead, start to employ elements from HTML5 gradually, as updates become necessary.

Summary

In this chapter, we examined a more precise way to create HTML markup, rather than a lot of new functionality. For example, rather than simply using the generic `<div>` element, you can now use elements such as `<section>`, `<nav>`, `<figure>`, and so forth. Clearer markup early makes for greater control and functionality later on.

Subsequent chapters will examine this new functionality. Beginning in Chapter 2, you will start to see the possibilities of this increased functionality.

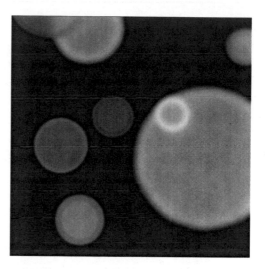

Chapter 2

HTML5 Markup

In Chapter 1, we explored many of the new structural tags associated with HTML5. By using additional structural tags, you can describe the parts of your document with greater detail and accuracy. You also learned that there are many attributes associated with tags. Some of these attributes are specific to particular tags, and some are global across all tags.

This chapter revisits many of the tags you might have used in earlier versions of HTML. However, you will see that these familiar tags have been greatly enhanced in HTML5. You will also learn in this chapter how HTML5 can assist you in linking up your application to the outside world and, importantly, to multimedia. Let's try to solve a few problems here.

Solution 2-1: Using the <hr> tag in HTML5

In previous versions of HTML, the <hr> tag was used strictly for creating horizontal lines on a page. In HTML5, it has changed semantically.

At first blush, the <hr> tag looks like it is doing exactly the same thing in HTML5 that it did in previous versions of HTML. However, the purpose of HTML is to describe the various parts of the document. Previously, the <hr> tag drew a horizontal line. While that line came in handy, it really did nothing to describe a part of the document other than a horizontal line.

The W3C has semantically changed the function of the <hr> tag. Officially, its purpose is now to define "the end of one section and the beginning of another." Here is where the confusion starts: as discussed in Chapter 1, HTML5 has a new tag called <section>, which is designed to separate sections. This is the

19

subject of ongoing debate among developers. As of this writing, the consensus is that perhaps the `<hr>` tag can be used to separate topics within a section. Since HTML5 is still a work a work in progress, and it is likely to remain so for a long time, perhaps a more final definition will come.

What's involved

Let's assume you have several paragraphs that you want to separate with a horizontal line. You may want it to look something like the simple example shown in Figure 2-1.

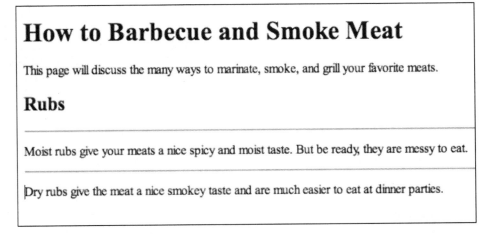

Figure 2-1. Using the `<hr>` tag

If you are scratching your head and wondering what is different, you are not alone. Many developers are doing exactly the same thing. While Figure 2-1 looks like it has the same functionality as previous HTML versions, it is really semantically separating the topics of moist rubs and dry rubs. In Figure 2-1, we are also using it to separate the descriptions from the heading, "Rubs."

How to build it

The example shown in Figure 2-1 is accomplished with the following code:

```
<!DOCTYPE html>
    <html>
        <head>
            <title>Using the <hr> tag</title>
        </head>
        <body>
            <h1>How to Barbecue and Smoke Meat</h1>
            This page will discuss the many ways to marinate, smoke, and grill your favorite➡
    meats.
            <h2>Rubs</h2>
            <hr>
```

```
        Moist rubs give your meats a nice spicy and moist taste. But be ready, they are→
messy to eat.
        <hr>
        Dry rubs give the meat a nice smokey taste and are much easier to eat at dinner→
parties.
    </body>
  </html>
```

According to the W3C, sections should be separated by the <hr> tag rather than the <p> tag. In this example, the <p> tag was not used, in order to bring this into compliance with HTML5 standards. Of course, the <p> tag can still be used to separate paragraphs within a section.

Expert tips

In order to accommodate the new semantic definition of the <hr> tag, you could use CSS to change what the <hr> tag produces. Note the following example:

```
hr
{
    height: 15px;
    background: url('decorative.gif');
    no-repeat 50% 50%;
}
```

You need to be careful about this, however. As of this writing, Safari and Firefox will replace the horizontal line with the graphic shown in the above code; but Internet Explorer will surround the graphic with horizontal lines.

Solution 2-2: Using the <iFrame> tag

You can use the <iframe> tag to create a browser within a browser and open documents from other sources. This can be seen in the example shown in Figure 2-2.

Using the iFrame tag

Figure 2-2. Opening two external websites using the <iFrame> tag

In Figure 2-2, two separate websites were opened using two <iFrame> tags. This tag has increased importance because HTML5 doesn't support the attributes of scrolling, frameborder, and marginheight, all of which were supported in previous versions of HTML.

What's involved

One of the proposed specifications of the <iFrame> tag in HTML5 is the seamless attribute. This allows the outside source to be incorporated into the host document without borders or scrollbars. That means that the outside source will look as if it is part of the hosting document. Unfortunately, as of this writing, no browsers support the seamless attribute.

How to build it

The following code is used to create the example shown in Figure 2-2:

```
<!DOCTYPE html >
   <html>
      <head>
         <title>Using the <iFrame> tag</title>
      </head>
```

```
      <body>
          <strong>Using the iFrame tag</strong><hr>
          <iframe src="http://www.apress.com/" width="600" height="250" seamless></iframe><br>
          <iframe src="http://www.friendsofed.com/" width="600" height="250" seamless➥
  ></iframe><br>
      </body>
    </html>
```

Notice that the `seamless` attribute is used in the above code, However, you still see the scrollbars and borders. This means that the browser does not support the use of the `seamless` attribute.

Expert tips

Security can be a factor when bringing in any sort of content from an outside source. In HTML5, the `<iFrame>` tag has a sandbox around it to help improve security. The sandbox's attributes include the following:

- *allow-scripts*: blocks or allows the execution of certain scripted content, including JavaScript.

- *allow-forms*: allows or blocks the submission of forms.

- *allow-same-origin*: forces the content of the outside document to originate from the same origin. Thus, a page cannot receive data from one origin and then write data to a different origin.

- *Allow-top-navigation*: allows or blocks navigation to top-level browsing content.

Solution 2-3: Embedding media into a page

Like the `<iFrame>` tag in the last section, the `<embed>` tag is used to embed outside content into a host web page. However, the focus here is on media such as photos, videos, sounds and, despite all the rumors to the contrary, Flash content. In Figure 2-3, for example, you would get the following result (assuming that a photograph was being brought in from an outside source):

Using the embed tag

Figure 2-3. Using the ⟨embed⟩ tag

What's involved

While you are probably thinking that you could do the same thing with the ⟨img⟩ tag, you can use the ⟨embed⟩ tag to bring a variety of media into web pages. For instance, you could bring in videos, sound files, and so forth. However, when dealing with video, things are in transition a bit at this time.

As of this writing, there seems to be a growing trend against the use of browser plug-ins such as Adobe Flash Player. Many mobile technologies do not support these plug-ins currently. For example, one of the most-used Flash Video formats is FLV. This requires the use of the aforementioned Adobe Flash Player. The ⟨embed⟩ tag seems to point to a possible solution; however, there is a caveat. Videos come in a variety of flavors — FLV, MOV, H.264, and so on. Each of these MIME types (file extensions) requires someone to take the original video and encode it. This means wrapping it in a special container called a CODEC (COmpression DECompression). In addition, the person seeing the video needs to have a copy of the video's CODEC installed on their computer. In the case of Flash Video, the CODEC is contained within the Flash Player.

As of this writing, there are two CODECS that support HTML5 video: H.264 and Theora. Keeping this in mind, and again as of this writing, there is the following browser support:

- Firefox 3.5 and above supports HTML5 with only Theora, not H.264.

- Internet Explorer 9 supports HTML5 video with only H.264 and not Theora.

- Safari 3 and above supports HTML5 video with only H.264 and not Theora.
- Chrome 3 and above supports HTML5 video with both H.264 and Theora.
- Opera 10.5 supports HTML5 video with only Theora and not H.264.

How to build it

The following code is used to create the example shown in Figure 2-3:

```
<!DOCTYPE html>
<html>
    <head>
        <title>Using the embed tag </title>
    </head>
    <body>
        <p><strong>Using the embed tag</strong></p>
        <embed type="jpg" src="002.jpg" height="250" width="350" />
    </body>
</html>
```

What distinguishes this tag is the type attribute. You probably associate the type attribute with tags such as <input>. In HTML5, however, the use of attributes has been made more consistent over tags. In most cases, the media's MIME type (file extension) is used as the type. As you will soon see, however, there is an alternate way of identifying video types.

The other unique attribute is the src. This can be any URL needed to connect to the source.

Expert tips

As illustrated above, different browsers support different encodings for HTML5 video. For that reason, it may be necessary to do two encodings of any given video: one for H.264 and one for Theora. Within the <embed> tag, you use the type attribute to identify which encoded video to open.

When using the type attribute with video, the type of video can be identified with the syntax video/type. For example, for a QuickTime video, identify the type as type = "video/Quicktime".

Solution 2-4: Using the <area> tag

While you may have used the <area> tag in previous versions of HTML, the version implemented in HTML5 presents some new and interesting possibilities. Let's begin by looking at some basics of using the <area> tag in HTML5.

What's involved

The <area> tag is used to create hyperlinks using image mapping. In other words, it takes an existing graphic and divides it up into sections, each with its own unique hyperlinks. HTML5, however, looks at links a bit differently than previous versions of HTML. It divides links into three categories:

- *Hyperlinks*: allow the user to navigate to a given resource.

- *External Resources*: links to resources that are processed automatically to augment the current document.

- *Annotations*: modifications to the automatic resources used in External Resources; they can also modify how a hyperlink works.

In previous HTML versions, the `rel` attribute is used to show the relationship between the current resource and the resource it is being linked to. For example, note the following:

```
rel = "stylesheet"
```

This shows that the document the resource is being linked to is a stylesheet. While this may not sound like much, it could have enormous implications for a search engine's understanding of the relationships of various documents within a website.

While the `rel` attribute is not new, HTML5 extends the relational definitions.

Table 2.1 shows the relationship with the external document of the `<area>` tag as of this writing. Since this specification is in transition, the information provided in the table may change. However, you will be surprised to see that the reference values now represent such diverse relationships as family, professional, and even romantic.

Table 2-1. Relationship to Referenced Document of the `<area>` Tag

rel value	Used with the `<area>` tag	Description
acquaintance	Yes	This indicates that the person represented in the referenced document is an acquaintance of the person represented in the current document.
alternate	Yes	Used to specify that the referenced document is to be used with the media specified. In HTML5, the media attribute can now be used with the `<area>` tag. This was not true in previous versions of HTML.
archives	Yes	A link to a document of historical interest.
author	Yes	This indicates that the referenced document provides additional information about the author.
bookmark	Yes	This indicates that the referenced document is an ancestor to the host document.
child	Yes	This indicates that the person represented in the referenced document is a child of the person represented in the current document.
colleague	Yes	This indicates that the person represented in the referenced document has a professional relationship with the person represented in the current document.
contact	Yes	Contact information.
co-resident	Yes	This indicates that the person represented in the referenced document shares an address with the person represented in the current document.

rel value	Used with the <area> tag	Description
co-worker	Yes	This indicates that the person represented in the referenced document is a co-worker of the person represented in the current document.
crush	Yes	This indicates that the person represented in the referenced document has a romantic interest in the person represented in the current document.
date	Yes	This indicates that the person represented in the referenced document is dating the person represented in the current document.
external	Yes	This shows that the referenced document is not part of the existing site as the host document.
first	Yes	This indicates that the referenced document is the first document in a series of documents.
friend	Yes	This indicates that the person represented in the referenced document is a friend of the person represented in the current document.
help	Yes	This shows that the referenced document is context-sensitive help.
icon	No	This imports an icon to represent the referenced document.
index	Yes	A link to an index or table of contents.
kin	Yes	This indicates that the person represented in the referenced document is a family member or extended family member of the person represented in the current document.
last	Yes	This indicates that the referenced document is the last document in a series of documents.
license	Yes	This is a link to the licensing information of the current document.
me	Yes	This indicates that both the current document and the linked document represent you.
met	Yes	This indicates that the person in the current document and the person in the referenced document have physically met.
muse	Yes	This indicates that the person represented in the referenced document gives inspiration to the person represented in the current document.
next	Yes	This indicates that the referenced document is next document in a referenced series of documents.
neighbor	Yes	This indicates that the person represented in the referenced document is a neighbor of the person represented in the current document.
nofollow	Yes	This means that the referenced document is not endorsed by the author of the hosting document, but instead is used as a reference or relationship.
noreferrer	Yes	This means that the HTTP header does not use the referrer property in the hyperlink.
parent	Yes	This indicates that the person represented in the referenced document is a parent of the person represented in the current document.

rel value	Used with the <area> tag	Description
pingback	No	Allows the referenced server to ping back to the current document.
prefetch	Yes	Allows the referenced document to be prefetched.
prev	Yes	Like the next ref, this indicates that this is a reference to a series of documents and that this is the previous document.
search	Yes	This links to a tool that can perform searches on the current or referenced documents.
sidebar	Yes	This will show the referenced document in the browser as a sidebar.
sibling	Yes	This indicates that the person represented in the referenced document is a brother or sister of the person represented in the current document.
spouse	Yes	This indicates that the person represented in the referenced document is a spouse of the person represented in the current document.
sweetheart	Yes	This indicates that the person represented in the referenced document is a close romantic interest of the person represented in the current document.
stylesheet	No	This indicates that the referenced document is a stylesheet.
tag	Yes	This indicates that a tag in the referenced document applies to the present document.

In all of the rel links listed in Table 2-1:

- Hyperlinks are created with the acquaintance, alternate, archives, author, bookmark, child, colleague, contact, co-resident, co-worker, crush, date, external, first, friend, help, index, kin, license, me, met, muse, neighbor, next, parent, prev, search, sidebar, sibling, spouse, sweetheart, and tag values.

- External Resources are referenced with prefetch.

- Annotations are used by nofollow and noreferrer.

Also, beginning with HTML5, the <area> tag can use the media attribute to indicate what media the link will target. In previous versions of HTML, you could not use the media attribute in the <area> tag. For the sake of consistency, HTML5 now allows its use.

How to build it

There are many different ways of using the <area> tag. The following example is one such way. Please note that this example is for demonstration only and does not represent a working site.

```
<!DOCTYPE html >
<html>
    <head>
        <title> Example For Area Tag href attribute </title>
    </head>
```

```
<body>
    <img src="usa.gif" width="350" height="299"  usemap="#usamap" />
    <map name="usamap">
        <area  coords="20, 80, 122, 230"  href="http://www.friendsofed.html" shape="rect"↵
hreflang="en" rel="license" media="screen" />
        <area  coords="123, 82, 288, 160"  href="http://www.apress.html" shape="rect"↵
hreflang="en" rel="license" media="print"/>
    </map>
  </body>
</html>
```

The <area> tag is used in conjunction with the <map> tag. Notice the usemap attribute in the <img> tag. The same identifier is used in the name attribute of the <map> tag. This associates the image with an image map.

The media attribute is used to show with which media the link is associated. As stated earlier, the ability to use this attribute in the <area> tag is new to HTML5.

Expert tips

When using the <area> tag, it is a good practice to use the hreflang attribute in conjunction with the href attribute. This will indicate the language of the target document or resource.

Summary

In this chapter, we looked at how HTML5 markup gives traditional HTML tags new functionality. We also examined how to link the HTML5 document to the outside world using tags such as <iFrame> and <area>.

In the following chapter, you will see how HTML5 uses the DOM API model. In the process, we revisit some concepts you learned in this chapter and in Chapter 1. However, you will see them in a more complex context.

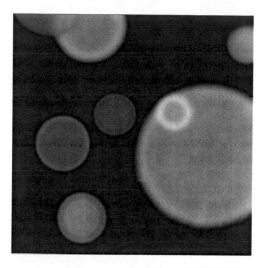

Chapter 3

HTML5 Structural and Semantic Elements

The term "semantic web" is definitely not new. The creator of the World Wide Web himself, Tim Berners-Lee, used it for the first time when talking about the transformation of the World Wide Web into an environment where published documents are associated with information and data that specify their semantic context in an interpretable format.

With HTML5, a lot of work has been done on this aspect of the World Wide Web, and a great number of new elements have been introduced to provide a better definition and structure to web pages. Still, there are more elements to address.

In this chapter, we focus on the techniques and elements used to create a semantic structure for a web page using microdata, the figure container, and the aside element.

Understanding microdata

HTML5 introduces the possibility of defining custom semantics in a web page using microdata.

Microdata enables you to specify machine-readable custom elements in a web page by using syntax made up of name-value pairs with existing content.

The custom elements that represent the subject are called items. The values that are assigned to these items are their properties. For these custom elements to be valid, you need to define a custom vocabulary that includes the list of named properties that represent the subject.

If, for example, you wanted to create microdata that represents the User subject, you would have to define its properties in a microdata vocabulary. This vocabulary would include the declaration of properties such as the name, surname, address, and social security number.

To create an item, use the itemscope attribute. To define a property of an item, use the itemprop attribute.

In particular, the itemscope attribute is the element that is associated with an HTML element, and it allows you to define the scope of the element. The itemscope attribute can be associated with any valid HTML element:

```
<div itemscope>
  <p>Name:<span itemprop="name">Marco</span>.</p>
  <p>Last Name: <span itemprop="lastname">Casario</span>.</p>
  <p>Photo: <img itemprop="photo" src="myPhoto.png"> </p>
  <p>Address: <span itemprop="address">Via Lazzaro Spallanzani</span>.</p>
  <p>Social Security Number: <span itemprop="ssn">000-0000-000</span>.</p>
</div>
```

In this example, we've defined an item with five properties:

- Name
- Last Name
- Photo
- Address
- Social Security Number

By using this structure, it is possible to create all the items you want. You can also associate multiple properties with an item that has the same name and different values:

```
<div itemscope>
  <p>Name:<span itemprop="name">Marco</span>.</p>
  <p>Last Name: <span itemprop="lastname">Casario</span>.</p>
  <p>Photo: <img itemprop="photo" src="myPhoto.png" > </p>
  <p>Address: <span itemprop="address">Via Lazzaro Spallanzani</span>.</p>
  <p>Address: <span itemprop="address">Via Ludovico di Breme </span>.</p>
  <p>Social Security Number: <span itemprop="ssn">000-0000-000</span>.</p>
</div>
```

Before creating an item, however, you need to create the custom vocabulary that will enable you to define the valid properties for the elements. The vocabulary shall therefore be a list of properties with their description, such as those shown in Table 3.1.

Table 3.1. The User Microdata Vocabulary

Property	Description
Name	The name of the user. Required.
Last Name	The surname of the user. Required.
Address	The address of the user.
Photo	An image in PNG, GIF, or JPG format of the user.
Social Security Number	The valid Social Security Number of the user. Required.

The custom vocabulary is associated with the elements of an itemtype attribute:

```
<div itemscope itemtype="http://www.my-vocabulary.org/user">
 <p>Name:<span itemprop="name">Marco</span>.</p>
 <p>Last Name: <span itemprop="lastname">Casario</span>.</p>
 <p>Photo: <img itemprop="photo" src="myPhoto.png" > </p>
 <p>Address: <span itemprop="address">Via Lazzaro Spallanzani</span>.</p>
<p>Social Security Number: <span itemprop="ssn">000-0000-000</span>.</p>
</div>
```

The values that are assigned to the itemtype attribute are identified as Uniform Resource Locators (URLs). In fact, in the example above, the itemtype attribute points to the URL: http://www.my-vocabulary.org/user.

The vocabulary also allows you to provide guidelines to developers who intend to use the same structure to describe the same subject.

Furthermore, another important aspect of microdata relates to search engines. In fact, search engines such as Google are designed to present to the user the most useful and informative search results. This information does not affect the content aspect of your pages, but allows search engines to understand the information coming from the web page and render it better. Therefore, microdata is also used as a method to make a web page more search-friendly for search engines.

Microdata is one of the three methods used to execute the markup of HTML content in a structured manner. (The other two methods are microformats and RDFs.)

Solution 3-1: Using the itemprop and itemscope attributes

The microdata introduced by HTML5 are a way to assign labels to content in order to describe a specific kind of information.

In this solution, you will create a web page containing recipes with HTML5 microdata.

What's involved

To create an element using the microdata syntax, you'll essentially declare three attributes to the standard HTML tags:

- *itemscope:* A Boolean attribute used to create an item
- *itemprop:* Used to add a property to an item or one of the item's descendants
- *itemtype:* Used to define a custom vocabulary

In this solution, we will use a custom vocabulary defined by Google for the item that we want to describe. There are some custom vocabularies that have already been defined and acknowledged by the well-known search engine at the URL: www.data-vocabulary.org/:

- Event
- Organization
- Person
- Recipe
- Product
- Review
- Review-aggregate
- Breadcrumb
- Offer
- Offer-aggregate

Therefore, all you have to do is point the itemtype attribute to the URL: www.data-vocabulary.org/ and add the element type. In the example, you will use the microdata that defines a recipe, which you can find at this address: www.data-vocabulary.org/Recipe/.

The valid properties are specified in Table 3-2.

Table 3-2. The Recipe Microdata Properties

Properties	Description
name	Contains the name of the dish. Required.
recipeType	The type of dish. For example, appetizer, entree, or dessert.
photo	Image of the dish being prepared.
published	The date the recipe was published in ISO 8601 (`http://www.iso.org/iso/date_and_time_format`) date format.
summary	A short summary describing the dish.
review	A review of the dish. Can include nested review information.
prepTime	The length of time it takes to prepare the recipe for dish in ISO 8601 duration format. Can use min and max as child elements to specify a range of time.
cookTime	The time it takes to cook the dish in ISO 8601 duration format. Can use min and max as child elements to specify a range of time.
totalTime	The total time it takes to prepare and cook the dish in ISO 8601 duration format. Can use min and max as child elements to specify a range of time.
nutrition	Nutrition information about the recipe. Can contain the following child elements: servingSize, calories, fat, saturatedFat, unsaturatedFat, carbohydrates, sugar, fiber, protein, and cholesterol. These elements are not explicitly part of the Recipe microformat, but Google will recognize them.
instructions	The steps to make the dish. Can contain the child element instruction, which can be used to annotate each step.
yield	The quantity produced by the recipe (for example, number of people served, number of servings, and so on.
ingredients	An ingredient used in the recipe. Can contain child item's name (name of the ingredient) and amount. Use this to identify individual ingredients.
author	Creator of the recipe. Can include nested Person information.

How to build it

The first thing to do when you want to create a new element using microdata is to specify the custom vocabulary to which it will refer. In this solution, we will use the vocabulary defined by Google at the URL: `www.data-vocabulary.org/Recipe/`, whose valid properties are those specified in Table 3-2.

Specify the vocabulary with the itemtype attribute:

```
<section itemtype="http://www.data-vocabulary.org/Recipe">
```

To create a new element, all you have to do is use the Boolean itemscope attribute:

```
<section itemscope itemtype="http://www.data-vocabulary.org/Recipe">
```

Now you can declare the properties identified by the custom microdata vocabulary for the Recipe type element.

Start by declaring the name of the recipe, a photo of the finished dish, and the author of the recipe:

```
<h1 itemprop="name">
Ciabatta Bread
</h1>
<p>
<a itemprop="author" href="http://groups.google.com/group/alt.bread.recipes➥
/browse_thread/thread/ad0e477790ef4f03/a644f520f4b3cd48?rnum=2#">Author's original URL</a>.
</p>

<p><img src="img/bread.JPG" itemprop="name"  />
</p>
```

Also insert a review of the dish by specifying a review property:

```
<span itemprop="review">
Ciabatta is an Italian white bread made with wheat flour and yeast. The loaf is somewhat
elongated, broad, and flattish. Its name is the Italian word for slipper. There are many
variations of Ciabatta.
Ciabatta in its modern form was developed in 1982. Since the late 1990s, it has been popular
across Europe and the United States. It is widely used as a sandwich bread.
From Wikipedia http://en.wikipedia.org/wiki/Ciabatta
</span>
```

Every recipe needs ingredients, so use the ingredients property to specify them:

```
<h3  itemprop="ingredients">
<ul>
<li>1 1/2 cups water </li>
<li>15 grams of salt </li>
<li>1 teaspoon sugar </li>
<li>1 tablespoon olive oil </li>
<li>3 1/4 cups all-purpose flour </li>
<li>20 grams of fresh yeast </li>
</ul>
</h3>
```

To insert the elements of our Recipe object, we used an unordered list and declared the itemprop attribute for an H3 element. In fact, the itemprop attribute can be declared for any HTML element.

Now add the instructions, this time using a numbered list:

```
<h4 itemprop="instructions">Instructions
<ol>
   <li>In Kitchen Aid style mixer, mix all ingredients roughly until combined with paddle. Let
it rest for 10 minutes.   </li>
   <li>With the paddle (I prefer the hook to prevent the dough from crawling into the guts of
the mixer), beat the living hell out of the batter. It will start out like pancake batter but,
in anywhere from 10 to 30 minutes, it will set up and work like a very sticky dough. If it
starts climbing too soon, then switch to the hook. </li>
   <li>You'll know it's done when it separates from the side of the bowl and starts to climb up
your hook/paddle, just coming off the bottom of the bowl. (I mean this literally about the
climbing—I once didn't pay attention, and it climbed up my paddle into the greasy inner
workings of the mixer. It was not pretty!) Anyway, it will definitely pass the windowpane
test.   </li>
   <li>Place into a well-oiled container, and let it triple! It must triple! For me, this takes
about 2.5 hours.
      Empty onto a floured counter (scrape if you must, however you got to get the gloop out),
and cut into 3 or 4 pieces. </li>
   <li>Spray with oil and dust with lots of flour. Let it proof for about 45 minutes, which
gives you enough time to crank that oven up to 500°F.
      After 45 minutes or so, the loaves should be puffy and wobbly; now it's iron fist, velvet
glove time. </li>
   <li>Pick up and stretch into your final Ciabatta shapes (~10" oblong rectangles), and flip
them upside down. This redistributes the bubbles, so that you get even bubbles throughout.
Then place the loaves on parchment or a heavily-floured peel. </li>
   <li>Try to do it in one motion and be gentle. It might look like you've ruined them
completely, but the oven spring is immense on these things.   </li>
   <li>Bake at 500°F until they are 205°F in the center (about 15-20 minutes), rotating 180-
degrees half way through. Some people like to turn the oven down to 450°F after 10 minutes—
whatever floats your boat. I usually bake in 2 batches.</li>
</ol>
</h4>
```

You also specify the estimated cooking time:

```
<p itemprop="cookTime">
Cook Time: 50 minutes approximately
</p>
```

By opening the file in a browser, you will obtain the result shown in Figure 3-1.

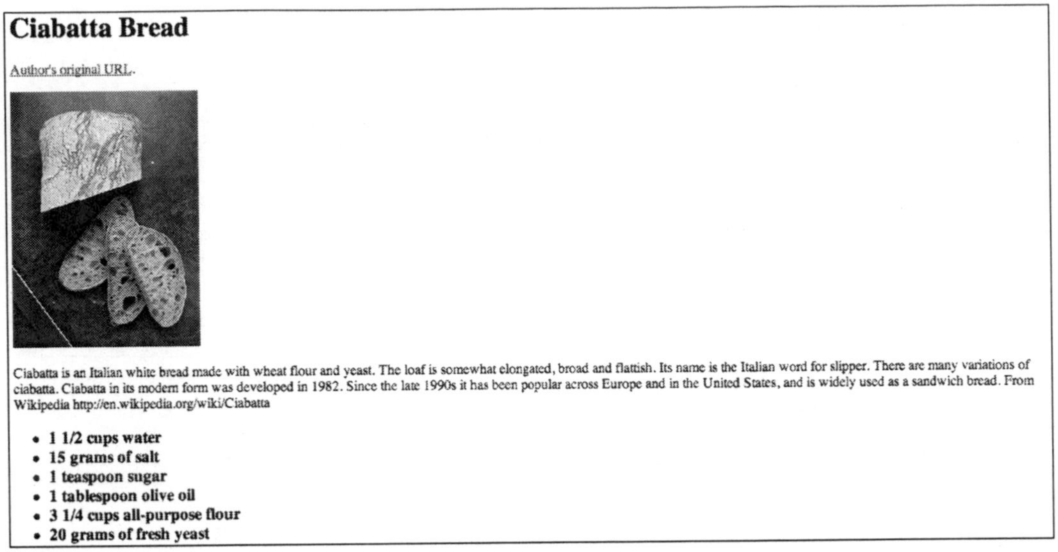

Ciabatta Bread

Author's original URL.

Ciabatta is an Italian white bread made with wheat flour and yeast. The loaf is somewhat elongated, broad and flattish. Its name is the Italian word for slipper. There are many variations of ciabatta. Ciabatta in its modern form was developed in 1982. Since the late 1990s it has been popular across Europe and in the United States, and is widely used as a sandwich bread. From Wikipedia http://en.wikipedia.org/wiki/Ciabatta

- 1 1/2 cups water
- 15 grams of salt
- 1 teaspoon sugar
- 1 tablespoon olive oil
- 3 1/4 cups all-purpose flour
- 20 grams of fresh yeast

Figure 3-1. The web page for the recipe using microdata

The user will not notice any difference due to microdata unless he or she opens the source code of the page. What you have done, however, is to create a robust semantic structure for your web page, and the search engine will definitely appreciate it.

Here is the complete source code for this example:

```
<!DOCTYPE HTML>
<html>
<head>
<meta http-equiv="Content-Type" content="text/html; charset=UTF-8">
<title>Solution 3-1: Using the itemprop and itemscope</title>
</head>

<body>

<section itemscope itemtype="http://www.data-vocabulary.org/Recipe">

<h1 itemprop="name">
Ciabatta Bread
</h1>
<p>
<a itemprop="author" href="http://groups.google.com/group/alt.bread.recipes/browse_thread↪
/thread/ad0e477790ef4f03/a644f520f4b3cd48?rnum=2#">Author's original URL</a>.
</p>

<p><img src="img/bread.JPG" itemprop="name"  />
```

```
</p>

<p itemprop="review">
Ciabatta is an Italian white bread made with wheat flour and yeast. The loaf is somewhat
elongated, broad, and flattish. Its name is the Italian word for slipper. There are many
variations of Ciabatta.
Ciabatta in its modern form was developed in 1982. Since the late 1990s, it has been popular
across Europe and the United States. It is widely used as a sandwich bread.
From Wikipedia http://en.wikipedia.org/wiki/Ciabatta
</p>

<h3  itemprop="ingredients">
<ul>
<li>1 1/2 cups water </li>
<li>15 grams of salt </li>
<li>1 teaspoon sugar </li>
<li>1 tablespoon olive oil </li>
<li>3 1/4 cups all-purpose flour </li>
<li>20 grams of fresh yeast </li>
</ul>
</h3>

<p itemprop="cookTime">
Cook Time: 50 minutes approximately
</p>

<h4 itemprop="instructions">Instructions
<ol>
  <li>In Kitchen Aid style mixer, mix all ingredients roughly until combined with paddle. Let
it rest for 10 minutes.   </li>
  <li>With the paddle (I prefer the hook to prevent the dough from crawling into the guts of
the mixer), beat the living hell out of the batter. It will start out like pancake batter but
in anywhere from 10 to 30 minutes it will set up and work like a very sticky dough. If it
starts climbing too soon, then switch to the hook. </li>
  <li>You'll know it's done when it separates from the side of the bowl and starts to climb up
your hook/paddle, just coming off the bottom of the bowl. (I mean this literally about the
climbing—I once didn't pay attention, and it climbed up my paddle into the greasy inner
workings of the mixer. It was not pretty!) Anyway, it will definitely pass the windowpane
test.   </li>
  <li>Place into a well-oiled container and let it triple! It must triple! For me, this takes
about 2.5 hours.
    Empty onto a floured counter (scrape if you must, however you got to get the gloop out),
and cut into 3 or 4 pieces. </li>
  <li>Spray with oil and dust with lots of flour. Let it proof for about 45 minutes, which
gives you enough time to crank that oven up to 500°F.
    After 45 minutes or so, the loaves should be puffy and wobbly; now it's iron fist, velvet
glove time. </li>
```

```
    <li>Pick up and stretch into your final Ciabatta shapes (~10" oblong rectangles), and flip
them upside down. This redistributes the bubbles, so that you get even bubbles throughout.
Then place the loaves on parchment or a heavily-floured peel. </li>
    <li>Try to do it in one motion and be gentle. It might look like you've ruined them
completely, but the oven spring is immense on these things.    </li>
    <li>Bake at 500°F until they are 205°F in the center (about 15-20 minutes), rotating 180-
degrees half way through. Some people like to turn the oven down to 450°F after 10 minutes—
whatever floats your boat. I usually bake in 2 batches.</li>
</ol>
</h4>


</section>

</body>
</html>
```

Expert tips

Some search engines, including Google, don't normally show the user elements that aren't visible, such as meta tags. However, this doesn't mean that search engines completely ignore this information.

In some situations, it can be useful to provide the search engines with more detailed information, even if we don't want visitors to see it. For example, if we allow the users to insert grades for our recipe on the site and the average grade is 8, then users (but not search engines) will suppose that the grade is based on a scale of 1 to 10. In this case, you can specify this aspect by using the meta element as follows:

```
<div itemprop="rating" itemscope itemtype="http://data-vocabulary.org/Rating">
    Rating: <span itemprop="value">8</span>
    <meta itemprop="best" content="10" />
</div>
```

In this code, the meta tag specifies additional information that cannot be seen in the page, but that is useful for the search engine to understand that the grading system is based on a scale of 1 to 10. The value of the property is specified using the content attribute.

Solution 3-2: Creating a custom vocabulary

The advantage of using microdata is that it allows you to create custom elements in your web page that are not otherwise included in the standard elements of HTML.

You need to create a custom vocabulary in order to enable the structure that you will create to define the name-value pair group to be reused by other developers and to be recognized by search engines.

A custom vocabulary is merely a list of the custom properties, which you create to define certain elements that will act as technical documentation for other developers and search engine designers.

Even if it isn't a compulsory practice, it is highly recommended that you create a custom vocabulary.

What's involved

As you have already seen in the previous solution, Google provides a website with some custom vocabularies for some custom elements. The custom vocabularies, which have already been defined and are recognized by the search engine, are available at the URL: www.data-vocabulary.org/.

To create a custom vocabulary, all you have to do is to document the properties that define your element, publish the web page, and point to it with the itemtype attribute.

How to build it

Creating a custom vocabulary means creating an HTML page that documents the properties that define the structure of a custom element. In this solution, you will create a custom vocabulary to describe a training course.

Therefore, create a new web page, which will then be published to a remote server:

```
<!DOCTYPE HTML>
<html>
<head>
<meta http-equiv="Content-Type" content="text/html; charset=UTF-8">
<title>Solution 3-2: Creating a custom vocabulary</title>
</head>

<body>
<h1>
Course
</h1>
<p>
When course information is marked up in web pages, use the following information in a
course.</p>
<p>To see an example, go to the <a href="http://www.comtaste.com/en/html-5-
training.htm">Comtaste Training page</a>: http://www.comtaste.com/en/html-5-training.htm</p>
<h2>
Course Properties
</h2>
<table width="100%" border="1" cellspacing="2" cellpadding="2">
  <tr>
    <th scope="col">Properties</th>
    <th scope="col">Description</th>
  </tr>
  <tr>
    <td>name</td>
    <td>The title of the course. Required.</td>
  </tr>
  <tr>
    <td>subtitle</td>
    <td>A short summary describing the course.</td>
```

```
</tr>
<tr>
  <td>summary</td>
  <td>A short description of the course.</td>
</tr>
<tr>
  <td>description</td>
  <td>A detailed description of the course and subjects.</td>
</tr>
<tr>
  <td>date</td>
  <td>The  published dates.</td>
</tr>
<tr>
  <td>hour</td>
  <td>The total duration of the course. </td>
</tr>
<tr>
  <td>location</td>
  <td>The location of the course.</td>
</tr>
<tr>
  <td>students</td>
  <td>The maximum number of students per course.</td>
</tr>
<tr>
  <td>prerequisites</td>
  <td> The skill required to participate to the course (if needed).</td>
</tr>
<tr>
  <td>objectives</td>
  <td>A short description of what you'll learn.</td>
</tr>
<tr>
  <td>HDrequirements</td>
  <td>Hardware and software requested for this course.</td>
</tr>
<tr>
  <td>book</td>
  <td>A list of course assets.</td>
</tr>
<tr>
  <td>outline</td>
  <td>The complete outline of the course.</td>
</tr>
<tr>
  <td>price</td>
  <td>The price of the course.</td>
```

```
    </tr>
    <tr>
      <td>instructor</td>
      <td>The name of the instructor that will lead the course.</td>
    </tr>
  </table>
  </body>
  </html>
```

Because it is a simple HTML file, you can open it with a common web browser, as shown in Figure 3-2.

Course

When course information is marked up in web pages use the following information in a course.

To see an example go to the Comtaste Training page: http://www.comtaste.com/en/html-5-training.htm

Course Properties

Properties	Description
name	The title of the course. Required
subtitle	A short summary describing the course.
summary	A short description of the course.
description	A detailed description of the course and subjects.
date	The published dates.
hour	The total duration of the course.
location	The location of the course.
students	The maximum number of students per course.
prerequisites	The skill required to partecipate to the course (if needed).
objectives	A short description of what you'll learn.
HDrequirements	Hardware and software requested for this course.
book	A list of course assets.
outline	The complete outline of the course.
price	The price of the course.
instructor	The name of the instructor that will lead the course.

Figure 3-2. The custom vocabulary page that documents the properties of the Course element

In order to use the vocabulary, you have to specify the address using the itemtype attribute after you have published the HTML page to a remote URL:

```
<div itemscope itemtype="http://www.comtaste.com/microdata/course">
```

To see an example of an HTML page that uses the microdata for a Course element, you can go to this URL: www.comtaste.com/en/html-5-training.htm, shown in Figure 3-3.

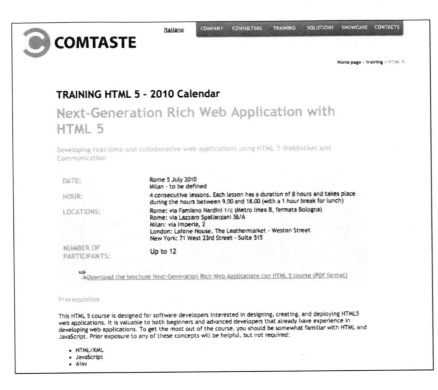

Figure 3-3. The Course microdata page

Expert tips

Google provides developers with an interesting tool, the Rich Snippets Testing Tool: `www.google.com/webmasters/tools/richsnippets`.

You can insert a valid URL to check if Google can correctly parse your structured data markup and display it in search results, as shown in Figure 3-4.

Figure 3-4. The Rich Snippets Testing Tool in action

Solution 3-3: Understanding link types and relations

Since the very first version of HTML, links have made simple text pages easy to navigate. With HTML5, however, a new concept is introduced: the link relation. The link relation allows you to tell the browser not only the page or the resource to which you are pointing, but also why you are pointing to it.

The link relations can be divided into two categories:

- *Links to external resources:* All links that point to resources that are processed by the browser, such as the style sheet, shortcut icon, pingback server, and so on

- *Hyperlinks:* Simple links that link to other documents

What's involved

Essentially, there are three tags you need to create a link relation in HTML5:

Using the `<link>` element within the `<head>` of a page

Using the `<a>` element

Using an `<area>` element

To determine which link types apply to a link or area element, the element's `rel` attribute must be split on spaces:

```
<a href="myTag/html5" rel="tag">html5</a>
```

In this code example, we created a tag link.

The `rel` attribute on `<a>` and `<area>` elements controls what kinds of links the elements create. The attribute's value must be a set of space-separated tokens.

The `rel` attribute has no default value. If the attribute is omitted, or if none of the values in the attribute are recognized by the user agent, then the document has no particular relationship with the destination resource other than there being a hyperlink between the two.

How to build it

It is quite simple to use link relations. Instead of providing a code example, it is more useful here to review a table with a list of the new `rel` values provided by HTML5.

Table 3-3 summarizes the link types that can be used with the `rel` attribute.

Table 3-3. New HTML5 Link Types

Property	Description
archive	Provides a link to a collection of records, documents, or other materials of historical interest.
	An example would be: `<a href="/archive" rel="archives">My Blog's Archive</a>`
author	Defines n hyperlink to a page that provides additional information about the author of the nearest article element, ancestor of the element defining the hyperlink if there is one, or of the page as a whole.
	For example: `This article has been written by <a href="http://www.linkedin.com/in/marcocasario" rel="author">Marco Casario</a>`
external	Indicates that the hyperlink leads to a resource outside the site.
first, last, prev, next, and up	Indicates that the hyperlink leads to the first, last, previous, or next resource of the sequence in which the current page appears.
	The up value indicates the "parent" document (in a hierarchy) compared to the current document.
	For example:

	`<a href="/firstArticle.htm" rel="first">First Part</a>`
	`  <a href="/nextArticle.htm" rel="next">Read the next article</a>`
	`    <a href="/lastArticle" rel="last">Last part of this series</a>`

icon	Defines an icon representing the page or site, and it should be used by the user agent when representing the page in the user interface.
	The sizes attribute gives the sizes of icons for visual media.
	For example:
	`<link rel=icon href="mac.icns" sizes="128x128 512x512">` `<link rel=icon href="gnome.png" type="image/png">`

Property	Description
license	Indicates that the referenced document provides the copyright license terms under which the main content of the current document is provided.
nofollow	Indicates that the link is not endorsed by the original author or publisher of the page, or that the link to the referenced document is included primarily because of a commercial relationship between people affiliated with the two pages. This keyword does not create a hyperlink. Rather, it annotates any other hyperlinks created by the element.
noreferrer	Indicates that no referrer information is to be leaked when following the link. This keyword does not create a hyperlink, but annotates any other hyperlinks created by the element.
pingback	The pingback system is a way for a blog to be notified automatically when other websites link to it. It allows you to get a notification when someone has linked to their document. For example: `<link rel-"pingback" href="pingback server url">`. For more information see the Pingback 1.0 specification `http://hixie.ch/specs/pingback/pingback-1.0`
prefetch	Indicates that fetching and caching the specified resource preemptively is likely to be beneficial, as it is highly likely that the user will require this resource.
search	Indicates that the referenced document provides an interface specifically for searching the document and its related resources. See this link for more information: www.opensearch.org/Specifications /OpenSearch/1.1#Autodiscovery_in_HTML_2FXHTML
sidebar	Indicates that the referenced document, if retrieved, is intended to be shown in a secondary browsing context (if possible), instead of in the current browsing context
tag	Indicates that the tag that the referenced document represents applies to the current document.
help	Link to a context-sensitive help page.

Expert tips

When thinking about the semantics of a web page, you cannot avoid considering the impact that your choices will have on Search Engine Optimization (SEO).

In fact, having a semantic table of the relationships between the links of your pages also helps their positioning on traditional search engines.

Google doesn't hide it—quite the opposite: It encourages the use of semantics and structures in your web pages.

To use the prev, next, last, and first relations, but also to improve searches and archives, means you're helping the search engine to index the pages of your site correctly by channelling search engine traffic towards more coherent content.

The tag relation is extremely useful in categorizing your pages by assigning a classification to the document that is more widely accepted, and thus is more useful and respected as compared to the old meta keywords system.

The external relation allows you to specify a link as "external," which in practical terms means to tell the search engine to assign a different weight (probably, a lower value) to that particular link as compared to the links that point towards the pages of your website.

Solution 3-4: The header and hgroup elements

In print, headers are an essential element to communicate article and section title information in a clear and immediate manner. This also has been a clear need on the Web since the early versions of HTML. Headers have always represented an important semantic element of the web page. Search engines, too, have made this tag important.

Figure 3-5 shows a classic example of a web page that uses headers to communicate the title and the subtitle of the course:

Figure 3-5. A classic use of the HTML headers

When we look at this page, however, we notice that there is a subtitle as well as the title:

Main title: TRAINING HTML5 – 2011 Calendar

Title: Next-Generation Rich Web Application with HTML5

Subtitle: Developing real-time and collaborative web applications using HTML5 WebSocket and Communication

With the previous versions of HTML, we could only use the <h1> to <h6> tags to distinguish the headers and define the page structure. If you looked at the source code of the web page in Figure 3-5, you would see the following HTML code:

```
<h2>TRAINING HTML5 - 2011 Calendar</h2>

<h1>Next-Generation Rich Web Application with HTML5</h1>

<h4>Developing real-time and collaborative web applications using HTML5 WebSocket and
Communication</h4>
```

You see three headers specified via the <h1>, <h2>, and <h4> tags, but this code isn't altogether correct from a semantic point of view. In fact, the subtitle and the main title are not sections of the page; rather, they are just subheadings and extra information.

HTML5 introduces new tags to avoid this problem: <header> and <hgroup>.

What's involved

A header element is usually intended to contain the section's heading, meaning the h1–h6 element or an hgroup element.

The <hgroup> element contains the heading of a section. It works as a wrapper for grouping a set of h1–h6 elements when the heading has multiple levels, such as subheadings, alternative titles, or taglines:

```
<header>
  <hgroup>
    <h1>Title</h1>
    <h2>Subheading</h2>
  </hgroup>
</header>
```

With this structure, we have created a semantic representation of the heading of a section with a title (<h1>) and a subtitle (<h2>).

It is also possible to create nested section content elements that use heading contents:

```
<header>
  <hgroup>
    <h1>Course Title</h1>
    <h2>Course Subtitles</h2>
  </hgroup>
```

```
<section>
<h3>Course Features</h3>
<section>
<h4>Prerequisites</h4>
    <p>This HTML5 course is designed for software developers interested in designing,
creating, and deploying HTML5 web applications.</p>
        <h4>Overview</h4>
        <p>HTML5 is the next major milestone in HTML, and it is not just another incremental
enhancement; it represents an enormous advance for modern web applications.</p>
</section>
</section>
</header>
```

How to build it

The use of the `<header>` and the `<hgroup>` tag may be confusing at first, but all you have to do is remember that:

- The `<hgroup>` can only contain a group of `<h1>` to `<h6>` elements

- The `<header>` can contain a `<h1>` to `<h6>` element or an `<hgroup>`

In this solution, you will use the headers to create a page that describes a training course, providing the information regarding the title, subtitle, a short description, and detailed information about the date, location, number of participants, and duration.

In the code below, the first heading content element inside a sectioning content element becomes that section's header.

Here is the complete code of the solution:

```
<!DOCTYPE HTML>
<html>
<head>
<meta http-equiv="Content-Type" content="text/html; charset=UTF-8">
<title>Solution 3-4: The header and hgroup elements</title>
<link href="Solution_3_4.css" rel="stylesheet">

</head>

<body>

<header class="training">
  <hgroup>
<h3>TRAINING HTML5 - 2011 Calendar</h3>
<h1>Next-Generation Rich Web Application with HTML5</h1>
<h4>Developing real-time and collaborative web applications using HTML5 WebSocket and
Communication</h4>
  </hgroup>
```

```
</header>
<section>
<table width="100%" border="0" class="training">
<tr>
<td><p>Rome TBC<br />
Milan TBC</p></td>
</tr>
 <tr>
<td class="caption_schede"><h4>HOUR:</h4></td>
<td><p>4 consecutive lessons. Each lesson has a duration of 8 hours, and it takes place during
the hours between 9:00 a.m. and 6:00 p.m. (with a 1-hour break for lunch)</p></td>
 </tr>
<tr>
<td class="caption_schede"><h4>LOCATIONS:</h4></td>
<td><p>Rome: via Famiano Nardini 1/c (Metro linea B, fermata Bologna)<br />
Rome: via Lazzaro Spallanzani 36/A<br />
Milan: via Imperia, 2<br />
 </tr>
 <tr>

<td class="caption_schede"><h4>NUMBER OF PARTICIPANTS:</h4></td>
<td>Up to 12</td>
 </tr>

</table>
</section>

</body>
</html>
```

You may notice that this HTML file is associated with an external CSS file, which applies simple style formats with the <link> tag. You will find the Solution_3_4.css file in the folder with the source code of this chapter.

The final result of the above file, rendered in a browser, is shown in Figure 3-6.

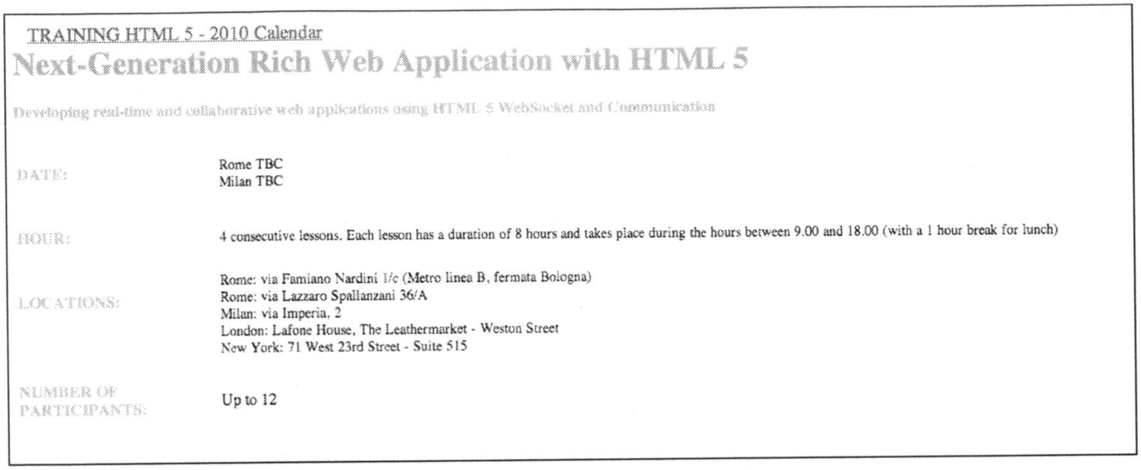

TRAINING HTML 5 - 2010 Calendar

Next-Generation Rich Web Application with HTML 5

Developing real-time and collaborative web applications using HTML 5 WebSocket and Communication

DATE:	Rome TBC Milan TBC
HOUR:	4 consecutive lessons. Each lesson has a duration of 8 hours and takes place during the hours between 9.00 and 18.00 (with a 1 hour break for lunch)
LOCATIONS:	Rome: via Famiano Nardini 1/c (Metro linea B, fermata Bologna) Rome: via Lazzaro Spallanzani 36/A Milan: via Imperia, 2 London: Lafone House, The Leathermarket - Weston Street New York: 71 West 23rd Street - Suite 515
NUMBER OF PARTICIPANTS:	Up to 12

Figure 3-6. The page structure uses the <header> and <hgroup> elements.

Solution 3-5: Connecting images with their captions

Traditionally, every image is associated with a caption, which may be a short text description or a legend for that image.

In the print publishing business, the image/caption pair is more than a best practice: this book, for example, uses this approach.

With HTML, two new semantic elements have been introduced that allow you to obtain this result by associating text with an image that acts as its legend.

What's involved

The elements that allow you to associate a caption to an image are <figure> and <figcaption>.

The <figure> tag is a container for images:

```
<figure>
  <img src="http://media02.linkedin.com/mpr/mpr/shrink_80_80/p/3/000/000/3d2/0f362fd.jpg"
alt="A photo of mine used in my LinkedIn profile">
</figure>
```
The <figcaption> is the text associated with the image that acts as a caption:
```
<figure>
  <img src="http://media02.linkedin.com/mpr/mpr/shrink_80_80/p/3/000/000/3d2/0f362fd.jpg"
alt="A photo of mine used in my LinkedIn profile">
<figcaption>Marco Casario as seen on TV !</figcaption>
</figure>
```

It's also possible to nest multiple images in a single caption:

```
<figure>
  <img src="http://media02.linkedin.com/mpr/mpr/shrink_80_80/p/3/000/000/3d2/0f362fd.jpg"↪
alt="A photo of mine used in my LinkedIn profile">
  <img src="http://www.flickr.com/photos/44124469126@N01/5431316371/" alt="Visiting Google's↪
headquarters">
<figcaption>Marco Casario as seen on TV !</figcaption>
</figure>
```

One of the advantages of using the <figure> and <figcaption> tags is that you can apply a CSS to them via an external or internal style sheet, just as you do for any other container tag.

How to build it

With HTML5, it is very important to plan the structure of the web page carefully. With all the new tags you have been provided, you can give an unambiguous semantic value to each element.

This planning phase is also important for images.

In this solution, you will create a simple business card with a picture, name, surname, and role, by specifying the text as a caption for the image. Then you will apply some simple style sheets, just to improve the final effect, shown in Figure 3-7.

Figure 3-7. The page structure uses the <header> and <hgroup> elements

Let's begin by declaring the container figure, where you will declare the image:

```
<figure>
<img src="http://media02.linkedin.com/mpr/mpr/shrink_80_80/p/3/000/000/3d2/0f362fd.jpg" alt=↪
"A photo of mine used in my LinkedIn profile">
</figure>
```

This image is loaded from the LinkedIn server. Add the caption by using the <figcaption> tag:

```
<figure>
<img src="http://media02.linkedin.com/mpr/mpr/shrink_80_80/p/3/000/000/3d2/0f362fd.jpg" alt=↪
```

```
"A photo of mine used in my LinkedIn profile">
<br /> <figcaption class="profile-header">Marco Casario - CTO Comtaste </figcaption>
</figure>
```

We've used a `<br>` to send the text of the caption as a new paragraph; otherwise it would have appeared next to the image.

Now you can create style sheets to re-create the border effects, define the margins, and set the background color for the image:

```
img
{
padding:2px;
border:1px solid #e6e6e6;
background-color:#fff;
}
```

Finally, add styles for the container and the caption text:

```
figure, figcaption {
        display: block;
        background-color:#ddf0f8;
        border:1px solid #666;
                text-align: center;


}
figcaption {
        font-face: Arial;
                font-size: 12px;
                font-style: italic;

        background-color:#ddf0f8;
        padding:2px;
        min-height:10px;
        margin:0 0 3px;
        border:1px solid #FFF

        }
```

Here is the complete code for this solution:

```
<!DOCTYPE HTML>
<html>
<head>
<meta http-equiv="Content-Type" content="text/html; charset=UTF-8">
<title>Solution 3-4: Connecting images with their captions </title>
<style>
```

```
img{padding:2px;border:1px solid #e6e6e6;background-color:#fff; margin:0 auto}

figure, figcaption {
        display: block;
        background-color:#ddf0f8;
        border:1px solid #666;
                text-align: center;

}
figcaption {
        font-face: Arial;
                font-size: 12px;
                font-style: italic;

        background-color:#ddf0f8;
        padding:2px;
        min-height:10px;
        margin:0 0 3px;
        border:1px solid #FFF

        }
</style>

</head>

<body>

<figure>
<img src="http://media02.linkedin.com/mpr/mpr/shrink_80_80/p/3/000/000/3d2/0f362fd.jpg" alt=
"A photo of mine used in my LinkedIn profile">
<br /> <figcaption class="profile-header">Marco Casario - CTO Comtaste </figcaption>
</figure>

</body>
</html>
```

Solution 3-6: Adding tangent content

HTML5 introduces a series of new tags that are useful in defining the semantic structure of your web pages more precisely. Among these tags there is one that, according to the W3C, represents content that is tangentially related to the content that forms the main textual flow of a document. This new element, the `<aside>` tag, allows you to associate additional text (a tangent) to an article or to the entire page.

What's involved

Starting with the definition of the `<aside>` tag, we can deduce that it has two characteristics: It is related to the main content, but only tangentially. It can also be considered separately from the main content.

To understand the use of the tag better, let's go back to the print publishing business. Figure 3-8 shows an example where a sidebar element is defined within two horizontal rules to provide additional information to the running text of the main article.

Deep-rooted problems

The National Audit Office (NAO) estimates that each individual aircraft is now 75% - more expensive than originally anticipated.

It says the joint management deal with Germany, Italy and Spain led to problems obtaining spares, and meant the RAF had problems fully training pilots.

The head of the NAO, Amyas Morse, said there were still "difficult and deep-rooted problems" to be overcome by the MoD.

"Key investment decisions were taken on an over-optimistic basis," he said, "and the department did not predict the substantial rate at which costs would rise. None of this suggests good cost control, a key determinant of value for money."

The NAO report says Typhoons are performing well in air-to-air missions, but that work on adapting the jets for ground attack is unlikely to be complete until 2018.

Until the jet's full multi-role capability is achieved, it says, the MoD will not have secured value for money.

"

(We) are working hard together to ensure project management continues to match the excellence of the Typhoon"

Peter Luff

Defence minister

Figure 3-8. The element on the right adds tangent content to the article. It's a perfect context to use the aside element. Source: www.bbc.co.uk/news/uk-12614995

How to build it

In this solution, you will create an article element that will contain the information from Marco Casario's profile from LinkedIn, and you will add two aside elements—one associated with the article, and one associated with the page.

Start by inserting the semantic elements for the article:

```
<article>
<h1>
Marco Casario Profile
</h1>
<p>
Marco has been passionate about information technology since he was little more than a child
and used to program games in BASIC for the Commodore 64 before dedicating himself, while still
very young, to innovative projects for the web using Flash and Director.
In 2001, he began to collaborate with Macromedia Italy. Since then, he has produced and headed
a long series of presentations, conferences, and articles, which you can find listed in detail
in his blog (casario.blogs.com), which currently receives several thousand unique visits every
day.
</p>
<p>

In 2005, Marco founded Comtaste (www.comtaste.com), a company dedicated to exploring new
frontiers in RIAs and the convergence between the web and the world of mobile devices.
MobyMobile (www.mobymobile.com) and YouThruBiz (www.youthrubiz.com) are representative of
their recent work.
        </p>

        <p>
        Another example of Marco's achievements is that he is founder of the biggest
worldwide Yahoo Flash Lite UG and of www.augitaly.com, a reference point for the Italian
community of Adobe users in which he carries out the role of Channel Manager for the section
dedicated to Flex (www.augitaly.com/flexgala.)
        </p>
        <p>
        Speaking Engagements:

FATC New York
TAC Singapore
Adobe MAX (Europe and US)
FlashOnTheBeach Brighton
FlexCamp London
MultiMania Belgium
FITC Amsterdam
360Flex
AJAXWorld Conference NY city
O'Reilly Web 2.0 Summit Berlin
Adobe MAX 2007
... and many others
</p>

        </article>
```

You need to add text in a lateral box to this content. The position of this lateral box and its style will be defined by CSS statements. First, insert an aside element into the article:

```
<article>
<h1>
Marco Casario Profile
</h1>
<p>
Marco has been passionate about information technology since he was little more than a child
and used to program games in BASIC for Commodore 64 before dedicating himself, while still
very young, to innovative projects for the web using Flash and Director.
In 2001, he began to collaborate with Macromedia Italy. Since then, he has produced and headed
a long series of presentations, conferences, and articles, which you can find listed in detail
in his blog (casario.blogs.com), which currently receives several thousand unique visits every
day.
</p>
<aside>
 <h4 id="quote">Marco is an Adobe Certified Instructor for Flex 3 and AIR (ACI) and an Adobe
Certified Expert for LiveCycle Platform, Flash, and Dreamweaver.
<p id="author">
<a href="http://casario.blogs.com">
Visit his personal blog !</a></p>
</h4>
</aside>

<p>

In 2005, Marco founded Comtaste (www.comtaste.com) a company dedicated to exploring new
frontiers in RIAs and the convergence between the web and the world of mobile devices.
MobyMobile (www.mobymobile.com) and YouThruBiz (www.youthrubiz.com) are representative of
their recent work.
        </p>


        <p>
        Another example of Marco's achievements is that he is founder of the biggest
worldwide Yahoo Flash Lite UG and of www.augitaly.com, a reference point for the Italian
community of Adobe users in which he carries out the role of Channel Manager for the section
dedicated to Flex (www.augitaly.com/flexgala.)
        </p>
        <p>
        Speaking Engagements:

FATC New York
TAC Singapore
Adobe MAX (Europe and US)
FlashOnTheBeach Brighton
FlexCamp London
MultiMania Belgium
```

```
FITC Amsterdam
360Flex
AJAXWorld Conference NY city
O'Reilly Web 2.0 Summit Berlin
Adobe MAX 2007
... and many others
</p>

</article>
```

Insert another aside element, but this time outside the article. With this in place, the content will relate to the entire page:

```
<aside>
<h4>He is author of the following books:</h4>
<ul>
<li>HTML5 Solutions: Essential Techniques for HTML5 Developers (Apress)
</li><li>Flex 4 Cookbook (O'Reilly)
</li><li>Professional Flash Catalyst (Wrox)
</li><li>AIR Cookbook (O'Reilly)
</li><li>Advanced AIR Applications (FOED)
</li><li>The Essential Guide to AIR with Flash CS4 (FOED)
</li><li>Flex Solutions: Essential Techniques for Flex 3 Developers (FOED)
</li></ul>

</aside>
```

The external aside element contains a list of elements; that is, all the books by the author.

All you have to do now is to create the CSS statements to add a bit of formatting and positioning.

Create a style block and insert the styles for the aside element into the article:

```
<style>

article aside {

  width: 270px;

  text-align: center;

  margin: 0;

  padding: 0;

  font-family: georgia, serif;

  font-size: 140%;
```

```
   letter-spacing: -1px;

   line-height: 1em;

   color: #555;
   float: right;
   }

#quote {

   margin: 0 10px 0 0;
   padding: 20px 20px 10px 20px;

}

#author {

margin: 0 10px 0 0;
padding: 0 0 10px 0;
color: #999;

font-size: 60%;
   }

#author a {

   margin: 0 10px 0 0;

   padding: 0 0 10px 0;

   color: #999;

   }

</style>
```

Save the file and open it in a browser. The final result, with the two aside elements, is shown in Figure 3-9.

Marco Casario Profile

Marco has been passionate about informatics since he was little more than a child and used to program games in Basic for Commodore 64 before dedicating himself, while still very young, to innovative projects for the web using Flash and Director. In 2001, he began to collaborate with Macromedia Italy. Since that year he has produced and headed a long series of presentations, conferences and articles, which you can find listed in detail in his blog (casario.blogs.com), which is currently receiving several thousands of unique visitors every day.

In 2005, Marco has founded Comtaste (www.comtaste.com) a company dedicated to exploring new frontiers in RIAs and the convergence between the web and the world of mobile devices—MobyMobile (www.mobymobile.com) and YouThruBiz (www.youthrubiz.com) are representative of their recent work.

Another example of Marco's achievements is that he is founder of the biggest worldwide Yahoo Flash Lite UG and of www.augitaly.com, a reference point for the Italian community of Adobe users, in which he carries out the role of Channel Manager for the section dedicated to Flex (www.augitaly.com/flexgala.)

Speaking Engagements: FATC New York TAC Singapore Adobe MAX (Europe and US) FlashOnTheBeach Brighton FlexCamp London MultiMania Belgium FITC Amsterdam 360Flex AJAXWorld Conference NY city O'Reilly Web 2.0 Summit Berlin Adobe MAX 2007 ... and many others

He is author of the following book project:

- HTML 5 Solutions (Apress)
- Flex 4 Cookbook (O'Reilly)
- Professional Flash Catalyst (Wrox)
- AIR Cookbook (O'Reilly)
- Advanced AIR Applications (FOED)
- The Essential Guide to AIR with Flash CS4
- Flex Solutions: Essential Techniques for Flex 3 Developers (FOED)

Marco is an Adobe Certified Instructor for Flex 3 an AIR (ACI) and an Adobe CertifiedExpert for: Livecycle Platform, Flash, and Dreamweaver.

Visit his personal blog!

Figure 3-9. The box on the right adds further content to the article, while the list on the bottom references the entire page.

The aside element is very useful in semantic terms for your web pages. Furthermore, search engines are better able to index the pages that use these new HTML5 tags.

Summary

Although talk of using semantic HTML has been around since HTML's birth, only HTML5 has implemented serious improvements in this area.

Instead of using HTML tags such as `<div>` and `<span>` for absolutely everything, it's now possible to use specific HTML5 tags for their implied meaning. In fact, a great number of new elements have been introduced in HTML5 to provide better definition and structure to web pages.

In this chapter, you've learned how to use these techniques and elements to create a semantic structure for a web page using microdata and vocabulary, which allows you to specify machine-readable custom elements in a web page by using a syntax consisting of name-value pairs with existing content. A custom vocabulary enables the structure that you create to define the name-value pair group that can be reused by other developers and that is recognized by search engines. You've also learned about link types and relations in this chapter. These allow you, not only to indicate the browser the page or the resource to which you are pointing, but also why you are pointing to it. Next, we covered the figure container, which associates text with an image that acts as its legend. Finally, you studied the `aside` element. This element represents content that is tangentially related to the content and that forms the main textual flow of a document.

In Chapter 4, you will study forms, which are used in all web applications.

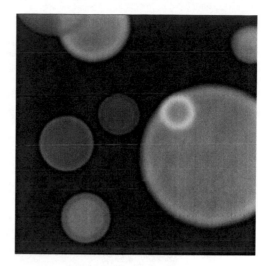

Chapter 4

HTML5 Forms

Forms are an essential part of any web application that requires input by the user.

Since first created with HTML 2.0 specifications, forms have allowed us to make web pages interactive. In fact, through form controls, it is possible for the user to interact with and insert various types of information, which can then be sent to the server to be processed.

HTML 4 provided pretty basic form controls, which were usually text fields and most of the interactivity happened on the server side. Validation of a type of data inserted onto a form control is a classic example of operations that were carried out on the server side with HTML 4, unless they used JavaScript or AJAX frameworks.

With HTML5 forms today, it is possible to develop applications with a high-level end user experience faster and more efficiently. Unfortunately, browser compatibility varies widely, and not all new form elements are supported yet. Figure 4-1 illustrates support for some of the new HTML5 form elements in various browsers and operating systems:

	MAC				WIN								
	OPERA	FIREFOX	SAFARI	CHROME	OPERA	FIREFOX		SAFARI	IE				CHROME	
	10.63	3.6	5	7	10.63	3.6	4.03	5	6	7	8	9	7	8
Form: Search	✘	✘	✔	✔	✘	✘	✔	✔	✘	✘	✘	✘	✔	✔	38%
Form: Phone	✘	✘	✔	✔	✘	✘	✔	✔	✘	✘	✘	✘	✔	✔	38%
Form: URL	✔	✘	✔	✔	✔	✘	✘	✔	✘	✘	✘	✘	✔	✔	38%
Form: Email	✔	✘	✔	✔	✔	✘	✘	✔	✘	✘	✘	✘	✔	✔	38%
Form: DateTime	✔	✘	✘	✘	✔	✘	✘	✘	✘	✘	✘	✘	✘	✘	4%
Form: Date	✔	✘	✘	✘	✔	✘	✘	✘	✘	✘	✘	✘	✘	✘	4%
Form: Month	✔	✘	✘	✘	✔	✘	✘	✘	✘	✘	✘	✘	✘	✘	4%
Form: Week	✔	✘	✘	✘	✔	✘	✘	✘	✘	✘	✘	✘	✘	✘	4%
Form: Time	✔	✘	✘	✘	✔	✘	✘	✘	✘	✘	✘	✘	✘	✘	4%
Form: LocalTime	✔	✘	✘	✘	✔	✘	✘	✘	✘	✘	✘	✘	✘	✘	4%
Form: Number	✔	✘	✘	✘	✔	✘	✘	✘	✘	✘	✘	✘	✘	✔	5%
Form: Range	✔	✘	✔	✔	✔	✘	✘	✔	✘	✘	✘	✘	✔	✔	37%
Form: Colour	✘	✘	✘	✘	✘	✘	✘	✘	✘	✘	✘	✘	✘	✘	

Figure 4-1.The Web Designers' HTML5 & CSS3 Checklist, published by www.findmebyip.com/litmus/. The checklist shows browsers support for some of the new HTML5 form elements.

As time passes, browser support will grow more and more consistent with HTML specifications, so all it will take is patience before we can make our forms visible to everyone.

Understanding the new input types

HTML5 forms introduce a new set of tools to make form development easier and richer.

Here are some of the new form elements introduced by HTML5:

- keygen element
- output element
- progress element
- meter element
- e-mail input type
- url input type

- date picker element

- time, datetime, month, and week elements

- number input type

- search input type

- range input type

- tel input type

- color input type

Other than input types, HTML5 introduces several new attributes that can be used within a form such as list, autofocus, placeholder, required, multiple, pattern, autocomplete, min and max, and step.

Even the grammar for the declaration of form elements changes with HTML5. In fact, now you can declare a form element at any point of the page and associate with a form object by using the form attribute of the element:

```
<form id="myForm" />
<input type="text" form="myForm" />
```

In this example, the text input is declared outside of the form tag (called form owner), but it is still associated with the myForm form with the form attribute.

In the following solutions, we show the potential of the new HTML5 forms.

Solution 4-1: Using the e-mail input type

The <input type="email"> tag creates a form element that expects to receive a valid e-mail address from the user. The form control obviously doesn't verify whether or not the e-mail address actually exists, only if the text the user inserts into the field uses valid syntax.

From the user's point of view, using this input type in the HTML form doesn't change the look and feel much. The element is, in fact, rendered in the browser as a normal text input (apart from Opera, which uses an e-mail icon next to the text field, as shown in Figure 4-2).

Figure 4-2. The Opera browser adds a small icon into the e-mail input type.

What changes is the validation operation that instead is executed in the background of the browser, which returns an error if the e-mail address isn't validated. This verification changes from browser to browser. With Opera, for example, including *@* in the input is enough for it to be accepted; whereas in Safari, Chrome, and Firefox, you need to enter at least *@-.- (a character before and after the @ symbol and a period followed by a character).

What's involved

To use the new e-mail input type, it's enough to use the following markup:

```
<input type="email" />
```

Table 4-1 shows a list of valid attributes for this input type.

Table 4-1. Valid Attributes Accepted by the E-mail Input Type

Attributes	Description
name	Contains the name of the name/value pair associated with this element for the purposes of form submission.
disabled	Sets a disabled control.
type	Specifies that its input element is a control for editing an e-mail address or list of e-mail addresses given in the element's value.
form	The container for all the form elements.
autocomplete	Stores the value entered by the user.
autofocus	Puts the focus on the element once it has been loaded.
maxlength	The maximum allowed value length of the element.
list	Specifies that the element represents a disabled control.
pattern	Specifies a regular expression against which the value will be checked.
readonly	Represents a control whose value is not meant to be edited.
required	Specifies if the element is mandatory.
size	The number of options meant to be shown by the control represented by its element.
placeholder	The text shown in the input element (intended to help the user when entering data into the control).
multiple	Allows you to specify multiple e-mail or file values for an input element.
value	Contains an e-mail address or a list of e-mail addresses.

How to build it

The following code example shows how to use the new e-mail input type:

```
<!DOCTYPE html>
<html>
  <head>
    <title>
     Solution 4-1: Using the email input type
    </title>
  </head>
```

```
  <body>

<form id="myForm">
<fieldset>
  <legend>Solution 4-1: Using the email input type</legend>

      <label for="name">Name</label>
      <input id="name" name="name" type="text"/><br/>
      <label for="email">Email</label>
      <input id="email" name="email" type="email"/><br/>
      <input type="submit" value="Submit"/>
</fieldset>
</form>
</body>
</html>
```

Right after the creation of the tag form, a fieldset tag has been declared. This element specifies a set of form controls, optionally grouped under a common name given by the first legend element.

In the code example, the name of the fieldset is:

```
<legend>Solution 4-1: Using the email input type</legend>
```

Then an input text is declared for the name of the user as well as one for the e-mail address. For both the input types, a label element is associated through the for attribute, referring to the id of the input:

```
<label for="name">Name</label>
<input id="name" name="name" type="text"/><br/>
<label for="email">Email</label>
<input id="email" name="email" type="email"/><br/>
```

The form ends with a button to submit the data.

If you open the file in Opera 12 and an invalid value is inserted for the e-mail address, an error message is returned and the form won't be submitted when the submit button is clicked, as shown in Figure 4-3.

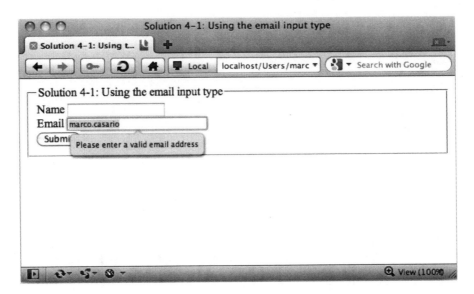

Figure 4-3. Opera shows an error message if the e-mail address is not accepted as being valid.

If the user inserts a valid e-mail address, no message will appear and the form will be submitted.

In Firefox, Internet Explorer, and Chrome, no error message will be shown to users.

In order to get an error message, we will have to wait for a future version of these browsers (or use JavaScript) before we can use this interesting feature, which will finally allow us to validate a client e-mail address on the client instead of server side.

Expert tips

Users of touch-screen mobile devices, such as iPhone, iPad, and Android OS devices, will have a pleasant surprise when they use the e-mail input type to navigate the web page.

For some of these devices, the browser is able to recognize the new HTML5 input types, and the devices change the on-screen keyboard to help users with that kind of input. This means a better user experience!

In fact, these devices show the virtual keyboard with the @ and period symbols included on the primary screen when inputting text, as shown in Figure 4-4.

Figure 4-4. The iPhone and iPad browser supports the new e-mail input types, and it shows an e-mail-enabled virtual keyboard.

Solution 4-2: Using the URL input type

Nowadays, the user is inserting web addresses into forms with increasing frequency. Whether it's the URL to his or her personal website, blog, or LinkedIn account, until now this element was normally managed with a simple text input. HTML5 now introduces a new input type to manage this type of text by respecting Internet address standards.

At the moment, support for the URL input element is pretty bad. For example, in the Opera browser, which appears to be the only web browser that recognizes the new tag, this element is only partially supported. Here is what it does:

- Opera automatically adds the `http://` suffix, even if you only insert a short form address such as `www.comtaste.com`.

- It shows a list of recently-visited sites (from browsing history).

- Unlike the e-mail input type, no validation is carried out for this kind of input.

- Safari on iPhone will dynamically display the ".com" button on the on-screen keyboard.

- Browsers that don't support this input type will treat the element like a normal text input.

What's involved

To create a URL input element, all you have to do is specify the attribute `type` of the tag input:

```
<input type="url" />
```

This way, the URL type will be used for input fields that contain a URL address.

The data type accepted by the control is an absolute URI (Universal Resource Identifier).

> Note: Oftentimes, people use the terms URI and URL (Universal Resource Locator) interchangeably. What you need to know is that a URL is a subset of the URI protocols, such as `http://`, `ftp://`, and `mailto:`. Therefore, all URLs are URIs.

How to build it

Starting from the example provided in the previous solution, add a URL type input control to the HTML page.

Here is the complete code:

```
<!DOCTYPE html>
<html>
  <head>
    <title>
      Solution 4-2: Using the URL input type
    </title>
  </head>

  <body>

<form id="myForm">
<fieldset>
  <legend>Solution 4-2: Using the URL input type</legend>

      <label for="name">Name</label>
      <input id="name" name="name" type="text"/><br/>
      <label for="email">Email</label>
      <input id="email" name="email" type="email"/><br/>

      <label for="blog">Blog</label>
      <input id="blog" name="blog" type="url"/><br/>

      <input type="submit" value="Submit"/>

</fieldset>
</form>

</body>
</html>
```

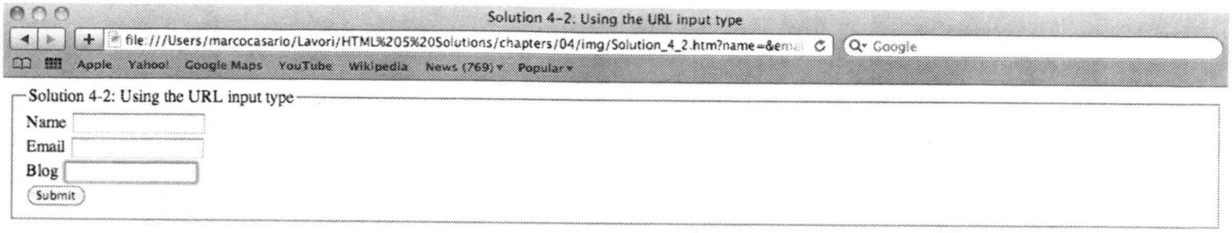

Figure 4-5. Safari doesn't support the URL input type, which it renders as simple text input.

When you open the file with Chrome, Internet Explorer, or Safari, you won't notice any difference compared to a simple text field, as shown in Figure 4-5.

Solution 4-3: Using a spinner control for numbers

Working with numbers is always more complex than you would imagine. For example, a user can very easily insert an undesirable value in a text field that expects to receive a number.

A classic example is a quantity field in an e-commerce website. When you pick an object to buy and click on the Add to Shopping cart button, you will also be asked to insert the quantity of the item to buy. Some websites have a simple text field for quantity, as shown in Figure 4-6.

Figure 4-6. The Quantity field requires a simple text input.

The user can insert any value in this field, so what happens if the user inserts a letter or a non-valid symbol by mistake?

The application will have to verify it on the client or server side to avoid passing invalid information that the e-commerce system rejects (or sends and invoices the incorrect quantity).

Some sites, such as Amazon, solves the problem of invalid data-type entry by using a combo box control, as shown in Figure 4-7.

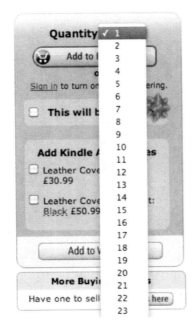

Figure 4-7. Amazon lets the user insert the quantity from a combo box.

HTML5 helps developers by adding a spinner control to the tool arsenal.

A *spinner control* is a text input control with up and down arrows. The result is a single-line text input that can be spun to display each number in the text field, as shown in Figure 4-8:

> Solution 4-3: Using the Number input type
>
> Choose your magic number: 2

Figure 4-8. The spinner control, rendered by Google Chrome

The user can click on the arrows to change the number value he or she wants to put into the form.

By using this form element, the user can't make a mistake when filling out the form because the numbers provided are all valid.

Browsers that don't support this new tag render the component like a simple text field.

What's involved

Regardless of the fact that the control you see has a built-in navigation mechanism that allows the user to change the numerical value in the text field (without being able to directly edit it), the developer doesn't have to do anything.

All you need to do is use the number value as the type attribute for this input in order to inherit all these functions:

```
<input type="number" />
```

The increase and decrease mechanism of the value will work automatically.

Some attributes allow you to customize the control. These properties allow you to set a maximum and minimum value and the unit to use for the increase and decrease mechanism. These specific properties are listed in Table 4-2.

Table 4-2. Valid Attributes Accepted by the Number Input Type

Attributes	Description
max	A floating-point number that contains the maximum numeric value to be used and shown in the input tag.
min	A floating-point number that contains the minimum numeric value to be used and shown in the input tag.
step	Contains the unit to increment the element's value.
value	A string representing a number.

Note: Using these properties, developers can determine how the number input element will behave and which values will be passed from the control to the server.

How to build it

Most of the work involved in the creation of a spinner control is done by the browser and its level of support for this tag.

All the developer has to do is insert a number type input.

Here is an example:

```
<!DOCTYPE html>
<html>
  <head>
    <title>
     Solution 4-3: Using a spinner control for numbers
    </title>
  </head>
  <body>
```

```
<form id="myForm">
<fieldset>
  <legend>Solution 4-3: Using a spinner control for numbers</legend>
      <label>Choose your magic number: </label>
      <input type="number" min="0" max="100" step="1" value="1"/>
</fieldset>
</form>

</body>
</html>
```

We created a number type input control with the following properties:

```
min="0"
max="100"
step="1"
```

This means that when the user clicks on the up or down arrows, the value will increase or decrease by one unit (step=1), but he or she cannot insert any value below zero or over 100.

How this control is rendered depends on the browser. In Figure 4-9, we show how Safari (left) and Opera (right) display this object.

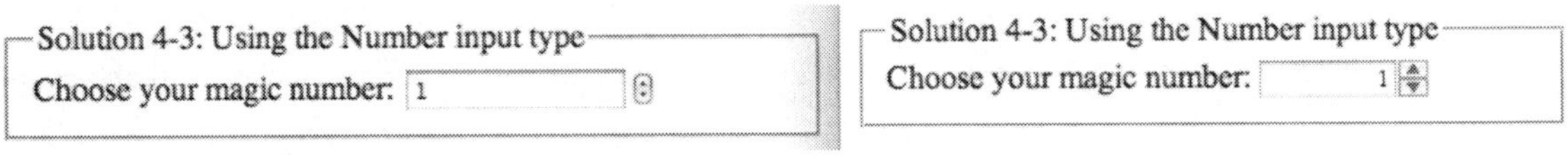

Figure 4-9. The number input type, rendered by Safari (left) and Opera (right)

The browsers in some tablets, however, behave differently. Figure 4-10 shows how the browser used by the 7-inch Samsung Galaxy Tab, based on Android 2.2, renders the input control as a simple text input. However, it dynamically displays the numeric on-screen keyboard:

Figure 4-10. The number input type, rendered by a Samsung Galaxy Tab tablet

Expert tips

There are a couple of interesting methods that you can use with JavaScript for the number input type. They are:

stepUp(n): increase the field's value by n

stepDown(n): decrease the field's value by n

valueAsNumber: return the value of the element, interpreted as a number

Solution 4-4: Adding a slider to your form with the range input type

Another interesting component HTML5 provides that is used to work with numbers and forms is the slider.

A *slider component* is a form control that allows the user to adjust values within a finite range along one or two axes. The user selects a value by sliding a graphical thumb between the end points of a track that corresponds to a range of values.

Like the spinner, this control also helps you avoid mistakes.

Sliders are very popular in web applications, especially in configurators such as the page in the Kayak.com website shown in Figure 4-11.

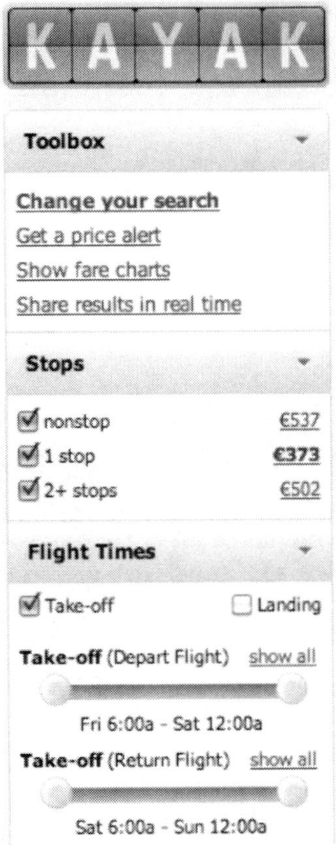

Figure 4-11. The slider controls are used to help the user to choose among a range of values.

The user interacts with the thumb object to change the numeric value in the input. In the case of Kayak.com, the user changes departure times for air travel.

Slider creation before HTML5 involved designing graphical elements for the user interface of the element and programming the behavioral logic of the control with JavaScript. With HTML5, this control is now native to the browser, including all aspects linked to accessibility for keyboard users (see Chapter 12).

What's involved

The markup to create a slider control in a form is very easy. You just need to specify the range as the input type and its attributes:

```
<input type="range" min="1" max="10" step="1" value="6"/>
```

Like the number input type, the properties allow you to set the minimum and maximum value as well as the units to use for the increase and decrease functions.

Table 4-3 lists these specific properties.

Table 4-3. Valid Attributes Accepted by the Range Input Type

Attributes	Description
max	It's a floating-point number that contains the maximum numeric value to be used and shown in the input tag.
min	It's a floating-point number that contains the minimum numeric value to be used and shown in the input tag.
step	Contains the unit to be used as the increment or decrement value of the element's value.
value	A string representing a number.

This new input type is supported by many browsers in their most recent versions: Opera, Safari, Chrome, and Internet Explorer.

How to build it

The developer doesn't have to do much for this solution either. Alternatively, you can use the <input> markup and assign the range value to the type attribute. The browser will do the rest.

Here is a complete example:

```
<!DOCTYPE html>
<html>
  <head>
    <title>
      Solution 4-4: Adding a slider to your form with the range input type
    </title>
  </head>

  <body>

<form id="myForm">
<fieldset>
  <legend>Solution 4-4: Adding a slider to your form with the range input type</legend>

    <label>Choose your magic number: </label>
    <input type="range" min="1" max="10" step="1" value="1"/>

    <br/>
</fieldset>
</form>

</body>
</html>
```

When you open this example in the browser, it will appear as shown in Figure 4-12.

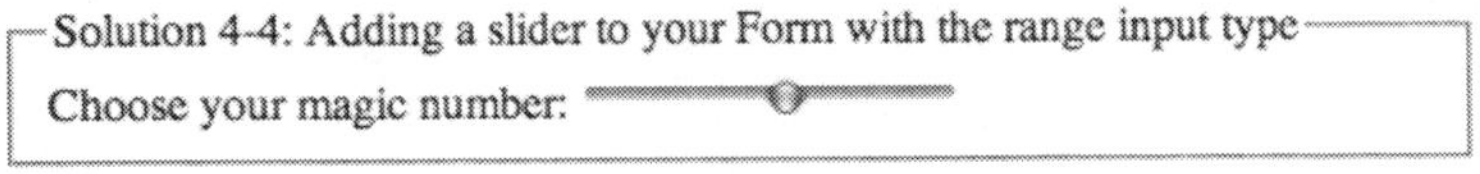

Solution 4-4: Adding a slider to your Form with the range input type

Choose your magic number: ▭▭▭▭O▭▭▭▭

Figure 4-12. The range input type, rendered by the Chrome browser

The interactivity of the control input is applied by the browser automatically, and the user can use the thumb element to change the value.

Expert tips

There is a new element in HTML5 that allows you to display calculated results: <output>. This element can be used, for example, to show the numerical value that the user has selected in the slider.

In the following example, we have changed the code of the solution so that the selected value is shown in the <output> element every time the user moves the slider:

```
<form id="myForm">
<fieldset>
  <legend>Solution 4-4: Adding a slider to your Form with the range input type</legend>

      <label>Choose your magic number: </label>
      <input type="range" min="1" max="10" step="1" value="6"
             onchange="myOutput.value=this.value"/>

      <br/>

      <label>This is the selected value: </label>
      <output name="myOutput"> 6 </output>


</fieldset>
</form>
```

In the <input type="range"> tag, we added the following statement in the onchange event, which is triggered each time the user moves the thumb element in the slider:

```
<input type="range" min="1" max="10" step="1" value="6"
       onchange="myOutput.value=this.value"/>
```

myOutput is the name of the output element declared in the following line:

```
<output name="myOutput"> 6 </output>
```

Strangely enough, browsers in mobile devices such as the iPhone, iPad, and Android devices do not support this form control currently; they render it as a simple text box.

The keyboard doesn't event change dynamically to be optimized for numeric input.

Solution 4-5: Sending multiple files

It was already possible to send any kind of file from your computer to a remote server with the older versions of HTML by using the form, and the <input type = file> in particular.

This form control, however, had the limit of being able to send only one file at a time. If the user wanted to upload a photo album and thus send several photos, the developer had to use other technologies, such as Flash or JavaScript, to provide this feature.

Now, with HTML5 and with the addition of an attribute, it is possible to manage everything without using any external language.

What's involved

HTML5 introduces a new attribute to the file input type, multiple, to improve file upload usability. Multiple is a Boolean attribute that indicates whether the user should be allowed to specify more than one value. It's specified inline to the markup input tag:

```
<input type="file" multiple />
```

This attribute is supported by the latest versions of Safari, Chrome, Firefox, Internet Explorer, and Opera.

The input control will be rendered according to the browser, with a simple text input with a button on the side to select the files (e.g., Opera), or with only a button (e.g., Chrome and Safari).

Opera also changes the label of the button if the multiple attribute is declared with "Add Files" text, as you can see in Figure 4-13 and Figure 4-14.

Figure 4-13. The button's label, shown in Opera and changed when the multiple attribute is set

Figure 4-14. The button's label for a file input type in Opera, if the multiple attribute is not specified

Other browsers, such as Chrome, use the same button label used for a simple file input type. However, they specify the number of selected files for the user (but not their file names, as Opera and Firefox do), as shown in Figure 4-15.

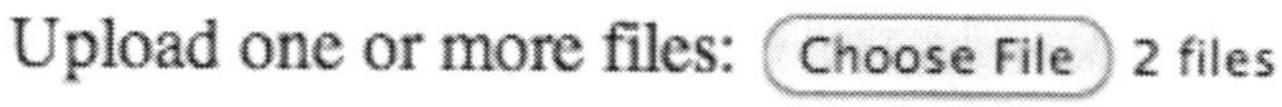

Figure 4-15. Chrome rendering the file input type for multiple attributes, with the same button label but specifying the number of selected files

To carry out a multiple selection, the user will use the SHIFT or CTRL or CMD keys after having clicked on the Choose Files or Add Files button.

How to build it

From a technical point of view, the only thing you need to be aware of to allow the user to upload multiple files is to add the multiple attribute in the declaration of the tag file input type.

Here is a complete example:

```
<!DOCTYPE html>
<html>
  <head>
    <title>
      Solution 4-5: Sending multiple files
    </title>
  </head>

  <body>

<form id="myForm">
<fieldset>
  <legend>Solution 4-5: Sending multiple files</legend>

    <label>Upload one or more files:</label>

     <input type="file" name="multipleFileUpload" multiple />

    <br />

</fieldset>
</form>

</body>
</html>
```

Expert tips

The files that the user selects will have to be sent to the server and processed using server-side language. Some programming languages, such as PHP, require you to add brackets to the name attribute of the tag to send multiple files:

```
<input name="filesUploaded[]" type="file" multiple />
```

By doing so, PHP will construct an array data type, which will contain the uploaded files on the server. If you don't specify the brackets, the programming language will process the files in order and only provide the last file in your script.

Solution 4-6: Creating a suggest-like autocomplete with the data list component

In this day and age, any user likes an autocomplete system that helps simplify their web experience.

In the past, creating such a system was a not so simple a task. It could require quite a few hours of work. You can find various solutions and libraries for free or at some expense by searching the Web.

With HTML5 the new <datalist> markup was introduced. This tag denotes a set of option elements that represent predefined options for other controls. Therefore, it can be associated with a form control, such as a text input. When the control gets the focus, it will provide a list of predefined options to the user as data is filled in, as well as enabling the user to type something in on their own.

Older browsers, or those that don't support datalists, will render a simple text field.

What's involved

To associate a <datalist> tag to an <input> control, you use a list attribute:

```
<input list="food" name="food"/>
<datalist id="food">

</datalist>
```

In the code snippet above, the list attribute links the <input> element to the <datalist> tag by the <datalist> tag's id.

Once you've associated the datalist element to the input control, you can specify the values that will be suggested when the user selects that input. To specify these values, you use the <option> tag within the <datalist> tag:

```
<input list="food" name="food"/>
<datalist id="food">

<option value="Spaghetti Aglio e Olio">
<option value="Lasagne">
<option value="Fusilli al pesto">
<option value="Rigatoni alla Carbonara">

</datalist>
```

There is nothing else to type. The browser will do the rest.

How to build it

Here is a complete example of how to use the datalist element:

```
<!DOCTYPE html>
<html>
  <head>
    <title>
```

```
    Solution 4-6: Creating a suggest-like autocomplete with the data list component
  </title>
</head>

<body>

<form id="myForm">
<fieldset>
  <legend>Solution 4-6: Creating a suggest-like autocomplete with the data list
 component</legend>

  <label> Enter your favorite movies:<br/>
  <input type="text" name="movies" list="movies"/>
  <datalist id="movies">
   <option value="Star Wars">
   <option value="The Godfather">
   <option value="Goodfellas">
  </datalist>
 </label>

 <p>

  <label> This is your favorite movie:
  <output name="myOutput" onforminput="this.value=movies.value" />
  </label>

 </p>
</fieldset>
</form>

</body>
</html>
```

The datalist is associated to a text input:

```
<input type="text" name="movies" list="movies"/>
  <datalist id="movies">
   <option value="Star Wars">
   <option value="The Godfather">
   <option value="Goodfellas">
  </datalist>
```

When the user goes to the text input control to insert a value, the browsers that support this new markup will pop up a menu right under the input control with the values suggested in the datalist. Figure 4-16 shows this functionality, implemented in Opera.

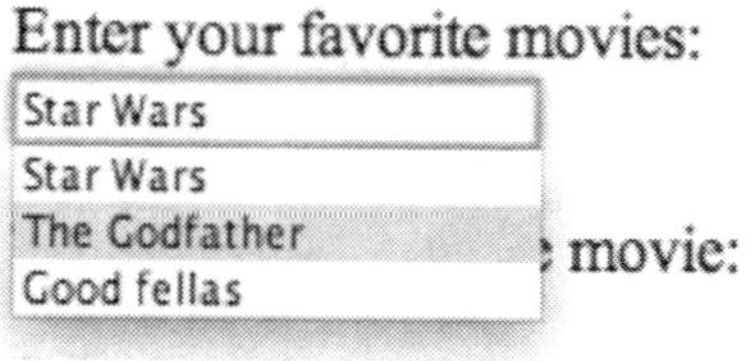

Enter your favorite movies:

| Star Wars |
| Star Wars |
| The Godfather |
| Good fellas |

movie:

Figure 4-16. The suggested options are shown right below the input text box.

Furthermore, when the user selects a value from the menu, this value will be displayed in the output element that has been associated with the following statement on the onforminput event:

```
<output name="myOutput" onforminput="this.value=movies.value" />
```

The onforminput event is executed when a form receives user input. The final result is shown in Figure 4-17.

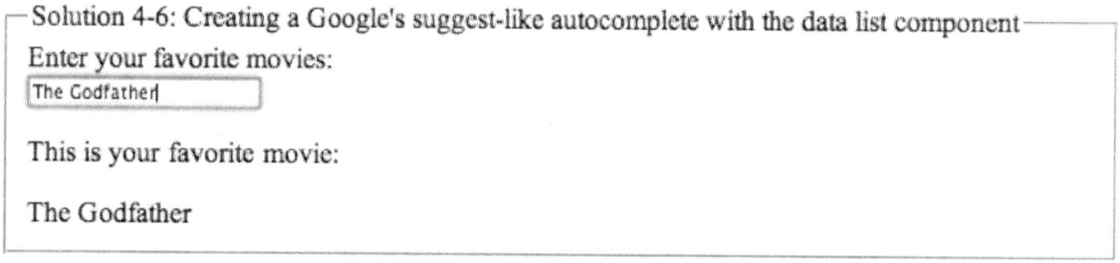

Solution 4-6: Creating a Google's suggest-like autocomplete with the data list component

Enter your favorite movies:

| The Godfather |

This is your favorite movie:

The Godfather

Figure 4-17. When the user selects one of the options, the value is written in the output element.

Expert tips

To make your code compatible with older browsers and with those that don't support datalist, you can use the <select> tag.

By doing so, this tag will only be displayed in browsers that don't support the datalist elements:

```
<label> Enter your favorite movies:<br/>
<input type="text" name="movies" list="movies"/>
<datalist id="movies">

<label> or select one from the list:
<select name="movies">
 <option value="Star Wars">
 <option value="The Godfather">
 <option value="Goodfellas">
</select>
 </label>

 </datalist>
</label>
```

Solution 4-7: Validating form controls

In the first solution in this chapter, we showed you how to use built-in mechanisms to validate an e-mail input type. This function is new to HTML5.

When you work with forms, validation of data is definitely an important aspect that may require quite a lot of effort. We often resort to mixed validation systems. With JavaScript or AJAX frameworks (such as JQuery, Dojo, and MooTools), you can make client-side validations and you can develop server-side validating procedures with server-side languages (PHP, Python, Java, and so on).

Thanks to the insertion of new attributes in HTML5, you can delegate some data verification functions to the browser and reduce the effort required for these kinds of operations (at least from the client side).

What's involved

Some form controls inherit validation systems without having to write any code. In Solution 4-1, we showed how the validation mechanism for an e-mail type text input works automatically by only declaring the markup:

```
<input type="email" />
```

The same can be said for the URL and number markups, `<input type="url">` and `<input type="number">`.

There is, however, an attribute that can be used to specify the presence of a compulsory field in a form, which you can't leave empty.

To request this kind of validation, you need to use `required` in the input control:

```
<input type="text" required />
```

This attribute is Boolean. When specified, the element is required.

Browsers that support this attribute display an error message or insert a red border on the field that generated the error and won't submit the form.

How to build it

For this solution, modify the code from Solution 4-2 by adding the `required` attribute for two of the three fields.

Here is the complete code:

```
<!DOCTYPE html>
<html>
  <head>


    <title>
```

```
      Solution 4-7: Validating form controls
    </title>

  </head>

  <body>

<form id="myForm">
<fieldset>
  <legend>Solution 4-7: Validating form controls </legend>

      <label for="name">Name</label>
      <input id="name" name="name" type="text" placeholder="Insert your first name" required↪
  /><br/>
      <label for="email">Email</label>
      <input id="email" name="email" type="email" placeholder="Insert your email" required↪
  /><br/>

      <label for="blog">Blog</label>
      <input id="blog" name="blog" type=url placeholder="Insert your blog"/><br/>

      <p>
       <input type-"submit" value-"Submit"/>
      </p>

</fieldset>
</form>

</body>
</html>
```

If you open the file and try sending the form without any data in the two required fields, the browser will not allow you to submit the form if the mandatory fields are empty, and you will obtain the result shown in Figure 4-18.

Figure 4-18. The browser shows an error message for mandatory field (Opera).

One important aspect regarding the usability of the form suggests that the mandatory fields have to provide the user with a visual or textual clue informing them of the required data. One convention is to insert an asterisk (*) symbol next to the required field.

You can add some text and graphic clues with CSS by using the pseudo-classes :valid, :invalid, :optional, and :required.

A form element is :required or :optional if a value for it is, respectively, required or optional before the form to which it belongs is submitted.

You can learn more about this topic by reading this article: www.w3.org/TR/css3-ui/#pseudo-validity. All you have to do is use these pseudo-classes to make the fields more stable. Change the code from before by adding a <style> block, as follows:

```
<!DOCTYPE html>
<html>
  <head>
    <style>

   #myForm .required:after { content: " * "; color:red;}

   #myForm input:required { background:red; color:white; }

    </style>

    <title>
     Solution 4-7: Validating form controls
    </title>

  </head>

  <body>

<form id="myForm">
<fieldset>
   <legend>Solution 4-7: Validating form controls </legend>

       <label for="name" class="required">Name</label>
       <input id="name" name="name" type="text" placeholder="Insert your first name" required↵
 /><br/>
       <label for="email" class="required">Email</label>
       <input id="email" name="email" type="email" placeholder="Insert your email" required↵
 /><br/>

       <label for="blog">Blog</label>
       <input id="blog" name="blog" type="url" placeholder="Insert your blog"/><br/>

       <p>
        <input type="submit" value="Submit"/>
       </p>

</fieldset>
</form>

  </body>
</html>
```

In the new style block, we have declared two CSS statements. The first acts on the required class and adds text after the selector with the pseudo-class :after; in our case, a * next to the label element:

```
#myForm  .required:after { content: " * "; color:red;}
```

The second statement, on the other hand, uses the required pseudo-class on the input tag changing the background color to red:

```
#myForm  input:required { background:red; }
```

The only change required in the code is in the tag label, with which you need to associate the :required class using the attribute class, so it will insert the *:

```
<label for="name" class="required">Name</label>
        <input id="name" name="name" type="text" placeholder="Insert your first name" required➙
/><br/>
        <label for="email" class="required">Email</label>
        <input id="email" name="email" type="email" placeholder="Insert your email" required
/><br/>
```

Once you've saved the file and executed it in a browser, you'll see that the CSS pseudo-classes is applied to the fields as shown in Figure 4-19.

Figure 4-19.The formatting styles are shown in the input fields (shown in Opera).

Expert tips

The built-in validation mechanism of the fields in HTML5 will be applied automatically by default. However, there are contexts in which it is necessary to use JavaScript to create more complex and robust validation routines.

In such cases, it is necessary to override the default validation system of the browser.

The novalidate attribute specifies that the form should not be validated when submitted:

```
<form id="myForm" novalidate>
<fieldset>
  <legend>Solution 4-7: Validating form controls </legend>

      <label for="name" class="required">Name</label>
      <input id="name" name="name" type="text" placeholder="Insert your first name" required➙
/><br/>
```

```
    <label for="email" class="required">Email</label>
    <input id="email" name="email" type="email" placeholder="Insert your email" required↵
/><br/>

    <label for="blog">Blog</label>
    <input id="blog" name="blog" type="url" placeholder="Insert your blog"/><br/>

    <p>
     <input type="submit" value="Submit"/>
    </p>

</fieldset>
</form>
```

You can specify this attribute at the form level, as in the example above, or within the following <input> types: text, search, URL, telephone, e-mail, password, date pickers, range, and color.

Solution 4-8: Creating custom input types using regular expressions

Regular expressions provide a powerful, concise, and flexible means for matching strings of text, such as particular characters, words, or patterns of characters. A regular expression is written in a formal language that can be interpreted by a regular expression processor, which is a program that either serves as a parser generator or examines text and identifies parts that match the provided specification. See Wikipedia for more information: http://en.wikipedia.org/wiki/Regular_expression.

HTML5 allows you to check the user's inputs and to match the input values against a regular expression.

What's involved

The code that you needed to write to use regular expressions with previous versions of HTML was as follows:

```
<input type="text" name="ssn"
onblur="if (!^\d{3}-\d{2}-\d{4}$this.value) alert(this.title+'\nAn error occurred. Please
verify your data.');" title="The Social Security Number"/>
```

On the onblur event of the input element, a JavaScript statement is executed. It controls the pattern to be applied to the data in the field, and it provides an error message if the validation wasn't successful.

With HTML5, a new attribute is available that allows you to associate a pattern of characters via regular expressions to a text input to be applied as validation of the data inserted in the field. The markup for this is really simple:

```
<input type="text" name="ssn" pattern="(!^\d{3}-\d{2}-\d{4}$"
```

The value specified in the pattern attribute must match the JavaScript pattern production as described in this document: www.ecma-international.org/publications/files/ECMA-ST/ECMA-262.pdf.

Note: Matching the JavaScript pattern implies that the regular expression language used for this attribute is the same as that used in JavaScript, except that the pattern attribute must match the entire value—not just any subset. (This is somewhat as if it implied a ^(?: at the start of the pattern and a)$ at the end.)

To provide the user with a description of the pattern, or an error reporting on the field if an invalid value is entered, you can use the attribute `title`:

```
<input type="text" name="ssn"
pattern="(!^\d{3}-\d{2}-\d{4}$"
title="The Social Security Number" />
```

How to build it

In the following solution, we use a regular expression to validate the American zip code:

```
(\d{5}([\-]\d{4})?)
```

This expression is inserted in the `pattern` attribute of the text input. Here is the complete code:

```
<!DOCTYPE html>
<html>
  <head>
    <title>
      Solution 4-8: Creating custom input types using regular expressions
    </title>

  </head>

 <body>

<form id="myForm">
<fieldset>
  <legend>Solution 4-8: Creating custom input types using regular expressions</legend>

<label> Insert a valid American Zip code:
<input type="text" name="ssn"
pattern="(\d{5}([\-]\d{4})?)"
title="Zip Code" />
</label>

<p><input type="submit" value="Check Zip code" /> </p>

</fieldset>
</form>

</body>
</html>
```

When you execute the file in a browser, such as Opera, that supports the pattern attribute, and click the submit button of the form, you will obtain the result shown in Figure 4-20.

89

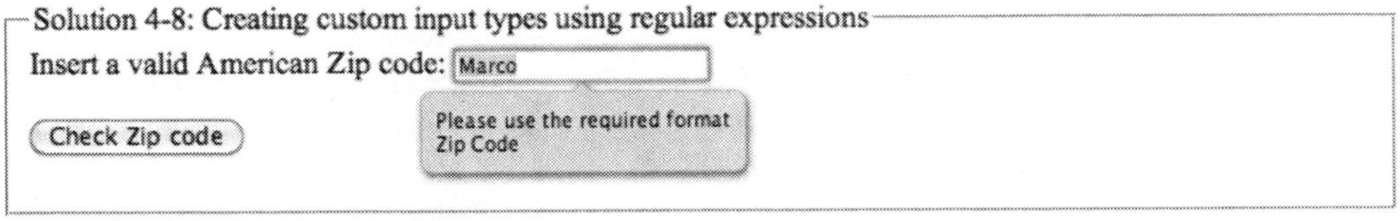

Figure 4-20. The error message shown in the text input that uses the regular expression pattern.

The browser provides control over the validity of the data that matches the regular expression specified in the attributes pattern. If it fails, it returns an error message.

Expert tips

Not all browsers support this powerful attribute yet. Fortunately, there is a library that fills this gap: Google's Web Forms 2, which you can find at the following address: `https://github.com /westonruter/webforms2`.

The project, as described on the site, is a cross-browser implementation of the WHATWG Web Forms 2.0 specification. If the library realizes when it is loaded that the browser is not compatible with some of the new HTML5 functions, such as the pattern attribute, it applies its own methods instead.

You need to import the JavaScript wbforms2_src.js library using the script tag to use the library:

```
<script type="text/javascript" src="YOUR_FOLDER/webforms2_src.js"></script>
```

It is also important for the webforms2.css and webforms2-msie.js both to be located in the same directory as webforms2.js or webforms2-p.js (whichever you decide to use).

The implementation has been tested and should work in the following browsers:

- Mozilla Firefox 1.0.8
- Mozilla Firefox 1.5.0.9
- Mozilla Firefox 2
- Internet Explorer 6
- Internet Explorer 7
- Safari 2.0.4
- Safari 3 (Windows)
- Opera 9 (native experimental implementation)

Solution 4-9: Setting placeholder text in an input field

Usability is a delicate and very important aspect of web applications and of forms in particular. Developers try to make the user experience with forms as smooth as possible by minimizing the possibilities of error when users input data. A simple but effective trick is to place text in an input field to provide a hint for the users.

Figure 4-21 shows the "Search with Google" hint text in the Opera search bar.

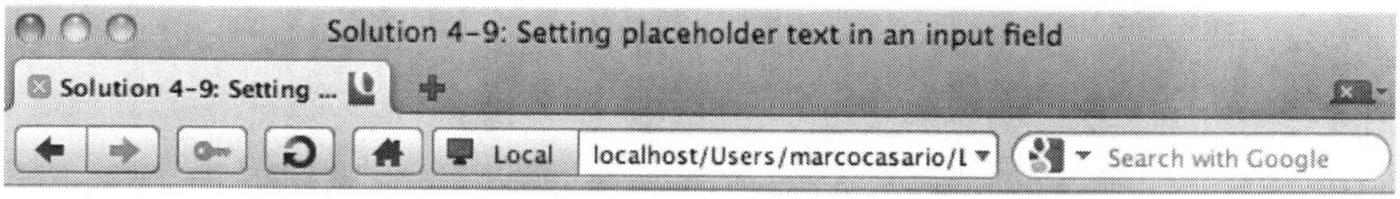

Figure 4-21. The Opera search bar uses "Search with Google" text as a hint for users.

Even if it was simple in the past to create this kind of feature, you still had to use JavaScript.

HTML5 introduces a new smart attribute associated with the input controls that inserts text in the input field, but disappears if the field gets the focus or makes it reappear if It loses focus. All of this is accomplished without JavaScript code.

What's involved

The attribute that allows you to implement this functionality is the `placeholder`. It is extremely easy to use the placeholder text in a web form:

```
<input type="text" placeholder="Insert your first name"/>
```

Browsers that don't support this attribute will simply ignore it and show nothing in the field.

The attribute only allows you to manage simple text—no line feed (LF) or carriage return (CR) characters are allowed, so you can't use HTML tags or images.

How to build it

In this solution, we have made slight changes to the code of Solution 4-2 by adding the `placeholder` attribute in the input fields:

```
<!DOCTYPE html>
<html>
  <head>
    <title>
     Solution 4-9: Setting placeholder text in an input field
    </title>
  </head>

  <body>
```

```
<form id="myForm">
<fieldset>
  <legend>Solution 4-9: Setting placeholder text in an input field</legend>

      <label for="name">Name</label>
      <input id="name" name="name" type="text" placeholder="Insert your first name"/><br/>
      <label for="email">Email</label>
      <input id="email" name="email" type="email" placeholder="Insert your email"/><br/>

      <label for="blog">Blog</label>
      <input id="blog" name="blog" type="url" placeholder="Insert your blog"/><br/>

</fieldset>
</form>

</body>
</html>
```

Expert tips

If you read the specification about this attribute (at this URL: www.w3.org/TR/html5/common-input-element-attributes.html#the-placeholder-attribute), you'll learn that a usability recommendation is to use the title attribute for a longer hint or other advisory text.

Solution 4-10: Creating date and time controls

Dates and times are used frequently in forms. If you think about how often we use this data, it won't take long to realize that their accurate and effective use can help determine the success or failure of an entire site. You think I'm exaggerating?

Think about booking a flight. The information you insert in a typical form for this query is: departure airport, arrival airport, date of departure, date of return, and preferred times for outbound and return flights.

So imagine how important it is to have a form that helps the user accurately insert the information on dates and times, reducing or even excluding the possibility of error.

One of my favorite sites to use to book flights is Kayak.com, which has a very efficient flight search system (used by most travel sites). From Figure 4-22, you can see that as soon as the Departure or Return field is selected, a date picker appears on top of your form and allows you to select a date.

Figure 4-22. The date picker allows the user to insert a date from a calendar to avoid typing errors.

Also, one must consider that the date format changes according to country. Anglo-Saxon countries, such as the US and the UK, use the Month-Day-Year format, whereas most European countries use the Day-Month-Year format.

Web developers take these issues into account when developing date picker functions by using JavaScript controls, which can be found in the most common AJAX frameworks (or from the various JavaScript libraries on the Web).

HTML5 introduced a series of markups to work with dates, leaving the hard task of managing dates and times up to the browser.

What's involved

HTML5 introduces a number of different input types for handling date/time pickers:

```
<input type="date" />
<input type="time" />
```

The date type creates a date picker with a built-in mechanism to select data by browsing a calendar, as shown in Figure 4-23.

Figure 4-23. A date control, rendered by the browser (shown in Mac OSX Safari)

The input type time text input containing a separator for hours, minutes, and seconds is shown in Figure 4-24.

Select a time: 11:02

Figure 4-24. A time control, rendered by the browser (shown in Mac OSX Safari)

There are also other controls that handle date and time.

The timedate type represents a control for setting the element's value to a string representing a global date and time (with time zone information).

Moreover, you can allow the user to select a value that is a month or a week instead of a complete date. In fact, there are week and month input types:

```
<input type="month" />
<input type="week" />
```

How to build it

Here's a complete example that uses all the date and time input types that HTML5 provides:

```
<!DOCTYPE html>
<html>
  <head>
    <title>
     Solution 4-10: Creating Date and Time Controls
    </title>

  </head>
```

```
  <body>

<form id="myForm">
<fieldset>
  <legend>Solution 4-10: Creating Date and Time Controls</legend>

<p>
<label> Choose a date from the  Date Picker control:
<input type="date" />
</label>
</p>

<p>

<label>Select a time:
<input type="time" />
</label>
</p>

<p>

<label>Select a date and a time:
<input type="datetime" />
</label>
</p>

<p>

<label>Select a month:
<input type="month" />
</label>
</p>

<p>

<label>Select a week:
<input type="week" />
</label>
</p>

</fieldset>
</form>

</body>
</html>
```

Summary

All web applications use forms. In fact, forms are an essential part of any web application that requires input by the user.

HTML Version 4 provided rather basic form controls, which were text fields for the most part. Also, most of the interactivity happened on the server side. Validation of a data type inserted onto a form control is a classic example of operations that were carried out on the server side in HTML 4, unless they used JavaScript or AJAX frameworks.

In this chapter, you've learned that with HTML5 forms, it is now possible to develop applications with a high level end-user experience faster and more efficiently. In Chapter 5, you will learn how to embed a video in a web page using the new HTML5 audio and video tags.

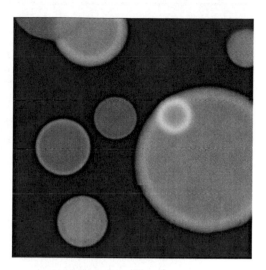

Chapter 5

HTML5 Media Elements: Audio and Video

Today the Web has truly gone multimedia. Audio and video have become an integral part of the content that we navigate through daily on the Web. Thanks to the continual increase of bandwidth and compression technologies for multimedia content, it is now common to watch a TV show on your mobile device, or a view a movie stream when you are comfortably seated in front of your TV thanks to devices enabled with Apple or Google TV technologies.

Furthermore, most TV networks offer free or fee-based content on their websites, not to mention the popularity of YouTube and similar video sharing sites.

Regardless of the great availability of multimedia content, before HTML5 there was no open standard for the delivery of multimedia on the Web. In fact, the delivery of multimedia content on the Web was (and is still) entrusted to third-party plug-ins such as QuickTime, Windows Media Player, Flash Player, and Real Player.

In the beginning it was chaos. The uneven availability of plug-ins caused those who wanted to publish videos on their websites to provide them in different formats that could be used with the most common players.

Multiple formats meant encoding the same video using different video codecs when publishing them on websites. A video codec is software that enables video compression and/or decompression for digital video. The compression usually employs lossy data compression methods. "Lossy" means that the software compresses data by losing some information from the original source. Read more about video codecs on Wikipedia at: http://en.wikipedia.org/wiki/Video_codec.

It was a bona fide war between plug-ins, and one emerged over the rest between 2005 and 2006: Adobe Flash Player.

Adobe Flash Player is a plug-in that was very popular in those early years and was installed on 90% of machines connected to the Internet. Before it was acquired by Adobe, Macromedia inserted the Flash Video format in Flash Player 7, and it didn't take long for the big companies in the industry to adopt this format so that virtually anyone could play Flash-based videos.

Flash Video is a container file format used to deliver video over the Internet using Adobe Flash Player versions 6–10. Flash Video content may also be embedded within SWF files.

There are two different video file formats known as Flash Video: FLV and F4V. The audio and video data within FLV files are encoded in the same way as they are within SWF files. Both formats are supported by Adobe Flash Player, and they are currently developed by Adobe Systems. FLV was originally developed by Macromedia.

The format has quickly established itself as the format of choice for embedded video on the Web. Notable users of the Flash Video format include YouTube, Hulu, Google Video, Yahoo! Video, Metacafe, Reuters.com, and many other news providers.

> Note: Although Flash Player and the Flash Video format are very popular and supported, Apple has decided not to support it for iOS devices (iPhone, iPad, and iPod Touch). Instead, these devices support HTML5.
>
> If you wish to investigate this topic further, start with "Thoughts on Flash" by Apple's CEO at: www.apple.com/hotnews/thoughts-on-flash/ and the Adobe CEO's reply at: blogs.wsj.com/digits/2010/04/29/live-blogging-the-journals-interview-with-adobe-ceo/.

For more information on Flash Video, visit Wikipedia at: http://en.wikipedia.org/wiki/Flash_Video.

During this time of extraordinary development, HTML offered little more than two tags to allow people to insert content that could be used by an external plug-in in a web page: the <object> and <embed> tags.

HTML5 introduced a native open standard for delivering multimedia content. Because the language specifications are still being defined, support for these new tags is only found in the versions of the browsers listed in Table 5-1.

Table 5-1. Browsers that Support the HTML5 Video and Audio Elements

Google Chrome	Internet Explorer	Safari	Firefox	Opera	iPhone	Android
3 or Up	9 or Up	3 or Up	3.5 or Up	10.5 or Up	1 or Up	2 or Up

The current problem isn't the adoption of the new markups HTML5 introduced, as HTML5 is the definition of a standard for the codecs to use (see Figure 5-1). Instead, the problem is that Ogg Theora, H.264, and VP8/WebM are currently the only formats that are supported by the video element. Which among them will be universally supported by browsers in the future? We don't yet have an answer to this question.

There is currently great debate on this issue and various points of view. The most discussed is the position of Google, which acquired On2 Technologies and has open-sourced the VP8/WebM video codec. In January 2011, Google also announced that it would remove its support for the H.264 codec from Chrome, but Apple and Microsoft will still continue to support this codec .

> Note: On2 Technologies produces the following video codecs: VP3, VP4, VP5, VP6, VP7, and VP8. Ogg Theora is derived from the proprietary VP3 codec released into the public domain by On2 Technologies.

In essence, a new battle has begun to establish the next video codec. As usual, we can only wait and see.

Browser	Latest stable release version date	Native video format support			
		Ogg Theora	H.264	VP8 (WebM)	Others
Internet Explorer	8.0 (March 19, 2009; 21 months ago)	No[note 1]	9.0[19]	No[note 2]	No[21]
Mozilla Firefox[22]	3.6.13 (December 9, 2010; 39 days ago)	3.5[23]	No[note 3]	4.0[25][26]	No
Google Chrome	8.0.552.237 (January 12, 2011; 5 days ago)	3.0[27][28]	Yes (3.0)[29] / No (deprecated)[30]	6.0[31][32]	No[33]
Chromium	N/A	r18297[34]	Depends[35]	r47759[36]	No[33]
Safari	5.0.3 (November 18, 2010; 60 days ago)	No[note 4]	3.1[37][38]	No	Depends[note 5]
Opera	11.00 (Build 1156) (December 16, 2010; 32 days ago)	10.50[40]	Depends[note 6]	10.60[42][43]	Depends[note 6]
Konqueror	4.5.5 (7 January 2011; 10 days ago)[44][45]	4.4[46]	No[note 7]	Depends[note 7]	Depends[note 7]

Figure 5-1 The status of video codecs on the Web and their browser support. (*Source:* Wikipedia, http://en.wikipedia.org/wiki/HTML5_video)

In this chapter, we present solutions on how to use the new HTML5 markups to work with audio and video multimedia content.

Solution 5-1: Embedding a video in a web page

With HTML5, publishing a video on a web page has become a truly simple operation. This era, in which we resorted to third-party plug-ins to make video accessible in an HTML page, is about to end.

Code such as this may become a distant memory:

```
<object width="640" height="480">
<param name="movie" value="your_video.swf">
<embed src="your_video.swf" width="500" height="500">
</embed>
</object>
```

The end user will no longer have to download additional plug-ins or update to the correct version of the ones they have installed in order to watch a video. Nor will they undergo brutal browser crashes due to the instability of some of the third-party plug-ins.

Let's see how things are changing with HTML5.

What's involved

With the introduction of the new `<video>` tag, all we have to do is declare this markup in the web page, specify the video to load, and the browser will do the rest (assuming it supports the video element):

```
<video src="your_video.ogg" />
```

The `src` attribute contains the address of the media resource (video or audio) to be shown in the page. In the code example above, we asked it to load the video in the Ogg Theora format.

Even if this code alone is enough to make the video usable, it is preferable to specify the dimensions of the video container using the width and height attributes:

```
<video width="640" height="360"
src="your_video.mp4" />
```

If you don't set these values, the browser will use the dimensions of the original video asset.

Other properties that are supported by the video tag are:

- *preload:* Tells the browser to preload the video content while the page is loading. This way the user won't have to wait for the video to load when playing the video.

- *autoplay:* Tells the browser to play the video automatically as soon as it's available. You need to be careful with this attribute because you aren't always sure that the user will want to see the video. This is especially true if the user is connected via a mobile device, and bandwidth is more expensive.

- *loop:* Re-executes the video as soon as it ends.

- *controls:* If specified, it tells the browser to display a built-in set of controls such as play, stop, pause, and volume.

- *poster:* Specifies an image file that the user agent (browser) can show when no video data is available.

How to build it

The following code example shows how to import and display a video in a web page:

```
<!DOCTYPE html>
<html>
  <head>
    <title>
     Solution 5-1: Embedding a video in a web page
    </title>

  </head>

  <body>
    <h1>Comtaste's Showreel</h1>
```

```
<video width="640"  height="360"
src="comtaste_showreel.mp4" autoplay />
```

```
</body>
</html>
```

If you open this example in a browser, the video will be executed immediately and occupy a space 640 pixels wide and 800 pixels high, as shown in Figure 5-2.

This is an HTML5 Video Element

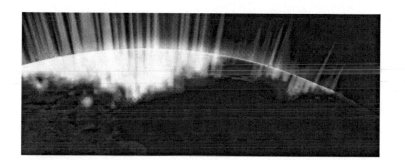

Figure 5-2. The video will play automatically in the web page.

> *Note: If you want to try this solution for loading a remote video, you can use the following code:*
>
> *<video width="640" height="360" src="http://www.youtube.com/demo/ google_main.mp4" autoplay />*

If a user opens the HTML file in a browser that does not support the video tag, a blank page is displayed. Therefore, it is good practice to provide alternative content in the page in case this happens. Use the poster attribute to display an image that could be a frame of the video (captured as an image). It can be local, or come from elsewhere on the Web.

Let's add this attribute to the video tag:

```
<video width="640" height="360"
src="comtaste_showreel.mp4" autoplay
poster="../img/Figure_5_3.png"> Video is not supported in this browser! </video>
```

If the video doesn't load, the browser will show the image specified in the poster attribute, as shown in Figure 5-3.

Figure 5-3. The browser shows the image specified in the poster attribute.

If the poster attribute is not specified and the browser isn't able to load the video, the first frame of the movie will be displayed by default.

Expert tips

For mobile Apple iOS devices (iPhones, iPod Touches, and iPads) and Android devices, there are some problems with HTML5 video support:

- If you use the poster attribute, iOS will ignore the video element. Apple has declared that this bug has been fixed in iOS 4.0.

- iOS only supports the H.264 format. If you use the <source> tag (see the next Solution), it will only recognize the first video format.

- Android devices, on the other hand, don't support the native controls of the browser and will therefore ignore them. Also, the operating system will get a bit confused with the type attribute, which is used to specify the video container.

Solution 5-2: Detecting video support across browsers

We have already discussed the wide range of video formats available on the Web these days earlier this chapter.

The first specifications of HTML5 established that browser support for video elements had to be based on two formats: Ogg Vorbis (for audio) and Ogg Theora (for video). This declaration caused quite a stir among the big players, such as Apple and Nokia, so much so that the WSC removed any reference to audio and video formats from the specifications.

This choice obviously led to format chaos on the Web. MPEG4 (H.264), Ogg Theora, AVI, and VP8/WebM are all ready to wage war in the hopes of becoming the standard of the future. Even the browsers have started taking sides. Figure 5-4 summarizes the support provided for video containers in the various browsers:

- Opera supports Ogg Theora, and in the future it will support WebM.

- Chrome supports Ogg Theora and WebM. (It has recently declared that it will no longer support H.264.)

- Firefox supports Ogg Theora and will support WebM in the future.

- Safari supports H.264.

- Internet Explorer supports H.264 and WebM.

	CHROME	EXPLORER	FIREFOX	OPERA	SAFARI
H.264- MP4	No Support	9	No Support	No Support	3.2 +
Ogg Theora - OMG	3 +	No Support	3.5 +	10.5 +	No Support
VP8 - WebM	6 +	9	4	10.6 +	No Support

Figure 5-4. Browser support for video containers

It is easy to understand why it is necessary, given the current situation, to conduct checks to verify the browser that is loading the page and to pick the right version of the video formats to load.

What's involved

There are various techniques to verify which video format is supported by the browser that is loading the page. This solution uses the Modernizr JavaScript library, from www.modernizr.com, which we introduced in Chapter 1.

We can also use the native functions of this video library to verify its support of the video tag and the codecs. Here is an example:

```
if (Modernizr.video) {
 if (Modernizr.video.webm) {
 // Support the WebM
}
else if (Modernizr.video.ogg)
{
// Support the Ogg Theora + Vorbis
} else if (Modernizr.video.h264){
// Support the H.264 video + AAC audio }
}
```

Basically, the library executes the video support verification by testing the canPlayType property of the video element.

The browser then returns one of three values:

- *empty string:* It does not support it.

- *maybe string:* It is not sure it isn't supported.

- *probably string:* It supports the combination of container and codec.

How to build it

To create an HTML page that verifies video tag support and loads the right code, use a mechanism that's similar to the previous solution but with some small differences.

Here is the complete code that uses the Modernizr library to detect video support across browsers:

```
<!DOCTYPE html>
<html>
  <head>
    <title>
      Solution 5-2: Detecting Video support across browser
    </title>

<script type="text/javascript" src="js/modernizr-1.0.min.js"></script>

    <style type="text/css">
      body { background: #f7f7f7; color: black; text-align: center; }
      .video #no-video,
      .no-video #video { display: none; }
    </style>

  </head>

  <body>

<h1>Comtaste's Showreel</h1>

    <div id="video">
<h1> This is an HTML5 Video Element </h1>
    <video width="640"  height="360"
src="comtaste_showreel.mp4" autoplay poster="../img/Figure_5_3.png" />

    </div>

</body>
</html>
```

> Note: At the time of this writing, the latest version of the Modernizr library is 1.7, but this solution works with older versions too.

We created two DIVs in the code: one that will contain the code for browsers that support the <video> tag (with id equal to #video), and the other for other browsers (with id equal to #no-video). We also inserted a style block with CSS statements to hide the necessary DIV with the command display: none.

In the first DIV (the one with id #video) block, we inserted the `<video>` tag, whereas on the second we will use a technique written by Kroc Camen, which doesn't use JavaScript and only requires two video encodes: one Ogg file and one MP4 file.

This technique is based on the assumption that, if the HTML5 video is not supported, Adobe Flash will be used instead.

This approach is compatible with HTML4, HTML5 (valid markup), and XHTML 1, and it also works when served as application/XHTML+XML.

Read more about this approach to a JavaScript-less way to use HTML5 video in "Video for Everybody," by Kroc Camen. You can find this article at: http://camendesign.com/code/video_for_everybody.

In the second DIV, the one that will load if the browser doesn't support the video tag, insert the following code:

```
<!-- fallback to Flash: -->
        <object width="640" height="360" type="application/x-shockwave-flash"➙
data="__FLASH__.SWF">
                <!-- Firefox uses the `data` attribute above, IE/Safari uses the param➙
below -->
                <param name="movie" value="comtaste_showreel.SWF" />
                <param name="flashvars" value="controlbar-over&amp;image=➙
comtaste_showreel.JPG&amp;file=comtaste_showreel.mp4" />
                <!-- fallback image. note the title field below, put the title of the➙
video there -->
                <img src="comtaste_showreel.JPG" width="640" height="360"
                    title="No video playback capabilities, please download the video➙
below" />
        </object>
```

Expert tips

There are other solutions for how to work with videos on the Web. One that is having a lot of success is the HTML5media project, at https://github.com/etianen/html5media.

This project detects the dual support of the video tag and video formats by using an HTML5 multimedia player. It supports both H.264 (MP4) and Ogg Theora formats.

If the browser doesn't support the HTML5 video tag, it uses Adobe Flash Player to provide the same functions as the original video. This is why we use the Flowplayer JavaScript library (http://flowplayer.org).

To enable the HTML5 video tag in all major browsers, all you have to do is recall the jQuery library and the script in the head of the document:

```
<script src="http://ajax.googleapis.com/ajax/libs/jquery/1.4.2/jquery.min.js"></script>
<script src="http://html5media.googlecode.com/svn/trunk/src/jquery.html5media.min.js">➙
</script>
```

Then you can insert the video in an HTML page with the following code:

```
<video src="video.mp4" autoplay autobuffer></video>
```

Other libraries on the same topic are: http://mediaelementjs.com/ and http://videojs.com/.

Solution 5-3: Creating a custom video controller

Any multimedia element, be it audio or video, has to provide the user with the option of interacting with the content using the classic play, stop, pause, and volume control buttons. HTML5 has an attribute that natively renders the above-mentioned buttons on a screen video controller.

However, it is possible (and often preferable) to create custom control buttons so that they match the graphics of the website where the video is published.

Audio and video elements are part of the HTML5 DOM media elements, which provide a powerful and very easy-to-use API to control movie playback. In this solution, we will see how to add custom controls to a video.

What's involved

It's simple to insert a video control in video content. In fact, there is a controls attribute for the `<video>` tag that takes advantage of the browser's built-in controls. All you need to do is to specify the attribute in the tag to show the controllers on the video:

```
<video width="640" height="360" src="comtaste_showreel.mp4" controls />
```

Every browser will use its own graphics for the design of the video controls. For example, in Figure 5-5, you can see the graphic used for the video controls in Safari.

Figure 5-5. The video controls rendered by Safari

This discrepancy will raise many designers' eyebrows, as they will want to control the look and feel of the video controls so that they match the graphics of the website.

In Figure 5-6, you can see the graphics used for the video controls in all the other major browsers.

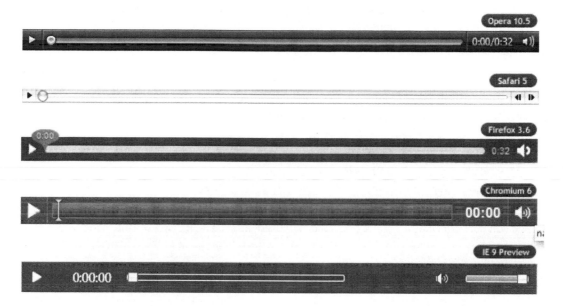

Figure 5-6. How the major browsers render video controls

It is possible, however, to create custom video controls using your own graphics, and to decide which functions to provide. For example, you could write a feature to synchronize subtitles in a video and activate them with video controllers, or a feature to allow the user to skip from one bookmark to another to see the segment in which he or she is most interested.

Because you are the one writing the functions of the video controller with JavaScript, you can really do as you please.

To do so, you have to use the HTML5 media attributes and DOM events for which you can listen, such as load progress, media playing, media paused, and media done playing. For example, for features that play video, there are the following attributes:

- *media.paused:* returns true if playback is paused; otherwise false.

- *media.ended:* returns true if playback has reached the end of the media resource.

- *media.defaultPlaybackRate [= value]:* returns the default rate of playback for when the user is not fast-forwarding or reversing through the media resource.

- *Media. playbackRate [= value]:* returns the current rate playback where 1.0 is normal speed.

- *Media.played:* returns a TimeRanges object that represents the ranges of the media resource that the browser has played.

- *Media.play():* sets the media.paused attribute to false, loading the media resource and beginning playback if necessary. If the playback had ended, it will restart it from the beginning.

- *Media.pause():* sets the media.paused attribute to true, loading the media resource if necessary.

- *Media.volume:* gets or sets the volume of the video's audio track. It takes a float value ranging from 0.0 (silent) to 1.0 (loudest).

- *Media.muted:* mutes a video.

- *Media.currentTime:* returns the current playback position in seconds, expressed as a float.

For a complete list of media attributes and events, refer to the following page: `http://www.whatwg.org/specs/web-apps/current-work/multipage/video.html`.

By using these methods and a few lines of JavaScript,, you can create a simple video controller:

```
if (video.paused)
{
        video.play();
 }
```

This condition controls whether or not the video is paused, and if it is, it executes the video with the `play()` method. If, on the other hand, the video has ended, we have to go back to the beginning by acting on the `currentTime` property and then play it again:

```
if (video.paused)
{
    video.play();
 } else if (video.ended)
{
video.currentTime=0;
video.play();
}
```

Basically, the deed is done with a few lines of code. Let's see how to create a complete example.

How to build it

Start by creating two DIV blocks. The first will contain the video element, and the second will contain the video controls.

Then create a new file and add a `<video>` tag in a DIV block to which you assign an id equal to a `video_container`. The id is important because you will access it later with JavaScript and CSS.

Here is the code snippet:

```
<div id="video_container">

<video width="320" height="176" src="comtaste_showreel.mp4" />

</div>
```

It loads a video in MPEG format and assigns a size of 320x176 pixels.

Insert a second DIV block, which will contain the video controls for play, pause, volume, mute audio, and timing. To do this, use <button> tags for the play, pause, and mute buttons, and then use a slider to control the volume. Information about the play time on the video is contained in a label:

```
<div id="video_controller">

<button id="btn_play"> Play </button>

<button id="btn_pause"> Pause </button>

<input type="range" min="0" max="1" step="0.1" id="volume">

<button id="btn_mute"> Mute </button>

<label id="time">-:--:--</label>

</div>
```

In this case, it is also important to pay attention to the names given to the id attributes of the tags, because you will need them later to reference the objects in JavaScript.

The final result for the user interface of the web page is shown in Figure 5-7.

Figure 5-7. The video element and its custom video controller

Now you have to write the logic of the video controller. Insert a script block and start with an event handler as soon as the web page is loaded. In the event handler, define a global variable that will contain the video element and local variables that contain the reference to the video controllers:

```
<script type="text/javascript">

var video;

window.onload = function(){

        video = document.getElementsByTagName("video")[0];

        var btn_play = document.getElementById("btn_play");

        var btn_pause = document.getElementById("btn_pause");

        var btn_mute = document.getElementById("btn_mute");

        var btn_volume = document.getElementById('volume');
```

We've used the getElementsByTagName method to access the video element, and the getElementById method to access the first element with the specified id to reference the other controls. This way, we can access, for example, the video element referring to the video global variable without having to recall the getElementById method.

For the buttons to execute the operations on the video, you have to associate their click events to an event handler (which is actually a method), where you can write the operations that the control button has to execute. We use the addEventListener() method to associate the event of an element to a method.

First, add the following lines to the code. (We are still writing code in the onload event of the window object.)

```
        btn_play.addEventListener('click', doPlay, false);

        btn_pause.addEventListener('click', doPause, false);

        btn_mute.addEventListener('click', doMute, false);
```

Three event handlers have been associated to the clicks of the buttons: doPlay(), doPause(), and doMute().

Finally, before closing the statements in the onload event of the page, add an event handler to deal with the volume of the video element that will work on the change event of the slider control.

Add the following code straight after the rest:

```
btn_volume.value = video.volume;
btn_volume.addEventListener('change',function(e) {

                    myVol= e.target.value;

                    video.volume=myVol;


        if (myVol==0) {
                    video.muted = true;
```

```
                        } else {

                                video.muted = false;

                        }
                        return false;
                }, true);
};
```

Let's analyze the code we've just written. As soon as you open the web page, the video element will inherit the volume from the user settings. This is why you had to set the value of the slider control to the current value of the video:

```
btn_volume.value - video.volume;
```

That way, you are sure that the user will change the volume of the video starting from its real initial value.

We then created an event handler for the change event, which happens when the user drags the slider thumb. This is how the user changes the volume of the video element, which will be equal to the value of the slider:

```
myVol= e.target.value;
video.volume=myVol;
```

We execute a condition to check if the volume is equal to 0. This setting sets the muted attribute on the video; otherwise, it's unmuted automatically on volume change:

```
if (myVol==0) {
video.muted = true;
} else {
video.muted = false;
}
```

With these few lines of code, you've written the volume control function for the video element.

Now we can start writing the event handlers for the buttons. Add the following code:

```
function doPlay(){
        if (video.paused){
                video.play();
        } else if (video.ended)
        {
          video.currentTime=0;
         video.play();
        };
};

function doPause(){
        if (video.play){
                video.pause();
        };
};
function doMute(){
    document.getElementById('volume').value = 0;
```

```
                video.muted = true;
};
```

With the `play()` and `pause()` methods and the `muted` property, we have provided the functions for the video controller buttons.

Now you can save the file and execute it in a browser. You will see how the play, pause, and mute buttons work, and you can also change the volume of the video by moving the slider thumb.

This is the complete code for this example:

```html
<!DOCTYPE html>
<html>
  <head>
    <title>
     Solution 5-3: Creating custom video controls
    </title>

<script type="text/javascript">

var video;

window.onload = function(){

        video = document.getElementsByTagName("video")[0];

        var btn_play = document.getElementById("btn_play");

        var btn_pause = document.getElementById("btn_pause");

        var btn_mute = document.getElementById("btn_mute");

        var btn_volume = document.getElementById('volume');

        btn_play.addEventListener('click', doPlay, false);

        btn_pause.addEventListener('click', doPause, false);

        btn_mute.addEventListener('click', doMute, false);

        btn_volume.value = video.volume;

        btn_volume.addEventListener('change',function(e) {

                    myVol= e.target.value;

                    video.volume=myVol;

            if (myVol==0) {
                                video.muted = true;

                    } else {
```

```
                                    video.muted = false;

                        }
                        return false;
                }, true);
};

function doPlay(){
        if (video.paused){
                video.play();
        } else if (video.ended)
        {
          video.currentTime=0;
      video.play();
        };
};

function doPause(){
        if (video.play){
                video.pause();
        };
};

function doMute(){
    document.getElementById('volume').value = 0;
        video.muted = true;
};

</script>

</head>

<body>

<div id="video_container">

<video width="320" height="176" src="comtaste_showreel.mp4" />

</div>

<div id="video_controller">

<button id="btn_play"> Play </button>

<button id="btn_pause"> Pause </button>

<input type="range" min="0" max="1" step="0.1" id="volume">

<button id="btn_mute"> Mute </button>

</div>

</body>
</html>
```

113

Expert tips

The video element exposes an event that allows you to trace the time left on the video execution.

The timeupdate event is executed when the current playback position changes as part of normal playback.

Let's add a markup label, which will contain the timing of the video when it is playing.

Insert the following code in the DIV block:

```
<button id="btn_play"> Play </button>

<button id="btn_pause"> Pause </button>

<input type="range" min="0" max="1" step="0.1" id="volume">

<button id="btn_mute"> Mute </button>

<label id="time">-:--:--</label>

</div>
```

We will insert the values of the video execution hours, minutes, and seconds in the label using JavaScript.

Add an event handler for the timeupdate event of the video element. Insert the following line of code in the function of the onload event of the window object:

```
video.addEventListener('timeupdate', updateTime, false);
```

You then declare the updateTime method, which will write the hour/minutes/seconds value in the <label> we created in the web page view:

```
function updateTime()
{
                    var sec= video.currentTime;
                    var h = Math.floor(sec/3600);
                    sec=sec%3600;
                    var min =Math.floor(sec/60);
                    sec = Math.floor(sec%60);

                    if (sec.toString().length < 2) sec="0"+sec;
                    if (min.toString().length < 2) min="0"+min;

                    document.getElementById('time').innerHTML = h+":"+min+":"+sec;

}
```

This function has only the task of splitting currentTime, expressed in seconds, into separate hour/minute/second strings, which it will then write in the label with id equal to time thanks to the innerHTML method:

```
document.getElementById('time').innerHTML = h+":"+min+":"+sec;
```

Then add a bit of CSS just to make the label field nicer:

```css
<style type="text/css">
#video_container {
        margin: 0;
        padding: 0;
}

#time {
        margin: 0;
        padding: 5px;
        width: 350px;
        font-family: Helvetica, Arial, sans-serif
        font-size: .7em;
        color: #000000;
        background-color: #ccc;
}

</style>
```

The final result is shown in Figure 5-8.

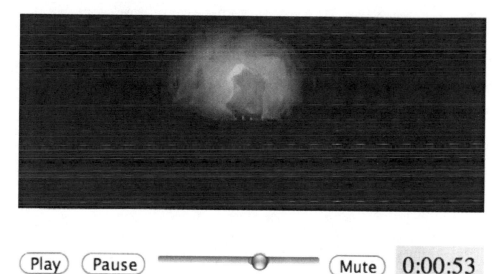

Figure 5-8. The video element and its working video controllers

Solution 5-4: Preloading a video

There are two main methods for delivering media over the Internet:

- streaming

- progressive download

A discussion of the differences between these two methods is beyond the scope of this solution. All we need to know is that the first method, streaming, uses a server and a protocol to allow the user to see any part of the video without having to wait for the video to load, throughout the entire length of the video.

The second method, on the other hand, uses the HTTP standard protocol to transmit the file. In this case, the user can't skip to a portion of the video that hasn't yet been loaded.

For a video that is delivered in progressive download, it is therefore important to manage the preloading operations. This allows you to load the video in the background even if the user still hasn't executed the movie.

What's involved

There is a preload attribute for the video element that allows you to load a video in the background. All you need to do is declare it in the video tag and specify one of the three values it can have:

- *auto (default value):* it starts downloading the video file as soon as the page loads.

- *none:* it does not start downloading the video file.

- *metadata:* it suggests that the browser prefetch the resource metadata, such as the size, duration, and so on.

However, you have to be very diligent with how you use this attribute. In fact, this attribute tells the browser to start downloading the video file as soon as the page loads. Even if the user never executes the video, in the background the page will ask for it to load anyway, wasting valuable bandwidth.

Here is an example of how to use the attribute:

```
    <video width="640" height="360"
src="comtaste_showreel.mp4" autoplay
preload
poster="../img/Figure_5_3.png" />
```

Note that the Safari browser on iOS ignores the preload attribute and never preloads videos.

How to build it

Create a new file for this solution, and start by inserting the video that you want to preload:

```
<!DOCTYPE html>
<html>
  <head>
    <title>
     Solution 5-4:  Preloading a video
    </title>

</head>

<body>

<video width="320" height="176" preload
```

```
            src="comtaste_showreel.mp4"  />

</body>
</html>
```

Because the auto value is the default value, you don't have to write preload="auto".

In this example, however, we specify that the browser shouldn't preload the video at all:

```
    <video width="640"  height="360"
src="comtaste_showreel.mp4" autoplay
preload="none"
poster="../img/Figure_5_3.png" />
```

Expert tips

Some browsers support the autobuffer attribute, which is used when autoplay is not used, and it forces the video to be downloaded in the background. The Safari browser on iOS ignores the preload attribute and never preloads videos. If both autoplay and autobuffer are used, then autobuffer is ignored.

Since the autobuffer attribute is no longer present in Firefox 4, and the preload attribute is not present in Firefox 3.5 and 3.6, if you want a video to download completely, you need to use both preload attribute set to "auto" and the autobuffer in the video element:

```
<video autobuffer preload="auto" width="640" height="360"
src="comtaste_showreel.mp4" />
```

Pay attention to this approach because the video will be downloaded, thereby using up bandwidth, even if the video will never be seen by the user. If you want the video only to be downloaded if the user actually plays it, you must omit either the preload or the autobuffer attribute.

Solution 5-5: Creating a custom seek bar for a video

Every decent video controller also provides the option to skip to certain points in the movie with a seek bar, as well as being able to manage the volume and play and pause the video.

YouTube allows the user to skip through a video quickly with a seek bar by dragging the thumb over the play and pause buttons of the video controller, as shown in Figure 5-9.

Figure 5-9. The seek bar used by YouTube

It is also possible to create this type of function with HTML5 by using some properties of the video element and writing a few lines of JavaScript.

What's involved

There are two properties and one event we will work on to create a seek bar: the currentTime and duration properties, and the timeupdate event.

We've already talked about these attributes in the previous solutions, but here is a quick reminder:

- The currentTime attribute returns the current time, in seconds, as a float value.

- The duration attribute returns the actual duration in seconds as a float value. If the duration is unknown, it returns NaN; if the video is streaming, it returns Infinite

- The timeupdate event is executed whenever the current position changes in any way.

By associating these attributes with a slider control, you can provide the user with the option to skip from one portion of the video to another.

For the slider control, use the new input type range of HTML5, which uses the built-in features that are native to the browser:

```
<input type="range" step="any" id="seekbar">
```

This input element will update its value when the timeupdate event is executed, and because it will be bound to the video's time value.

Let's see how it works.

How to build it

For this solution, let's take the example we created in the previous solution, to which you will add a slider control that will act as a seek bar for the video element.

Start by adding the only new user interface element for this example: the slider.

In the DIV block with id equal to video_controller, add a range input type between the mute button and the label containing the video timing:

```
<div id="video_controller">

<button id="btn_play"> Play </button>

<button id="btn_pause"> Pause </button>

<button id="btn_mute"> Mute </button>

<input type="range" step="any" id="seekbar">

<label id="time">-:--:--</label>

</div>
```

We haven't dealt with the max property, which allows us to specify the highest value for the slider control for this input element. We will use JavaScript to assign a value to this attribute.

But first, let's work on the script block of our code.

Start by adding the following lines of JavaScript code to the onload event of the object window.

Create a local variable containing the reference of the slider using the getElementById method of the document object:

```
var seekbar = document.getElementById('seekbar');
```

declare three event handlers on the change events of the slider control and the timeupdate and durationchange of the video element:

```
video.addEventListener('timeupdate', updateTime, false);
video.addEventListener('durationchange', initSeekBar, false);
seekbar.addEventListener('change', changeTime, false);
```

So the function on the onload event becomes the following:
```
window.onload = function(){

        video = document.getElementsByTagName("video")[0];
```

```
    var btn_play = document.getElementById("btn_play");

    var btn_pause = document.getElementById("btn_pause");

    var btn_mute = document.getElementById("btn_mute");

    var seekbar = document.getElementById('seekbar');

    btn_play.addEventListener('click', doPlay, false);

    btn_pause.addEventListener('click', doPause, false);

    btn_mute.addEventListener('click', doMute, false);

    video.addEventListener('timeupdate', updateTime, false);

  video.addEventListener('durationchange', initSeekBar, false);

    seekbar.addEventListener('change', changeTime, false);
```

Now let's set the min and max properties of the slider by associating them with the startTime and duration properties of the video element. In particular, set the min attribute to 0 and the max attribute to duration. We write this statement on the initSeekBar() event handler, which is invoked when the durationchange event of the video is executed:

```
function initSeekBar() {
  seekbar.min = 0;
  seekbar.max = video.duration;
}
```

To make sure the video changes its timing when the user moves the thumb of the slider, and that the seek bar is synchronized with the timing of the video, we have to write code on the event handlers so that they execute on the updateTime event of the video and on the change event of the slider control, respectively. We have registered the event handlers with the addEventListener method with the following functions:

```
seekbar.addEventListener('change', changeTime, false);
video.addEventListener('timeupdate', updateTime, false);
```

In the first video's event handler named updateTime(), we associate the value of the slider control to the currentTime of the video:

```
function updateTime()
{
  seekbar.value = video.currentTime;
}
```

Whereas on the second event handler, changeTime, we do the opposite, meaning we associate the currentTime of the video to the value of the slider:

```
function changeTime() {
  video.currentTime = seekbar.value;
}
```

Save the file and open it in the browser. You will see that the slider control is perfectly synchronized with the video and, if you drag the thumb, you can see that the current time of the video changes accordingly, as shown in Figure 5-10.

Figure 5-10. The seek bar is perfectly synchronized with the current time of the video element.

For the sake of clarity, here is the complete code for this example:

```
<!DOCTYPE html>
<html>
  <head>
    <title>
      Solution 5-5: Browsing the video with a seek bar
    </title>

<style type="text/css">

#video_container {
        margin: 0;
        padding: 0;
}


#time {
        margin: 0;
        padding: 5px;
        width: 350px;
        font-family: Helvetica, Arial, sans-serif
        font-size: .7em;
        color: #000000;
        background-color: #ccc;
```

```
}


</style>
<script type="text/javascript">
var video;
window.onload = function(){
        video = document.getElementsByTagName("video")[0];
        var btn_play = document.getElementById("btn_play");
        var btn_pause = document.getElementById("btn_pause");
        var btn_mute = document.getElementById("btn_mute");
        var seekbar = document.getElementById('seekbar');
        btn_play.addEventListener('click', doPlay, false);
        btn_pause.addEventListener('click', doPause, false);
        btn_mute.addEventListener('click', doMute, false);
        video.addEventListener('timeupdate', updateTime, false);
    video.addEventListener('durationchange', initSeekBar, false);
    seekbar.addEventListener('change', changeTime, false);

        btn_volume.value = video.volume;
        btn_volume.addEventListener('change',function(e) {
                    myVol= e.target.value;
                    video.volume=myVol;

        if (myVol==0) {
                            video.muted = true;
                    } else {
                            video.muted = false;
                    }
                    return false;
```

```
            }, true);



};


function initSeekBar() {
  seekbar.min = 0;
  seekbar.max = video.duration;
}



function changeTime() {
  video.currentTime = seekbar.value;
}


function updateTime()
{

                var sec= video.currentTime;
                var h = Math.floor(sec/3600);
                sec=sec%3600;
                var min =Math.floor(sec/60);
                sec = Math.floor(sec%60);

                if (sec.toString().length < 2) sec="0"+sec;
                if (min.toString().length < 2) min="0"+min;

                document.getElementById('time').innerHTML = h+":"+min+":"+sec;

  seekbar.min = video.startTime;
  seekbar.max = video.duration;
  seekbar.value = video.currentTime;

}


function doPlay(){
        if (video.paused){
                video.play();
        } else if (video.ended)
        {
          video.currentTime=0;
      video.play();
        };
};

function doPause(){
        if (video.play){
                video.pause();
        };
```

```
};

function doMute(){
    document.getElementById('volume').value = 0;
        video.muted = true;
};

</script>

</head>

<body>

<div id="video_container">

<video width="320" height="176" src="comtaste_showreel.mp4"  />

</div>

<div id="video_controller">

<button id="btn_play"> Play </button>

<button id="btn_pause"> Pause </button>

<button id="btn_mute"> Mute </button>

<input type="range" step="any" id="seekbar">

<label id="time">-:--:--</label>

</div>

</body>
</html>
```

Expert tips

There is one case in which the example as written above won't work correctly. In fact, if the video were streaming, the duration property would become infinite and the video would begin its execution with a startTime equal to 0. Therefore, we have to change the code for it to behave properly in this situation as well.

The startTime property of the video comes to the rescue. It normally returns 0, but for streaming videos it could return a different value.

Therefore, we have to make two changes in our code. The first is in the initSeekBar() event handler and has to do with the min and max attributes:

```
function initSeekBar() {
  seekbar.min = video.startTime;
```

```
    seekbar.max = video.startTime + video.duration;
}
```

Basically, the value of the min attribute isn't zero anymore; instead, it inherits the value contained in the startTime property, whereas the max value is equal to the startTime plus the value contained in the duration property.

The second change is in the event handler, updateTime(), in which we will use another property: the buffered property. It returns a TimeRanges object that contains a length property, a start() and an end() method.

We get the position of buffered data accessing the end time of the last range in the buffered property.

Change the code in the updateTime() handler as follows:

```
function updateTime()
{
    var bufferPosition = video.buffered.end(video.buffered.length-1);
    seekbar.min = video.startTime;
    seekbar.max = bufferPosition;
    seekbar.value = video.currentTime;

}
```

Solution 5-6: Using multiple source video elements

Current browser support for the various video containers and formats is as follows:

- Safari can read any video that is compatible with the H.264/AAC/MP4 formats.

- Microsoft still hasn't specified if the support of WebM will be native or available with a separately installable component in Internet Explorer. In any case, it supports the H.264/AAC/MP4 formats.

- Google supports the WebM codec, and it has announced that future versions of Android will support the WebM format. It has also recently stated that, as of March 2011, Chrome will no longer support the H.264 codec.

- Firefox, Opera, and Chrome support the Ogg/Theora/Vorbis format.

In this colorful scenario, it is necessary to publish the video in different formats to be able to guarantee the use of the video for the highest possible number of users.

It will then be up to the browser to understand which of these formats it is able to reproduce.

What's involved

These are the steps that will allow you to increase the probability that your video will be executed by users:

- Encode your video in the following formats: WebM (VP8 + Vorbis), H.264 video and AAC audio in an MP4 container, and Theora video and Vorbis audio in an Ogg container.

- Declare these three video files from a <video> element, and fall back to a Flash-based video player (see Solution 5-1).

To enable the browser to understand which video format it needs to load, you can use the source element, as follows:

```
<video controls autoplay>
 <source src="comtaste_showreel.ogv">
 <source src="comtaste_showreel .mp4">
 Sorry, your browser does not support the Video element
</video>
```

The browser will read the first video source and try to load and play comtaste_showreel.ogv. If it's not able to play it, it will try the next source element.

By default, the browser would also try to load the video in a format it wouldn't be able to reproduce. This would be an enormous waste of bandwidth. To save precious bandwidth, you can specify the MIME type of each video. The MIME type communicates which video container is being used, but it does not provide any information on the codec being used. Therefore, in the type attribute of the source, you also need to specify the codec.

By doing so, the browser doesn't need to download the video because it knows if that MIME type is supported or not:

```
<video controls>
 <source src="comtaste_showreel.ogv" type="video/ogg;codecs='theora, vorbis'">
 <source src="comtaste_showreel.mp4" type="video/mp4; codecs="avc1.42E01E, mp4a.40.2"'>
Sorry, your browser does not support the Video element
</video>
```

How to build it

Here is a complete code example that uses the source tag to expose different video formats to the browsers:

```
<!DOCTYPE html>
<html>
  <head>
    <title>
     Solution 5-7:  Using multiple source video elements
    </title>

  </head>

  <body>

      <video controls autoplay >

<source src="comtaste_showreel.webm" type='video/webm; codecs="vorbis,vp8"' />
<source src="comtaste_showreel.ogv" type='video/ogg;codecs="theora, vorbis"'>
 <source src="comtaste_showreel.mp4" type='video/mp4; codecs="avc1.42E01E, mp4a.40.2"'>
```

```
      Your browser does not support the new HTML5 video element
      </video>

  </body>

</html>
```

Pay attention to the codecs parameter that uses double quotes. It means that you have to use single quotes for the attribute value:

```
<source src="comtaste_showreel.webm" type='video/webm; codecs="vorbis,vp8"' />
```

Expert tips

Using mobile devices for navigation is becoming more and more popular. An increasing number of web developers optimize their designs with CSS so that their websites can be used by devices with lower-screen resolutions compared to standard notebook computers. Thus, it also becomes necessary for video providers to think about who will be using their content on handheld devices, as higher quality may be an undesirable feature—in terms of the bandwidth that is consumed by loading the video.

HTML5 provides the media attribute, which is declared in the source attribute of the video element. This attribute asks the browser for the screen size on which the media will be reproduced. Based on the response, the video tag is able to send different files that are optimized for different screen resolutions:

```
<video controls autoplay >
<source src="comtaste_showreel_mobile.ogv"
type='video/ogg;codecs="theora, vorbis"'
media="(min-device-width:480px)">
```

This way, the browser is asked if the minimum device width is 480px. If it is, then it loads the comtaste_showreel_mobile.ogv video that was optimized for mobile devices during the encoding phase.

> Note: You can read more about the media attribute at: http://www.whatwg.org/specs/web-apps/current-work/multipage/video.html.

Solution 5-7: Opening a video in full screen

Video quality on the Web has improved dramatically in recent years. Thanks to the ever-increasing availability of high-performance bandwidth, today multimedia content is spreading over the Internet with quality equal to television.

YouTube already lists a multitude of videos in HD quality, as shown in Figure 5-11.

Figure 5-11. YouTube allows you to select the quality of the video you want to load.

With this quality, it is possible to see videos in full screen, exactly as we watch videos on our laptops, only now we are watching these videos on the Web.

Several versions of Flash Player have already provided the possibility of reproducing a video in full-screen mode. HTML5 and its video element also provide methods to obtain this same effect.

What's involved

Some browsers already provide a button on the video controller to switch to full screen natively, for example Safari 5.0 and iOS 3.2 and greater. Other browsers, on the other hand, support the full-screen mode by accessing it through the right-context menu, such as Firefox 3.6.

You can verify that the current video is capable of being played in full-screen mode using the `webkitSupportsFullscreen` Boolean property, and you can launch the video in full-screen mode using the `webkitEnterFullscreen()` method The first thing you have to do is check if the browser supports full-screen mode:

```
if (video.webkitSupportsFullscreen)
    {
    }
```

Then execute the `webkitEnterFullscreen()` method of the video element:

```
video.webkitEnterFullscreen();
```

To exit full-screen mode in a video, press Esc to return to the normal view just like you would do with Flash Player.

How to build it

It's very easy to create a full-screen video feature.

Start by creating the user interface elements which, in our example, will be only a video element and a simple button:

```
<div id="video_container">
<video width="320" height="176" src="comtaste_showreel.mp4" id="myVideo" autoplay />
</div>
<br/>
<button type="button" id="btn_fullscreen" style="visibility:hidden">
Go Fullscreen
</button>
```

The button won't be visible when the page is loaded. In fact, specify a CSS element inline that makes the button invisible:

```
style="visibility:hidden".
```

Only after having checked that the browser supports the function will you make this button visible.

Now you can insert a JavaScript block where you will associate an event handler with the click of a button that will launch the video in full-screen mode, but only after having checked if the browser supports that function. Carry out this check when the `loadedmetadata` event of the video is executed, or when the browser knows the duration and dimensions of the media resource. In fact, the `webkitSupportsFullscreen` property is not valid until the movie metadata is fully loaded.

Write these statements in the onload event of the window object:

```
<script type="text/javascript">
var video;

window.onload = function()
{
    video = document.getElementById("myVideo");

    btn_fullscreen.addEventListener("click", forceFullScreen, false);

    video.addEventListener("loadedmetadata", makeVisible, false);
}
```

Now you are ready to write the event handlers declared in the `addEventListener()` method: `forceFullScreen()` and `makeVisible()`.

Here is the complete code for this example:

```
<!DOCTYPE html>
<html>
  <head>
    <title>
     Solution 5-8:  Full-screen video
    </title>
```

```
<script type="text/javascript">
var video;

window.onload = function()
{
    video = document.getElementById("myVideo");

    btn_fullscreen.addEventListener("click", forceFullScreen, false);

    video.addEventListener("loadedmetadata", makeVisible, false);
}

function makeVisible()
{
    if (video.webkitSupportsFullscreen)
    {
        document.getElementById("btn_fullscreen").style.visibility="visible";
    }
}

function forceFullScreen() {
        video.webkitEnterFullscreen();
}

</script>

</head>
<body>

 <div id="video_container">

<video width="320" height="176"  src="comtaste_showreel.mp4" id="myVideo" autoplay  />

</div>

    <br/>

    <button type="button" id="btn_fullscreen"  style="visibility:hidden">
    Go Fullscreen
    </button>

</body>
</html>
```

Figure 5-12 shows the video in full-screen once the Go Fullscreen button has been clicked.

Figure 5-12. The video in full-screen mode.

Expert tips

If you want to know which video players support full-screen mode, visit this web page: http://praegnanz.de/html5video/

Solution 5-8: Applying a mask to a video

You often see videos appear in a non-rectangular or discontinuous area on the Web. One of the earliest examples of this occurrence, which later became famous, was published by Vodafone; the videos showed movies playing in futuristic bracelets (see Figure 5-13).

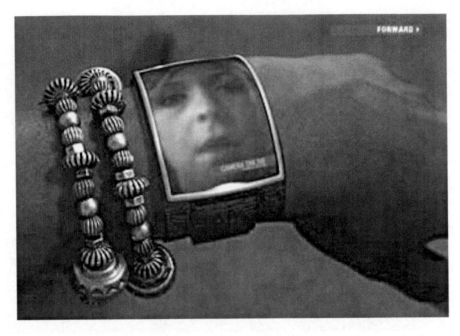

Figure 5-13. The masked video that plays in Vodafone's Visual Bracelet

The visual effect was catchy and took advantage of a new Flash Player function that supported the alpha channel for videos. The alpha channel served as nothing more than an image that acts as a mask for the video. This special image defines the only active area where the video appears.

It is also possible to recreate a similar effect with HTML5 by using a specific property of the browsers based on the WebKit engine and applying an image to use as a mask.

WebKit (http://webkit.org/) is an open-source web browser engine. WebKit is also the name of the Mac OS X system framework version of the engine that is used by Safari, Dashboard, Mail, and many other OS X applications. Chrome is based on WebKit, too.

For now, this solution is only supported by Safari and Chrome in their latest versions.

What's involved

The property that allows us to specify which image to use as a mask is: -webkit-mask-box-image.

All the specific properties of WebKit are prefixed with -webkit-. There are also WebKit properties for CSS. Currently, these properties are still not a part of the HTML5 standard described by the WSC, but they could be added in the near future.

The -webkit-mask-box-image property is specified directly in the video tag:

```
<video src = "comtaste_showreel.mp4" autoplay
 -webkit-mask-box-image: url(yourMaskImage.png) ;">
```

The url() parameter is specified in the property where you specify the image.

The mask image is usually a PNG file with the same dimensions as the video. The area of the image where the video is to be shown must be transparent; the area where the video is to be hidden needs to be opaque.

How to build it

To create and apply a mask to a video, simply use the specific tag and a mask image.

Creating a mask image, also known as alpha channel for a video, is a truly simple task. It is possible to use any graphic tool, such as Photoshop, Illustrator, Fireworks, and so on. There are many online tutorials that provide step-by-step instruction on how to carry out this operation. In this example, we use an image that was created previously and that you can find in the source code of the examples provided in this chapter.

A simple and well-made video tutorial is published on Adobe TV at: http://tv.adobe.com/ watch/photoshop-for-video/straight-alpha-channels/.

Here is the complete solution:

```
<!DOCTYPE html>
<html>
<head>
    <title>
     Solution 5-9:  Masking  a video
    </title>
</head>
<body>

    <img src="digitalScreenImage.jpg" width="430" height="365">

    <video src = "comtaste_showreel.mp4" autoplay
    style = "position:relative ; top: -325px ;
    -webkit-mask-box-image: url(maskImage.png) ;" />

</body>
</html>
```

We've used an image to create a frame for the video (digitalScreenImage.jpg). To make sure that the video element that will act as a frame is placed exactly at the right height of the image, we used relative positioning via CSS. In fact, we declared the style attribute in the video tag by placing the video element at a 325 pixel distance from the upper edge of the browser so that it stays inside the image. Finally, we applied the mask image with the -webkit-mask-box-image attribute:

```
<video src = "comtaste_showreel.mp4" autoplay
style = "position:relative ; top: -325px ;
-webkit-mask-box-image: url(maskImage.png) ;" />
```

All you have to do now is save the file and execute it in a WebKit-based browser, such as Google Chrome or Safari, to see the mask applied to the video.

Expert tips

In addition to the `-webkit-mask-box-image` attribute, there is another native property for WebKit-based browsers that allows you to apply a graphic effect to a video. It is in fact possible to add a reflection of a video by using the `-webkit-box-reflect` property.

The reflection is a copy of the video element that can appear on the left, right, above, or below the video. The offset space between the video and the reflection can be customized. The attribute is declared as a property of the style attribute as shown in the code snippet below:

```
<video src = "comtaste_showreel.mp4" autoplay
    style = "position:relative ; top: -325px ; "-webkit-box-reflect: below 0px;"
/  >
```

This code adds a reflection effect below the video.

Solution 5-9: Using the audio element

Audio is a multimedia element that is also commonly used on the Web. Just like video content, audio suffered from the lack of an open standard for delivery on the Web in the past. This is why using audio content on the Web was, and still is, entrusted to third-party plug-ins.

QuickTime, Windows Media Player, Flash Player, and Real Player are the most common plug-ins used by developers to play audio content. Again, in the end, Flash Player was declared the winner. With market penetration of close to 99% of computers connected to the Internet, Flash has guaranteed that any site can publish audio content compatible with this format.

By using Flash Player, it is possible to play audio in the following formats: AIFF, WAV, and MP3.

Now HTML5 has introduced an `<audio>` markup, which allows you to insert audio elements without having to distribute any third-party plug-in.

As far as formats are concerned, there are no restrictions described by the HTML5 specifications about the audio codec, or container format, you can use.

MP3, AAC, or OGG audio files are fine. What changes is the support provided to these formats by the various browsers. To guarantee the broadest possible compatibility, it is therefore good practice to provide different formats of the same audio element through the source attribute. It will then be up to the browser to pick the first listed source that it can play.

What's involved

The `<audio>` tag inherits most of the attributes and events of the `<video>` tag. In fact, to insert an audio element, all you need to do is declare the tag and specify the `src` attribute:

```
<audio controls autoplay src="audio.mp3">
```

The attributes you can use with this markup are:

- src: a URL, local or remote, that contains the source.

- autoplay: specifies whether the file should play once loaded.

- loop: specifies whether the file should be repeatedly played.

- controls: specifies whether the browser should display its default media controls.

- preload: specifies whether the audio has to be preloaded by the page. It accepts the following values: none, metadata, and auto.

- play() : plays the audio.

- pause() : pauses the audio.

- canPlayType() : tells whether the given MIME type can be played.

- buffered() : Specifies the start and end time of the buffered part of the audio.

Because not all types of audio are supported by all devices and browsers, it is a best practice to list as many <source> elements as you like:

```
    <audio controls autoplay >
<source src="mySong.aac" type="audio/mp4">
<source src="mySong.oga" type="audio/ogg">
<source src="mySong.mp3" type="audio/mp3">
</audio>
```

It is also important to specify the type attribute that declares the MIME type to the browser.

By doing so, the browser recognizes if it is able to play that format without having to load the file.

How to build it

Here is an example of how to use the audio element:

```
<!DOCTYPE html>
<html>
  <head>
    <title>
    Solution 5-10: Using the Audio element
    </title>

  </head>

<body>

    <audio controls autoplay >
<source src="your_audio.aac" type="audio/mp4">
<source src="your_audio.oga" type="audio/ogg">
<source src="your_audio.mp3" type="audio/mp3">

    Your browser does not support the new HTML5 audio element
```

```
        </audio>
    </body>

</html>
```

We've declared an audio element, for which we've used the native audio controller of the browser, which is played automatically as soon as the user loads the web page (see Figure 5-14).

Figure 5-14. The native audio controller, rendered by the Opera browser

The same audio file was encoded in different formats to allow all browsers to play it. To do so, we used the source tag to declare the different formats:

```
    <audio controls autoplay >
<source src="your_audio.aac" type="audio/mp4">
<source src="your_audio.oga" type="audio/ogg">
<source src="your_audio.mp3" type="audio/mp3">
```

The browser recognizes which format it is able to play starting with the first one declared. Once it understands which file it can execute, it will stop loading the other formats.

Summary

Media elements are very popular on the Web today. That's why there's a lot of attention being paid to the brand-new HTML5 audio and video tags. Although embedding a video in a web page is very easy, in this chapter you've learned that you face with two different problems as a developer: the definition of a standard for the codecs to use by the video element and the adoption of video codecs by browsers. Ogg Theora, H.264, and VP8/WebM are currently the only formats that are supported by the video element. Moreover, each browser supports only one of those video codecs making the developers' life difficult.

In this chapter, you've learned how to embed and play a video on a web page, customize the video controller, and publish a video in different formats in order to guarantee the video's availability to the largest number of users possible. You also learned how to open a video in full screen format and how to apply a mask to a video.

In the next chapter, you will learn about the HTML5 canvas drawing API, which provides you with many possibilities for drawing directly inside your web pages and applications.

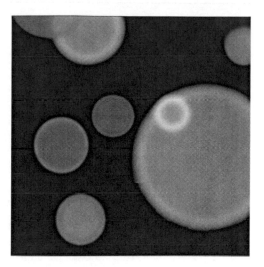

Chapter 6

HTML5 Drawing APIs

A cool feature of HTML5 is that you have the option to dynamically render 2D shapes and bitmap images on the fly, as it now has its own native drawing API. This is a huge move for HTML, which remained fairly static and limited in this area since its creation. Now those days are over, and a new realm of possibilities is here to deal with graphics created within the HTML page itself. It is now possible to build shapes, graphs, animations, and even games without needing to rely on any external plug-in (like Flash). This brings great value when it comes to developing web pages and applications, but even more so when it comes to compatibility with mobile devices.

The drawing API is part of the new HTML5 canvas element, and it provides an API for 2D drawing. More recently, the possibility of 3D drawing via HTML5's WebGL support seems to be on its way. At the time of this writing, few browsers are compatible with 3D drawing, but it's very likely that it will become part of the HTML5 options in the near future.

All major browsers that support HTML5 are compatible with the canvas element, and are therefore compatible with the 2D drawing API. However, when it comes to Internet Explorer, HTML5 compatibility will not come until version 9.0. Browser and mobile device compatibility for the canvas element and the 2D API is shown in Table 6-1.

Table 6-1. Browser and Mobile Device Compatibility with the Canvas Element and 2D API

Firefox	IE	Chrome	Safari	Opera	iPhone	Android	BlackBerry
3.0+	9	3.0+	3.0+	10.0+	1.0+	1.0+	OS 6.0

Note: Internet Explorer 7 and Internet Explorer 8 are not compatible with the HTML canvas element. It is possible, however, to overcome this problem and have canvas support in IE by using the 'ExplorerCanvas' extension. You can download the extension on Google Code at this address: http://excanvas.sourceforge.net/. You just need to include the following JavaScript code:

```
<!--[if IE]><script src="excanvas.js"></script><![endif]-->
```

Solution 6-1: How to draw with HTML5 using the canvas element's drawing API

The canvas element is a rectangular area that you can add to your HTML5 page, and it offers a wide range of graphic possibilities, as you can control every pixel through its 2D drawing API. By itself, the canvas element has no drawing abilities; everything you will create in it will be drawn programmatically using the JavaScript language.

In this solution, we will define a canvas element and make it ready for use so that you can take advantage of its drawing API.

What's involved

Setting the basis and background to be able to draw in HTML5 is pretty straightforward. You just have to define a canvas element, `<canvas></canvas>`. The canvas tag is really simple, and has only three attributes: width, height in pixels, and an ID to identify which canvas you're drawing in.

```
<canvas id="canvasID" width="300" height="200"></canvas>
```

You can position your canvas in your HTML5 page and apply CSS to it as you would do with any other tag.

Your `<canvas>` is initially empty—a plain area—unless you put a border or background color on it through CSS. However, it won't appear on the page until you draw something inside it. A canvas is simply a plain rectangle which will constitute the environment where you will be able to draw graphics, make animations, and so on.

To use your canvas and draw in it, you'll need to use JavaScript. If you have already drawn programmatically with languages like ActionScript 3 or Java, you will find a lot of similarities here.

Once the canvas is created, the first thing you need is to gain access to it. You can do that just like with any other element of the Document Object Model (DOM):

```
var myCanvas=document.getElementById("canvasID");
```

You can then access the canvas rendering context, which provides the access to the drawing API and its methods. To retrieve the context object, the canvas element uses the DOM method `getContext()`, which has only one parameter: the type of context. At the time of this writing, the 2D context is the only one available. We expect a 3D context to be available in the most popular browsers over the coming years, however, for now we must work with the 2D versions.

```
var context=myCanvas.getContext('2d');
```

Now that you have your canvas and access to its context object, you are ready to start using the drawing API and its methods to create some good pieces of art in your HTML page.

How to build it

Start by creating a new HTML5 page with your favorite code editor:

1. Create a blank HTML5 page.

```
<!DOCTYPE HTML>
<html>
<head>
<meta http-equiv="Content-Type" content="text/html; charset=utf-8">
<title>solution 6-1/title>
</head>
<body>
</body>
</html>
```

2. Create a canvas by inserting the canvas tag into your page, and set its width and height in pixels. (If you don't set any size, it will default to 300×150 in any browser.)

```
<canvas id="myCanvas" width="300" height="200"></canvas>
```

3. Give it a one-pixel grey border through CSS, as shown in Figure 6-1.

```
<canvas id="myCanvas" width="300" height="200" style="border:solid 1px #ccc;"></canvas>
```

Figure 6-1. Plain canvas with a one-pixel border

139

A canvas is a plain area until you draw in it, but you can use CSS properties as on any other HTML element and it will apply background color, image, brush stroke, and so forth.

4. Now you can add fallback content that you might want to show for non-supported browsers. An example of fallback content where canvas is not browser-supported is shown in Figure 6-2.

```
<canvas id="myCanvas" width="300" height="200" stye="border:solid 1px #ccc;">
Your browser doesn't support the HTML5 canvas element.
<img src="fallbackPicture.jpg" alt="fallback picture"/>
</canvas>
```

Figure 6-2. Fallback content from a non-canvas-compliant browser

Note: Canvas doesn't have an accessibility feature. You can use the fallback content to some extent to mask that problem, but it won't do so completely.

5. Access your canvas through the DOM with JavaScript.

```
<script type="text/JavaScript" language="JavaScript">

        var canvas=document.getElementById('myCanvas');

</script>
```

6. Retrieve your canvas context object.

```
<script type="text/JavaScript" language="JavaScript">

var canvas=document.getElementById('myCanvas');

var context = canvas.getContext("2d");
</script>
```

You can also optimize your code and access your canvas context in a single line, as follows:

```
var context= document.getElementById('myCanvas').getContext('2d');
```

Now your canvas is ready to be drawn in its 2D context. Here is the complete code for this example:

```
<script type="text/JavaScript" language="JavaScript">
        var canvas=document.getElementById('myCanvas');
        var context=canvas.getContext("2d");
</script>

<!DOCTYPE HTML>
<html>
<head>
<meta http-equiv="Content-Type" content="text/html; charset=utf-8">
<title>solution 6-1</title>
</head>
<body>
<canvas id="myCanvas" width="300" height="200" style="border:solid 1px #ccc;">
        Your browser doesn't support support the HTML5 canvas element.<br /><br />
            <img src="fallbackPicture.jpg" alt="fallback picture"/>
</canvas>
</body>
</html>
```

Expert tips

You can have several <canvas> elements on the same page, but you cannot have more than one context per canvas. Thus, if you were to try to retrieve another context object from your canvas, you would actually reset it.

```
<script type="text/JavaScript" language="JavaScript">

var canvas=document.getElementById('myCanvas');
var context = canvas.getContext("2d");
another_context= canvas.getContext("2d");

</script>
```

The first context variable will now return null, and you have access to the canvas context through the other context variable.

Solution 6-2: Using paths and coordinates

Now that you have set up your canvas and drawing context, let's see how to actually draw in it. The canvas drawing API gives you the option to draw with tools common to almost all graphics programs: strokes, fills, gradients, lines, primitives, arcs, or Bezier curves. Canvas drawing is vector-graphics based; the actual drawing is done in vectors. Once drawn, however, it becomes a bitmap format and you can interact with it at the pixel level. You will deal with paths when it comes to draw in it.

It is a pretty simple API, and it provides several methods to allow you to draw custom shapes.

What's involved

When it comes to drawing with paths, the process is divided into two major steps:

1. Define the path—where it starts, where it ends inside the canvas, and its style (colors, line width, strokestyle, fillstyle, and so on). This involves using the coordinate system of the canvas.

2. Render it by adding its stroke and/or fill.

Let's first have a look at the coordinate system of the canvas element to understand how to draw paths in it.

The canvas coordinates system

A canvas is a 2D grid and its coordinates are based on a regular 2D coordinate system: a vertical Y-axis, a horizontal X-axis, and an origin point that is positioned at x=0,y=0.

The coordinates of a canvas are always determined in pixels. The origin point, "0,0", is in the upper-left corner, and the pixel values increase as you go along the x- and y-axes. As you recall from Solution 6-1, when you defined a canvas, you gave it a height and a width (if not, the values default to 300 by 150 pixels). The dimensions of the drawing grid are determined by the canvas tag size values.

Whenever you want to place an element in the context, you first have to give its position on the canvas. You do this by passing x and y values, defined as shown in Figure 6-3. A positive x value will move to the right, and positive y value will move down the grid.

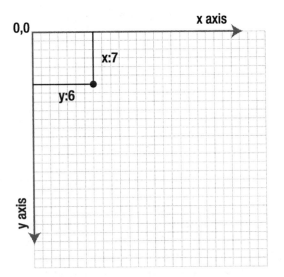

Figure 6-3. The coordinate system of a canvas and the coordinate and position of a point (7,6).

Drawing paths

Drawing with a path in HTML5 consists of drawing the general outline of a shape (it can be any shape). When it's over, you'll make it appear in the context by defining its stroke and/or fill color. Once your path is done and your shape is rendered, if you want to draw another shape just start over with a new path. It is important to note that there can be only one path per canvas, so creating a path will automatically close the previous one, if there is any.

When creating a path, you can connect multiple subpaths and draw complex shapes. You can use different methods to construct each subpath: lineTo(), quadraticCurveTo(), bezierCurveTo(), and arc(). The ending point of each successive subpath becomes the new starting point on the context grid, and this will continue until you finally close the path.

The path-drawing process always follows this sequence:

1. Start the path by calling the beginPath() method.

2. Define the coordinate where you want to start your path inside your canvas grid with the MoveTo(x,y) method, and pass the x and y coordinates that you wish to start the path. (With arc, you will pass those coordinates as parameters of the method itself and you won't need to use MoveTo()).

3. Use the API's methods to draw your shape with as many subpaths as you need to complete it. Each time you add a subpath, you must define the coordinate of the last point of the previous one using the MoveTo()method.

4. End the path by using the closePath () method. This will complete the shape. (If the methods that you used in the above step completes the path, then closePath () method does nothing.)

5. Finally, call the stroke () or the fill() methods to add a stroke or a fill, or both, to your shape. Note that if you are using the fill() method, it automatically closes the path and then fills the shape, so there is no need to invoke the closePath() method in this case.

> Tip: Although the canvas context defaults to a new subpath, it's a good practice to use the beginPath() method before creating each new path.

The 2D API offers the following methods to draw paths on a canvas. Again, remember that the actual drawing is done in the canvas context.

- *Drawing a line path.* You will define the starting point of your line with the moveTo() method and pass the coordinate of the ending point of your line by using the lineTo() method (see Figure 6.4).

  Method: context.lineTo(x,y);

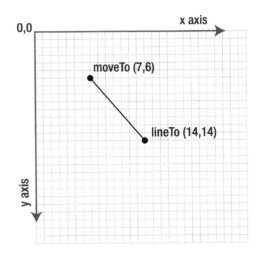

Figure 6-4. Drawing a line path

- *Drawing a Bezier curve.* A Bezier curve is normally defined by a starting point, an end point, and two control points. You set the starting point with the moveTo() method. You then have to add the coordinates of the two control points and of the ending point as parameters of the bezierCurveTo() method (see Figure 6.5).

    Method: context.bezierCurveTo(controlPoint1X, controlPoint1Y, controlPoint2X, controlPoint2Y, endPointX, endPointY);

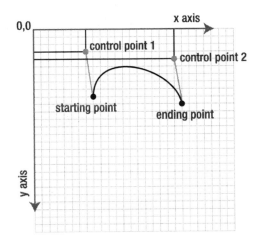

Figure 6-5. Drawing a Bezier curve

- *Drawing a quadratic curve.* Here you only have one control point, which will define the required curve by creating two invisible tangents connected to the starting point and the ending point, as shown in Figure 6.6. Thus, the parameters of the quadraticCurveTo()method will be the coordinates of the control point and the ending point. The starting point is, like the other paths, defined through the MoveTo( ) method.

Method: context.quadraticCurveTo(controlPointX, controlPointY, endingPointX, endingPointY);

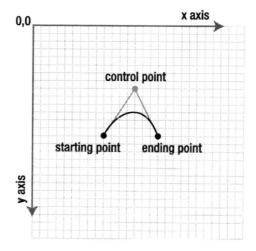

Figure 6-6. Drawing a quadratic curve

- *Drawing an arc.* You need to provide first the x and y coordinates of the center of your arc on the canvas context, then the starting angle and ending angle of your arc (they are set in radians), and finally whether you want to draw it counter-clockwise (true) or not (false), as shown in Figure 6-7.

Method: arc(centerX, centerY, radius, startingAngle, endingAngle, counter-clockwise;

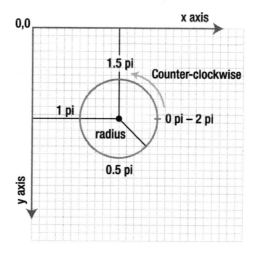

Figure 6-7. Drawing an arc

Setting styles for your shapes

A couple of canvas context properties are available to let you apply custom styles to your shapes, lines, and strokes.

Line properties and styles

- *Line join style.* If you want to draw a shape with several subpaths, there is a line property that addresses the rendering of the line connections: lineJoin. Paths can have three possible line joins: miter, round, or bevel, as shown in Figure 6-8. By default, it's set to miter.

miter **bevel** **round**

Figure 6-8. Line joins

- *Line width style.* You can also set the width of your line with the lineWidth property. The size should be given in pixels. By default, it's set to 1, and shown in Figure 6-9.

Line width Style : 1 pixel   Line width Style : 12 pixels

Figure 6-9. Line width styles

- *Line end style:* You can also add a cap at then end of any Canvas line through the lineCap property. Lines can have three different cap styles: butt, round, or square, as shown in Figure 6-10. By default, it is set to the butt cap style.

You may notice that two of these end styles look similar. This is because the butt property adds a flat edge perpendicular to the direction of the line, while the square value adds a rectangle with the length of the line width and the width of half of the line.

butt   square   round

Figure 6-10. Line end styles

How to build it

To see how to use paths and coordinates with the canvas API, we will show you how to draw the *friendsofED* logo (see Figure 6-11) because it requires the use of the different kind of paths to render in the canvas you already created in Solution 6-1.

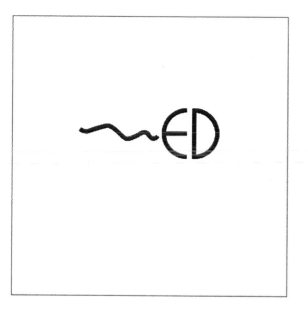

Figure 6-11. The *friendsofED* logo

1. Create a blank HTML5 page and add a canvas with a width and height of 500 pixels and with the ID "myCanvas". You should add some fallback content for users who don't have a browser supporting the HTML5 canvas element.

```
<!DOCTYPE html>
<html lang="en">
<head>
<meta charset="UTF-8" />
<title>solution 6-2/title>
</head>
 <body onload="drawLogo()">
 <canvas id="myCanvas" width="500" height="200">Your browser does not have support for HTML 5
Canvas.</canvas>
  </body></html>
```

2. From now on, everything will be done in JavaScript. You'll need to write a drawLogo() function that will contain the code with the drawing process. (In this solution, we include the script in the <head> tag page, but you could also choose to externalize your scripts like this: <script scr="yourcode.js"></script>). The first thing you'll do is to create an access to your canvas and its context.

```
<script type="text/JavaScript" language="JavaScript">
function drawLogo() {

var canvas = document.getElementById("myCanvas");
var context = canvas.getContext("2d");
```

3. Now that you have your context object, you can start drawing the designed mouse of the logo. When decomposing it, you have half a line crossing it at its center, and opposite to it a closed half circle.

```
context.lineWidth=4;

context.beginPath();
context.moveTo(190, 100);
context.arc(190,125,25,Math.PI*1.5,Math.PI*.5,true);
context.stroke();

context.beginPath();
context.moveTo(165,125);
context.lineTo(190,125);
context.stroke();

context.beginPath();
context.moveTo(198, 100);
context.arc(198,125,25,Math.PI*1.5,Math.PI*.5,false);
context.closePath();
context.stroke();
```

In this drawing, you want the same line width for any shape you draw. You just defined the lineWidth property to 4 pixels after defining your context. As such, all lines will have this width and you won't need to specify it for each shape you draw. If you want different line widths for each shape, you would just define a different lineWidth for each path you create.

In the above code, you opened a new path to draw each shape. You can also see why closing the path yourself can be important. In the case of the first shape, you drew a half-arc, but you want the stroke to appear only on the circumference and not the radius. So, you called the stroke() method after defining your arc circumference. This closes the path and draws a stroke only on the circumference. In the case of the second arc, by closing the path you connected the starting and ending point, adding a subpath between them. As a result, your stroke also includes the line between your starting and ending points.

4. Now draw the mouse wire shape, which is composed of several Bezier curves.

```
context.beginPath();
context.moveTo(73.3, 121.0);
context.bezierCurveTo(73.3, 121.0, 76.7, 123.7, 81.3, 123.3);
context.bezierCurveTo(81.3, 123.3, 100.3, 116.5, 104.0, 117.0);
context.bezierCurveTo(112.0, 118.0, 120.0, 131.3, 125.3, 131.0);
context.bezierCurveTo(129.0, 130.8, 136.7, 127.0, 136.7, 127.0);
context.bezierCurveTo(136.7, 127.0, 144.7, 120.3, 148.3, 126.3);
context.bezierCurveTo(153.5, 134.8, 158.0, 128.0, 158.0, 128.0);
context.stroke();
        }
```

```
    </script>
    </head>
```

Here again you started a new path, then you defined the subpaths you require to make this multicurve shape, and then you called the `stroke()` method. You now have all the shapes, and you can close your function and script.

5. To have your shape rendered when the page loads, add a call to the 'drawLogo()' function on the page load in the body tag.

```
<body onload="drawLogo()">
```

This is the complete code for this example:

```
<!DOCTYPE html>
<html lang="en">
<head>
<meta charset="UTF-8" />
<title>solution 6-2</title>
<script type="text/Javascript" language="Javascript">

function drawLogo() {
                var canvas = document.getElementById("canvas");
                var context = canvas.getContext("2d");
                context.lineWidth=4;
                context.beginPath();
                context.moveTo(190, 100);
                context.arc(190,125,25,Math.PI*1.5,Math.PI*.5,true);
                context.stroke();

                context.beginPath();
                context.moveTo(165,125);
                context.lineTo(190,125);
                context.stroke();
                context.beginPath();
                context.moveTo(198, 100);
                context.arc(198,125,25,Math.PI*1.5,Math.PI*.5,false);
                context.closePath();
                context.stroke();
                context.beginPath();
                context.moveTo(73.3, 121.0);
                context.bezierCurveTo(73.3, 121.0, 76.7, 123.7, 81.3, 123.3);
                context.bezierCurveTo(81.3, 123.3, 100.3, 116.5, 104.0, 117.0);
                context.bezierCurveTo(112.0, 118.0, 120.0, 131.3, 125.3, 131.0);
                context.bezierCurveTo(129.0, 130.8, 136.7, 127.0, 136.7, 127.0);
                context.bezierCurveTo(136.7, 127.0, 144.7, 120.3, 148.3, 126.3);
                context.bezierCurveTo(153.5, 134.8, 158.0, 128.0, 158.0, 128.0);
                context.stroke();
        }
    </script>
    </head>
    <body onload="drawLogo()">
      <canvas id="myCanvas" width="300" height="300" style="border:solid 1px #ccc"></canvas>
    </body>
</html>
```

149

Expert tips

Drawing with the Bezier curves can become very tedious when you want to make more complex shapes, as this involves calculation of what you draw. One way to avoid this is to draw your shape with any vector graphics program and then export the file in SVG format. You can then open it with any code editor to see the coordinates of your curves. You can then easily use them in your JavaScript code.

Also, if you are working with Adobe Illustrator, there is a great plug-in that will save you all the hard work. It is called AI2Canvas, and it lets you export your file directly as an HTML5 file with a canvas element and the corresponding JavaScript code. It will convert colors and gradients as well. You might want to rework the code to optimize it, of course, but this is a great plug-in for working with designers and for avoiding heavy calculations. You can download the plugin here: `http://visitmix.com/labs/ai2canvas/`.

Solution 6-3: Drawing shapes: rectangles and circles

In this solution, you will see how to draw circles and rectangles with the HTML5 drawing API. We already covered the use of paths for custom shapes in Solution 6-2, and now you will see methods provided by the API for specific shapes.

What's involved

The specific methods for circles, or perhaps we should say arcs, and rectangles also use the canvas path. This means it follows the same routine that you saw in Solution 6-2:

1. Setting the coordinates on the context canvas grid

2. Setting styles for filling and strokes

3. Applying the fill and/or stroke to complete the process and render the drawing.

We already mentioned in Solution 6-2 that there is only one path per canvas at a time, so you will just create a new path for each circle or rectangle, just as you did for each custom shape. These will be rendered through the context object of the canvas element, just like anything else drawn in the canvas. Let's start with rectangles.

Drawing rectangles

Unlike SVG, HTML5 canvas knows how to draw only one primitive shape—the rectangle. All other shapes must be created by combining one or more paths. There are four different methods that allow you to draw a rectangle in the canvas context; the method you select depends on your goal.

You can use the `rect()` method, which takes these parameters: the x and y position on the canvas context grid of the upper-left corner of the rectangle, and the desired width and height of the rectangle. The syntax is as follows:

```
rect(x, y, rectangle width,  rectangle height);
```

- The rect() method actually adds a rectangular path to the drawing context path. You don't need to call the beginPath() method here, as the rect() method does this itself. Then the stroke() or fill() method will render it on the context.

- You can draw a filled rectangle directly by calling the fillRect() method, which takes the same parameters as the rect() method. It's like having both the rect() and fill() methods in one.

```
fillRect(x, y, rectangle width,  rectangle height);
```

- Calling the StrokeRect() method will draw a stroked rectangle directly. It takes the same parameters as the two previous methods.

```
strokeRect(x,y,rectangle width, rectangle height);
```

- The last method is clearRect(). Primarily, this method does not draw a rectangle shape, but rather subtracts a rectangular shape from another shape. (If you are familiar with Illustrator, it's just like using the substract option of the 'pathfinder' tool). clearRect()takes the same parameters as the rect() method.

```
clearRect(x,y, rectangle width, rectangle height);
```

Drawing circles

For circles, you will need to use the arc method that we worked with in Solution 6-2, and then draw an arc with a starting angle of 0° and ending angle of 2×pi radians, drawing a complete rounded arc.

The method for drawing an arc is arc(), and it takes the following parameters:

1. The x,y coordinates of the center of the circle on the canvas grid

2. The start angle and end angle values, specified in radians. Since you want to draw a circle, you start from 0 and end at 2×pi (the equivalent in radians to 360 degrees)

3. A Boolean parameter indicating whether you want to draw your arc counter-clockwise (true) or not (false). In the case of a circle, it will work either way of course, so you can set it to either of these

```
arc(x center coordinate, y center coordinate, 0,Math.pi*2,true)
```

As it creates a path, the arc() method will only set the circle shape that you want to draw. To render it, you have to call the stroke() or fill() method, depending on your needs. (As you have drawn a complete arc here, the closePath() method is not necessary).

How to build it

To demonstrate this solution, you will draw a circle and two rectangles programmatically as illustrated in Figure 6-12. The inner rectangle will be a square, filled and stroked. It's a pretty basic drawing, but it covers the methods related for those two shapes. Remember that the drawing API is itself simple, but that doesn't mean that you can't draw complex things with it—far from that. It all depends on how you construct complex shapes by adding together several simple ones. The result of the following code will come out as follows:

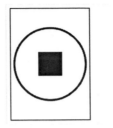

Figure 6-12. Drawing a complex shape

1. Open a basic empty HTML5 page, as in Solution 6-1, with a canvas and access to its drawing context.

```
<!DOCTYPE HTML>
<html>
<head>
<meta http-equiv="Content-Type" content="text/html; charset=utf-8">
<title>solution 6-3</title>
</head>

<body>
<canvas id="shapes" width="300" height="300" style="border:solid 1px #ccc"></canvas>
</body>
</html>
```

2. Create a drawShapes() function that will be called on the load page event. The first thing to do is to access your canvas and its context object.

```
<script type="text/JavaScript" language="JavaScript">
function drawShapes(){
var canvas=document.getElementById("shapes");
var context=canvas.getContext("2d");}
context.beginPath();
context.lineWidth="2";
context.strokeRect(10,10,200,280);
```

You have here a rectangle with a width of 200 pixels and a height of 280 pixels, with the upper-left corner at the coordinate (10,10) on your canvas. The stroke of the rectangle has a width of 2 pixels.

3. Draw your circle.

```
context.beginPath();
context.lineWidth="5";
context.arc(110,150,90,0,Math.PI*2,true);
context.stroke();
```

Your circle will have its center at the point 110,150, which is the center of your rectangle (itself placed at 10,10 of the canvas). It has a radius of 90 pixels and a stroke of 5 pixels.

4. To finish, draw a filled square at the center of your circle.

```
context.beginPath();
context.fillRect(80,120,60,60);
```

You started a new path and, with the `fillRect()` method, you drew a small black square positioned at the center of the circle. (A filled shape, unless otherwise defined, will always be black.)

5. To have your shape rendered when the page loads, add a call to your `drawShapes()` function on the page load in the body tag.

```
<body onload="drawShapes()">
```

Here is the complete code for this example:

```
<!DOCTYPE HTML>
<html>
<head>
<meta http-equiv="Content-Type" content="text/html; charset=utf-8">
<title>solution 6-3</title>
<script type="text/Javascript" language="Javascript">

function drawShapes(){
        var canvas=document.gettlementById("shapes");
        var context=canvas.getContext("2d");
        context.beginPath();
        context.lineWidth="2";
        context.strokeRect(10,10,200,280);
        context.beginPath();
        context.lineWidth="5";
        context.arc(110,150,90,0,Math.PI*2,true);
        context.stroke();
        context.beginPath();
        context.fillRect(80,120,60,60);
}
</script>
</head>
<body onLoad="drawShapes()">
        <canvas id="shapes" width="300" height="300" style="border:solid 1px #ccc"></canvas>
</body>
</html>
```

Expert tips

If you are not familiar with JavaScript or with drawing programmatically with other languages like ActionScript or Java, this may be a bit puzzling at first. Canvas Console is a great online tool to help you try all the methods of the canvas drawing API and to get familiar with their use (see Figure 6-13). This tool was coded by John Allsopp, a leading HTML5 and CSS expert (www.johnfallsopp.com), and it lets you draw anything in a context and see the result instantly. It also has a small cheat sheet of all the methods and properties. You can try it at this address: http://westciv.com/tools/canvasConsole/

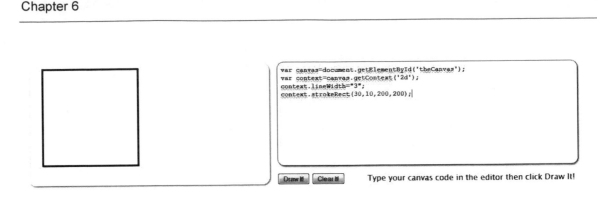

```
var canvas=document.getElementById('theCanvas');
var context=canvas.getContext('2d');
context.lineWidth="3";
context.strokeRect(30,10,200,200);|
```

Draw It   Clear It   Type your canvas code in the editor then click Draw It!

Figure 6-13. Canvas Console

Solution 6-4: Filling shapes with solid colors

In the two previous solutions, we covered drawing custom and basic shapes. You used only the default line and fill styles, which came out black, the default filling color. We will now explore the drawing API's options for filling your drawings, and you will see how you can add some solid colors.

What s involved

First let's see how to simply fill your shapes with basic colors.

Setting the *fillStyle* property

To fill an HTML5 canvas shape, you need to use the fillStyle property of the canvas context. With it, you can define the specific color which you want to fill your shape with. Then the fill() method, or fillRect() in the case of a rectangle, will apply this property and render your shape with your defined style.

The color property can be defined by referring to its RGB color value:

canvasContext.fillStyle = "rgb(255,0,255)";

or its hexadecimal value:

canvasContext.fillStyle = "0xcccccc";

If you call the fill() method without defining any fillStyle, the default color, black, will then be applied.

> Note: As you saw in Solutions 6-3 and 6-4, shapes, whether custom or not, are made up of subpaths of the canvas context path. As there is only one path per canvas, calling the fill() method closes the path automatically. This means that, if your combination of subpaths doesn't connect itself, the path will close anyway and connect the last end point with the starting path point and fill this area. Thus you should be careful about where you want this to happen, but it can also spare you some drawing code. For example, to draw a filled triangle you'll need to draw just two lines and, at the time of rendering, the API will create the last line to close the path.

Blending colors

When you fill your shape with solid colors, the drawing API will also add an alpha blend value to the mix that can be used. Instead of the rgb() property we discussed above, you must use the property rgba(), with 'a' standing for the alpha value and being the last parameter. The alpha value is to be defined from 0 (no transparency; that is, solid color) to 1(100% or complete transparency). This is illustrated in Figure 6-14.

Figure 6-14. Two rectangles overlapping, each with an alpha value of 0.5

Filling strokes

You can also set a solid color fill for the stroke of your shapes and the text drawn in the canvas context by using the strokeStyle property and then calling the stroke() method, which will render the stroke of your shape according to the style you defined (size, color, and so on).

Just as for fillStyle, the fillStroke color property can be defined by referring to its RGB color value:

```
canvasContext.fillStroke="rgb(255,0,255)";
```

or its hexadecimal value:

```
canvasContext.fillStroke="0xcccccc";
```

> Note: If you set both the fill and stroke for a shape, call fill() before stroke().
> Otherwise, the fill will overlap half of the stroke.

How to build it

In the previous solution, you drew several shapes inside your canvas. You will now fill them with some solid colors.

1. Open the previous solution code. You'll have your HTML5 page with a canvas of 300 by 300 pixels. Upon load, you already drew several shapes in it: a circle inside a rectangle.

```
<!DOCTYPE HTML>
<html>
```

```
<head>
<meta http-equiv="Content-Type" content="text/html; charset=utf-8">
<title>solution 6-4/title>
</head>
<body on load=drawShapes()>
<canvas id="myCanvas" width="300" height="300"></canvas>
</body>
</html>
```

2. Add your JavaScript code and write your function to draw your shapes, starting with accessing the context object of your canvas.

```
<script type="text/JavaScript" language="JavaScript">
function drawShapes(){
var canvas=document.getElementById("myCanvas");
var context=canvas.getContext("2d");
```

3. Inside the function drawShapes that you created, now draw your rectangle by first defining the fillStyle property. In this example, use the red color to fill it. You can either use its hexadecimal value (#ED1C24), or rgb (237,28,36).

```
context.fillStyle="#ED1C24";
context.fillRect(0, 0,200,200);
```

For this one, you didn't use any stroke color, so no stroke will appear. You have here a square shape of 200 by 200, and its upper-left corner will be placed at the upper-left corner of your canvas, as the coordinates are set to 0,0.

You would have had the same result with the following code:

```
context.beginPath();
context.fillStyle="#ED1C24";
context.rect(0, 0,200,200);
context.fill();
```

4. Now you can start a new path and draw your circle.

```
context.beginPath();
context.lineWidth="4";
context.strokeStyle="#1B1464";
context.fillStyle="#29ABE2";
context.arc(100,100,50,0,Math.PI*2,true);
context.stroke();
context.fill();
}
```

Here, you defined your circle's style properties (the stroke width, the stroke color, and the filling color), then its position and size, and finally you rendered it as usual by calling the fill() and stroke() methods.

5. You can now close your script tag.

```
</script>
```

As in previous solutions, call your drawShapes() function upon loading your page to load your canvas context. (Alternatively, you could just call it at the end of your script and it would have the same result.). The result is seen in Figure 6-15.

```
<body onload=drawShapes()>
```

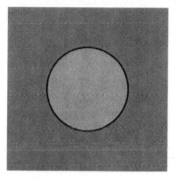

Figure 6-15. Shapes filled with plain colors

This is the complete code for this example :

```
<!DOCTYPE HTML>
<html>
<head>
<meta http-equiv="Content-Type" content="text/html; charset=utf-8">
<title>solution 6-4</title>
<script type="text/Javascript" language="Javascript">

function drawShapes(){
        var canvas=document.getElementById("myCanvas");
        var context=canvas.getContext("2d");
        context.fillStyle="#ED1C24";
        context.fillRect(0, 0,200,200);
        context.beginPath();
        context.lineWidth="4";
        context.strokeStyle="#1B1464";
        context.fillStyle="#29ABE2";
        context.arc(100,100,50,0,Math.PI*2,true);
        context.stroke();
        context.fill();
}
</script>
</head>

<body onLoad="drawShapes()">
<canvas id="myCanvas" width="300" height="300"></canvas>
</body>
</html>
```

Expert tips

Thus far, we have been dealing with very simple shape combinations without any real purpose other than drawing. When you start to build more complex canvas drawings and use them in an interactive way, however, you will have to be really careful with the performance of your code. Drawing can be quite processor-expensive, and once you have drawn something in your canvas you can't really separate it out from other drawn objects; that is, you are creating a single bitmap graphic as you go. Thus, any change will mean redrawing all of it. It can therefore be beneficial to combine CSS and the drawing API in some come cases.

If you have drawn a background, let's say, that you know you don't want to change on each interaction, it can be a good idea to have it as a background image of your canvas through CSS. As such, your context will redraw only what has to be changed and save your application some rendering expense.

Solution 6-5: Using gradients to fill shapes

Now that we know how to draw shapes filled with solid colors, let's see how we can fill them with gradients.

What's involved

As with any standard drawing programs, the API provides two types of gradients: linear and radial.

Using a linear gradient

To create a linear gradient with HTML5 Canvas, you need to call the `createLinearGradient()` method, which requires four parameters defining the direction of the gradient by creating an invisible line (See Figure 6-16).

```
var myGradient=context.createLinearGradient(lineStartingPointX, lineStartingPointY,↪
  lineEndingPointX, lineEndingPointY);
```

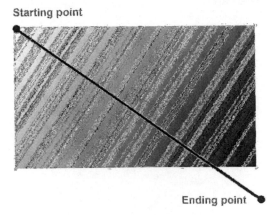

Figure 6-16. A linear gradient

Once you have created your gradient direction and set its coordinates, you can insert its colors using the addColorStop property. You can add as many colors as you need to your gradient and create subtle gradient-filled shapes and strokes with the following method using two parameters, offset and color value:

```
myGradient.addColorStop(offset value, color1);
myGradient.addColorStop(offset value, color2);
```

Using a radial gradient

To create a radial gradient with HTML5 canvas, you will use the createRadialGradient() method.

It has six parameters as follows, and as listed in Table 6-2:

```
var gradient=context.createRadialGradient(startCircleX, startCircleY, startCirlceRadius,↪
 endCircleX, endCircleY, endCirleRadius);
```

Table 6-2. Parameters and Values of the createRadialGradient () Method

Parameter	Value
startCircleX	X coordinate of the first gradient circle
startCircleY	Y coordinate of the first gradient circle
startCirlceRadius	Radius of the first gradient circle, in radians
endCircleX	X coordinate of the second gradient circle
endCircleY	Y coordinate of the second gradient circle
endCirleRadius	Radius of the second gradient circle, in radians

These parameters are the coordinates and radius of two imaginary circles that define the location and gradation of the gradient. Just as with the linear gradient, you can then add as many colors as required to fill your needs with the addColorStop method.

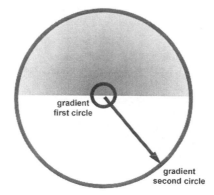

Figure 6-17. Radial gradient

You can see an example of a radial gradient with two colors in a semicircle shape, and the two invisible circles defined in the gradient parameters in Figure 6-17. The gradient starts from the first circle, which has a radius of 40 pixels, and moves radially toward the second circle (with a radius of 300 pixels), deploying the colors according to their offset value (0 and 1). The code to define this radial gradient is as follows:

```
var gradient=context.createRadialGradient(350,310,40,350,310,300);
gradient.addColorStop(0,"#6699cc");  //light blue color
gradient.addColorStop(1,"#cee7fa");  //darker blue color
```

Filling strokes with gradient

In the same way, you can fill the stroke of your shapes with gradient by defining the Fillstyle with a gradient and then using the strokeFill() method. The following example would fill a square stroke with a gradient.

```
gradient=context.createLinearGradient(20, 120, 160, 120);
gradient.addColorStop(0, "rgb(0, 0, 0)"); // black color
gradient.addColorStop(1, "rgb(255, 255, 255)"); // white color
context.strokeStyle=gradient;
context.rect(10, 10,200,200);
context.stroke();
```

How to build it

1. Start, as in other solutions, by setting up your canvas in an HTML5 page. Upon load, call the function drawGradientShapes() that will contain your JavaScript for drawing two shapes filled with gradients.

```
<!DOCTYPE HTML>
<html>
<head>
<meta http-equiv="Content-Type" content="text/html; charset=utf-8">
<title>solution 6-5</title>
</head>
<body onLoad="drawGradientShapes()">
<canvas id="myCanvas" width="300" height="300" style="border:solid 1px #ccc"></canvas>
</body>
</html>
```

2. Now to the JavaScript part and the drawGradientShapes() function. First, access your canvas and its context object. Then proceed by drawing a custom shape.

```
<script type="text/JavaScript" language="JavaScript">
function drawGradientShapes() {
    var canvas=document.getElementById("myCanvas");
    var context=canvas.getContext("2d");

    context.beginPath();
    context.moveTo(126.7, 185.6);
    context.bezierCurveTo(116.5, 192.0, 85.4, 160.2, 85.4, 160.2);
    context.bezierCurveTo(85.4, 160.2, 50.5, 187.6, 41.2, 179.9);
```

```
context.bezierCurveTo(31.9, 172.1, 52.5, 132.8, 52.5, 132.8);
context.bezierCurveTo(52.5, 132.8, 15.7, 108.1, 20.2, 96.8);
context.bezierCurveTo(24.7, 85.6, 68.4, 93.1, 68.4, 93.1);
context.bezierCurveTo(68.4, 93.1, 80.6, 50.4, 92.7, 51.2);
context.bezierCurveTo(104.7, 52.0, 111.2, 95.9, 111.2, 95.9);
context.bezierCurveTo(111.2, 95.9, 155.5, 94.3, 158.5, 106.0);
context.bezierCurveTo(161.5, 117.7, 121.7, 137.4, 121.7, 137.4);
context.bezierCurveTo(121.7, 137.4, 136.9, 179.1, 126.7, 185.6);
context.closePath();
```

3. Your shape path is now complete, and you can now define its `fillStyle`. Here you'll use a linear gradient with two colors.

```
gradient=context.createLinearGradient(19.8, 118.8, 158.7, 118.8);
gradient.addColorStop(0.00, "rgb(122, 226, 28)");
gradient.addColorStop(1.00, "rgb(200, 255, 47)");
context.fillStyle=gradient;
```

You just defined your linear gradient, giving it the coordinate of that invisible line you wish your gradient to follow. Then define the gradient colors and finally apply it to your context `fillStyle`.

4. You define the `lineWidth` and the color of your stroke as usual.

```
context.lineWidth=2;
context.strokeStyle = "rgb(127, 127, 127)";
```

5. Call the `stroke()` and `fill()` methods to complete the process and render your shape on the context.

```
context.stroke();
context.fill();
```

6. You will now draw a circle with a radial gradient.

```
context.beginPath();
context.arc(240,190,50,0,2*Math.PI,true);
context.closePath();
gradient=context.createRadialGradient(240,190,10,240,190,50);
gradient.addColorStop(0.00, "rgb(100, 181, 251)");
gradient.addColorStop(0.5, "rgb(139, 203, 253)");
gradient.addColorStop(1.00, "rgb(178, 224, 255)");
context.fillStyle = gradient;
context.fill();
```

You begin a new path, define your circle, and then its style. Here it's a radial gradient with three colors. The coordinate of the final gradient circle is at the center of your shape, and the second gradient circle has the same coordinates and radius of your actual circle. It will produce a gradient with three colors starting at the center of your circle and radiating toward its edge.

To render the final result you call the `fill()` method.

7. You can now close your function and script, and admire your handiwork (see Figure 6-18).

```
}
</script>
```

Figure 6-18. Custom shapes filled with gradients

This is the complete code for this example:

```
<!DOCTYPE HTML>
<html>
<head>
<meta http-equiv="Content-Type" content="text/html; charset=utf-8">
<title>solution 6-5</title>
<script type="text/Javascript" language="Javascript">

function drawGradientShapes(){
     var canvas=document.getElementById("myCanvas");
     var context=canvas.getContext("2d");
     context.beginPath();
     context.moveTo(126.7, 185.6);
     context.bezierCurveTo(116.5, 192.0, 85.4, 160.2, 85.4, 160.2);
     context.bezierCurveTo(85.4, 160.2, 50.5, 187.6, 41.2, 179.9);
     context.bezierCurveTo(31.9, 172.1, 52.5, 132.8, 52.5, 132.8);
     context.bezierCurveTo(52.5, 132.8, 15.7, 108.1, 20.2, 96.8);
     context.bezierCurveTo(24.7, 85.6, 68.4, 93.1, 68.4, 93.1);
     context.bezierCurveTo(68.4, 93.1, 80.6, 50.4, 92.7, 51.2);
     context.bezierCurveTo(104.7, 52.0, 111.2, 95.9, 111.2, 95.9);
     context.bezierCurveTo(111.2, 95.9, 155.5, 94.3, 158.5, 106.0);
     context.bezierCurveTo(161.5, 117.7, 121.7, 137.4, 121.7, 137.4);
     context.bezierCurveTo(121.7, 137.4, 136.9, 179.1, 126.7, 185.6);
     context.closePath();

     gradient=context.createLinearGradient(19.8, 118.8, 158.7, 118.8);
     gradient.addColorStop(0.00, "rgb(122, 226, 28)");
     gradient.addColorStop(1.00, "rgb(200, 255, 47)");
     context.fillStyle=gradient;
     context.lineWidth=2;
     context.strokeStyle = "rgb(127, 127, 127)";
     context.fill();
     context.stroke();
     context.beginPath();
     context.arc(240,190,50,0,2*Math.PI,true);
```

```
        context.closePath();
        gradient=context.createRadialGradient(240,190,10,240,190,50);
        gradient.addColorStop(0.00, "rgb(100, 181, 251)");
        gradient.addColorStop(0.5, "rgb(139, 203, 253)");
        gradient.addColorStop(1.00, "rgb(178, 224, 255)");
        context.fillStyle=gradient;
        context.fill();
}
</script>
</head>
<body onLoad="drawGradientShapes()">
        <canvas id="myCanvas" width="300" height="300" style="border:solid 1px #ccc">
    Your Browser doesn't support HTML5 Canvas !
    </canvas>
</body>
</html>
```

Solution 6-6: Drawing texts in a canvas

The canvas drawing API allows you to manipulate and draw text in the canvas element. In this solution, we show you how to do this.

What's involved

Drawing text isn't much different from drawing shapes and paths. It follows a similar process except that, instead of first describing a path or shape, you specify the font and font size you want to be used through the attribute font and then render the text with stroke and/or fill methods.

All the rendering styles we saw previously, color, gradient, and so on, can apply to text the same as they do to any other shape. CSS styles can also be used on text drawn through the canvas id.

Managing text inside a canvas is not as customizable as it is for regular text with CSS. But let's look at the several attributes that you can use.

Font attributes

Text drawn inside the canvas inherits the font size and style of the <canvas> element itself, if there are any, but you can override them by setting the font property and its attributes in your drawing context.

The font attributes that you can define there are the same as the ones you would set in CSS—font style, font weight, font size, and font family. The syntax is as follows:

context.font="bold 14px Arial" ;

The default font is 10 pixel sans-serif.

Aligning text attributes

You can set the textAlign property to align your text in a canvas context. The alignment is set relative to the x and y position that you established for your text. It can have these values: left, right, start(default

163

value), end, and center. Start and end attributes are based on the direction of the text of the canvas markup, left-to-right or right-to-left.

The text baseline attributes

Without going into a deep explanation, let's say that text alignment is based on a line box containing the text, and that every line box has a baseline. (You can see a figure representing this by opening the HTML5 specifications link below.) The baseline determines where your text will be positioned in the line box, and its values can be: top, hanging, middle, alphabetic(default), ideographic, and bottom.

For Latin-based alphabets, top, bottom, middle, and alphabetic will most likely only be used. If you have to deal with other alphabets, you can refer to the complete baseline description on the HTML5 specifications web page:

```
www.whatwg.org/specs/web-apps/current-work/multipage/the-canvas-element.html#dom-context-2d↵
-textbaseline
```

It is important to understand that text rendering on a canvas is treated the same way as any other path. Therefore, text can be stroked and filled, and all rendering styles can apply to text just as they do to any other shape. This being said, as you might expect the text drawing routine follows the same process as for any path:

1. Define your text style. Optionally, as with other shapes, you can specify the `fillStyle`, `strokeStyle`, `lineStyle`, and `lineWidth` attributes, and they will apply in the same way as for other shapes.

2. Call the `strokeText()`, or `fillText()` method to render the text on the canvas.

Those two methods each take three parameters: the x and y coordinates of your text on the canvas, and the string you want to draw. As you would guess, `strokeText()` will draw only the stroke of the font and `fillText()` will draw the text filled.

```
context.fillText(x,y,"string");
context.strokeText(x,y,"string");
```

> Note: As you may know, CSS3 now provides the @font-face property that allows you to load a specific font from a remote location. You may be tempted to use this with your canvas text by setting the canvas font properties through CSS. However, as drawing on the canvas has to happen immediately when you call the fillText() or strokeFill() method, the browser normally won't have loaded the font from its location at the time of context rendering. So most likely, it will just fall back to the default font.
>
> Whenever you want to use text in your canvas, several things have to be taken in consideration. First of all, anything that is rendered in the canvas is not accessible, and that goes for text as well. As it is, text drawn in it won't be selectable either. You may be tempted to use the canvas fallback content to overcome this problem, but it doesn't really fit this need.

How to build it

1. Create a basic HTML5 page with a canvas element.

```
<!DOCTYPE html>
<html>
<head>
<meta charset="utf-8">
<title>solution 6-6/title>
<script>
</script>
</head>
<body>
<canvas width="500" height="300" id="myCanvas" style="border:1px solid #ccc"></canvas>
```

2. In the head of your page, add a JavaScript tag and write a drawText() function that will contain your code for rendering text in your canvas. As in previous solutions, you start by accessing your canvas and its rendering context.

```
<script type="text/JavaScript" language="JavaScript">
function drawText() {

  var canvas=document.getElementById("myCanvas");
  var context=canvas.getContext("2d");

}

</script>
```

3. You can start to draw your text inside your function. First, define your text styles.

```
context.strokeStyle = "#993300";
context.fillStyle=" #ffff09";
context.font="bold 80px arial";
context.textAlign="center";
context.lineWidth="5";
context.lineJoin="round";
```

You have set the font, its size, the text stroke, and fill colors. Here you left the baseline to default.

4. Call the methods to draw the actual stroked and filled text and close your function.

```
context.strokeText("TML5",220,90);
context.fillText("HTML5",220,90);
}
```

As you are drawing, you have to draw both the stroke and the text fill to have stroked text.

5. Call your function upon loading your page inside the body tag of your page.

```
<body onLoad="drawText()">
```

6. The result will be as shown in Figure 6-19:

Figure 6-19. Background- filled text

This is the complete code for this example:

```
<!DOCTYPE html>
<html>
<head>
<meta charset="utf-8">
<title>solution 6-6</title>
<script type="text/Javascript" language="Javascript">

function draw_text() {
        var canvasObj=document.getElementById("myCanvas");
        var context=canvasObj.getContext("2d");
        context.font="bold 15px arial";
        context.strokeStyle = "#993300";
        context.fillStyle=" #ffff09";
        context.font="bold 80px arial";
        context.textAlign="center";
        context.lineWidth="5";
        context.lineJoin="round";
        context.fillText("HTML5",220,140);
        context.strokeText("HTML5",220,140);
}
</script>
</head>
<body onLoad="draw_text()">
        <canvas id="myCanvas" width="500" height="300" style="border:1px solid #ccc"></canvas>
</body>
```

Expert tips

You may find that the text possibilities in the canvas element are a bit limited. Jim Studt, a great JavaScript developer, has created an interesting JavaScript plug-in, named "canvas text," that extends the canvas context and adds some extra methods to deal with text. It adds the following methods to the canvas:

- `context.drawText` / `context.drawTextRight` / `context.drawTextCenter`: This will draw text in the specified font and size at the position (baseline).

- `context.measureText`: This will return the width of the text.

- `context.fontAscent / ctx.fontDescent`: returns the ascent/descent from the baseline.

Having these additional methods increases the possibilities for manipulating your text size and its position. They can be really useful in the case of dynamic rendering for applications, for example. You can learn more about these methods and read the documentation at: `http://jim.studt.net/canvastext/`

Solution 6-7: Working with relative font sizes to draw text on a canvas

Whenever you add text, you have to set its size. It can be fixed in pixels, but you can also set it relatively just as you can do with CSS.

What's involved

Just like every other element on your page, the `<canvas>` has a font size that is based on what you defined in your CSS. It's not different from what you are used to when dealing with your HTML4 page. Let's have a small recap of relative font size notions to understand how it works in canvas.

Font-size, em, and relative text content

There are two ways you can set the font size in your HTML page, either with an absolute value that could be in pixels (px) or points (pt), or with a relative value—the "em" value..

Em gives you the possibility of setting your font with a size relative to its parent element. In CSS, this is most useful for adapting your styles according to the rendering media.

You can use em values for your canvas text. What does this mean? Giving an em size to a font is designating its size proportionally to the font size of its parent element. Thus if your canvas font has been set to 10 px, and you then draw a text of a size of 2 em, this text will be twice as large as any other text on your canvas that doesn't have a specific font size defined.

```
context.font="2em Arial";
context.fillText("Arial with a 2em size", 100, 50);
```

Now, if you want to get rid of absolute value completely, you'll have to set the parent element font size in % (your canvas), and you'll have a complete relative rendering of your text. Nowadays, especially with the advent of smartphones and now tablets, taking care of the different configurations is crucial if you want your web content to be available on any platform.

How to build it

1. Create a basic HTML5 page, and add a canvas element to it.

```
<!DOCTYPE HTML>
<html>
```

```
<head>
<meta http-equiv="Content-Type" content="text/html; charset=utf-8">
<title>solution 6-7/title>
</head>
<body onLoad="drawText()">
<canvas id="textCanvas" width="400" height="300" style="font-size:100%"></canvas>
</body>
</html>
```

When adding the canvas element, set the CSS font-size to 100%. As such, your canvas font size will adjust the font size to the parent of the canvas.

2. You can now add your JavaScript code to draw your text. Here you'll write a drawText() function that will be called upon page load to have your text rendered immediately when loading the page in your browser. As seen in previous solutions, you'll first access your canvas through the DOM and then its context object in which to draw. Then you'll start to define and draw your text.

```
<script type="text/JavaScript" language="JavaScript">

function drawText(){
var canvas=document.getElementById('textCanvas');

var context=canvas.getContext('2d');
```

3. Now you want to write some text that's 0.8 times the size of the standard canvas text. To do this, you redefine the context font properties to override the one you just used, set the size to 0.8em, and then draw your new string with the fillText() method.

```
context.font="0.8em Arial";
context.fillText("Canvas Text Arial size 0.8em", 10, 50);
```

4. If you want to write text twice as high of the one defined in the canvas, you override the context.font properties according to your needs:

```
context.font="2em Arial";
context.fillText("Canvas Text Arial size 2em", 10, 100);
```

5. To use pixel sizes in the same context, you would do the following:.

```
context.font="14px Arial";
context.fillText("Canvas Text Arial size 14 pixels", 10, 140);

}

</script>
```

You can now close your function. When loading the page, you should have the following visual result:

Canvas Text Arial size 0.8em

Canvas Text Arial size 2em

Canvas Text Arial size 14 pixels

Figure 6-20. Text drawn with relative font sizes

This is the complete code for this example:

```
<!DOCTYPE HTML>
<html>
<head>
<meta http-equiv="Content-Type" content="text/html; charset=utf-8">
<title>solution 6-7</title>
<script type="text/Javascript" language="Javascript">
function drawText(){
        var canvas=document.getElementById('textCanvas');
        var context=canvas.getContext('2d');
        context.font="0.8em Arial";
        context.fillText("Canvas Text Arial size 0.8em", 10, 50);
        context.font="2em Arial";
        context.fillText("Canvas Text Arial size 2em", 10, 100);
        context.font="14px Arial";
        context.fillText("Canvas Text Arial size 14 pixels", 10, 140);
}
</script>
</head>
<body onLoad="drawText()">
<canvas id="textCanvas" width="400" height="300" style="font-size:100%"></canvas>
</body>
```

Expert tips

If you want your font size to adjust to the default value of the client browser, just do as you did in HTML4; that is, set the default font size of your page to 100% in your CSS file. The canvas, being a child element, will now base its font size on this value.

Solution 6-8: Saving a shape as a PNG file

Say that you made a small application in HTML5 using canvas and the drawing API, where the user can produce some custom results (generating a custom graph, or a design through a drawing application, for example), and you want him or her to be able to save it. The canvas object provides a method that will let you convert your canvas context into a PNG format file. (There are other image formats as well, but PNG is the only one with support required by the HTML5 specifications, so we will focus on it.)

What's involved

To retrieve the image data from the canvas, you will the use `toDataURL()` method of the canvas object.

When called, this method returns a URL containing a representation of the canvas content as a PNG file.

```
var canvas=document.getElementById('myCanvas');
var imageDate=canvas.toDataURL();
```

The content of the `dataUrl` retrieved will be retuned in the format `data:image/png;base64`, and a base64 string of your PNG image data. If the canvas has no pixels (that is. its height and width are null), then the method just return the string `data`. You can then retrieve and save it.

How to build it

1. Create an HTLM5 page with a canvas, as you have for other solutions in this chapter.

```
<!DOCTYPE html>
<html lang="en">
 <head>
  <meta charset="UTF-8" />
  <title>solution 8-1/title>
 </head>
 <body onload="init()">
   <canvas id="canvas" width="400" height="400"></canvas>
</body>
  </html>
```

2. Add a button in the body of your page with the call to the function `saveCanvas` on its click event.

```
<button onclick="saveCanvas();">Save PNG</button>
```

That's about it for the HTML5 itself. You will deal only with JavaScript from now on for this solution.

As you want your canvas and context to be available to several functions you are going to code, start by defining their respective variables. You then retrieve your canvas and context objects in a separate function that you will call upon load of your page. Finally, you will call a function (that you will write just after this) that will deal with drawing a simple shape, and that you'll call `drawShape()`.

```
<script type="text/Javascript" language="Javascript">
var canvas;
var context;
function init(){
canvas=document.getElementById('canvas');
context=canvas.getContext('2d');
drawShape();
}
```

3. For your function `drawShape()`, make it really simple and just draw a red square 200 pixels wide in the canvas.

```
function drawShape(){
        context.fillStyle="red";
        context.fillRect(10,10,200,200);
}
```

4. Use the function called on your button's click event, saveCanvas(), where you will retrieve the PNG image data of your canvas.

```
function saveCanvas(){
        urlData=canvas.toDataURL();
        window.location=urlData;

}
```

The urlData variable will now contain the base64 string of your PNG image data.

5. Call your init() function upon the loading of your page.

```
<body onload="init()">
```

When you launch your page, you'll see the red square and your button, "Save PNG." If you click on the button, it will open a new page whose URL is your canvas as a PNG file, and therefore your PNG in the browser. You might object that it's not really saving your image, and that's quite right. However, if you want to use only JavaScript, it's as far as you can go if you need a reliable solution, as JavaScript is a client-side language. In the following Expert tips section, you will see how you can do this through PHP and HTML5.

Expert tips

If you combine the Save PNG button with AJAX and PHP, you can retrieve the PNG from your canvas and force the download so that the client can save the PNG file. You can take the same code as above, but you will proceed differently when it comes to the saveImage() function.

As you saw, by calling the dataToURL method, you retrieved your canvas in a PNG format encoded as a base64 string. You can do several things with this variable by sending it through the POST method (GET won't work most of the time as it is limited in character size, and images can produce really long strings): you can save it on the server side and allow the user to download it. First let's see how you can send your image through a POST variable through AJAX. For this, you will rewrite your saveCanvas() function.

```
function saveCanvas(){
                var dataUrl=canvas.toDataURL();
                var xtr=new XMLHttpRequest();
                xtr.open("POST",'saveImage.php',true);
                xtr.setRequestHeader('Content-Type','application/upload');
                xtr.onreadystatechange=function(){
                        if(xtr.readyState==4  &&  xhr.responseText=="ok"){
                                window.location="download.php";
                        }
                }
                xtr.send(dataUrl);
        }
```

171

If you are not familiar with AJAX, let's go quickly through this code. What you are doing here is sending your PNG DataURL as a POST variable to a PHP script in 'saveImage.php'. To send the canvas context dataURL, you will use the AJAX XMLHttpRequest object.

When your PHP script receives this variable, it will decode the base64-encoded file, create a PNG file, name it "canvas.png," and save it on the server. If everything went well, it will send back the string "ok." (Note that in this example, you won't deal with all error messages.)

The XMLHttpRequest object has a property called readyState. This is where the status of your server's response is stored. With it, you can listen to the server response through the onreadystatechange property. If the readyState changes, meaning that we have server response, and it is equal to 4 (which means that the response from the server is complete), you can then check the responseText value sent back by your PHP script. If it's the string "ok" (the string sent by your PHP script to notify that your PNG as been correctly created), you can go to the next and last step: forcing the PNG's download through another small PHP script in 'download.php'.

Now let's see the PHP scripts. First, let's look at the saveImage.php page, which is saving the canvas image on the serve side:.

```php
<?php
if(isset($GLOBALS["HTTP_RAW_POST_DATA"])){
        $imageData=$GLOBALS['HTTP_RAW_POST_DATA'];
        $filteredData=substr($imageData,strpos($imageData,",")+1);
        $decodedData=base64_decode($filteredData);
        $fp=fopen('canvas.png','wb');
        if(fwrite($fp,$decodedData)){
                fclose($fp);
                echo 'ok';
        }

}
?>
```

This script is decoding the base64 data through the PHP function base64_decode(,)and then saving the decoded data into a PNG file named "canvas.png" on the server. It will return the string "ok" if the file was correctly created and saved.

The PHP script called with the download.php page will then force the download of the saved canvas.png file, and it appears as follows:

```php
<?php
$fsize=filesize('canvas.png');
header('Content-Disposition:attachment;filename="canvas.png"');
header('Content-type:application/force-download');
header('Content-type:image/png');
header('Content-length:'.$fsize.'');
readfile('canvas.png');
?>
```

Now when the user clicks on the Save PNG button, it will first create a PNG out of the canvas, name it "canvas.png," and if this is successful, it will open up a save dialog window allowing the user to save it to his or her own system.

This is the complete code for this example:

The HTML5 page:

```
<html lang="en">
<head>
<meta charset="UTF-8" />
<title>solution 6-8-2</title>
<script type="text/Javascript" language="Javascript">
var canvas;
var context;
    function init() {
      canvas=document.getElementById("canvas");
      context=canvas.getContext("2d");
      draw();
    }
    function draw() {
                context.strokeStyle="#993300";
                context.fillStyle="#ffff09";
                context.font="bold 40px arial";
                context.textAlign="center";
                context.lineWidth="2";
                context.lineJoin="round";
                context.fillText("Saved Image",220,140);
                context.strokeText("Saved Image",220,140);
    }

        function saveCanvas(){
                var dataUrl=canvas.toDataURL();
                var xtr=new XMLHttpRequest();
                xtr.open("POST",'saveImage.php',true);
                xtr.setRequestHeader('Content-Type','application/upload');
                xtr.onreadystatechange=function(){
                if(xtr.readyState==4 && xtr.responseText=="ok"){
                                window.location="download.php";
                }
        }
        xtr.send(dataUrl);
        }
  </script>
</head>
 <body onload="init()">
   <canvas id="canvas" width="400" height="400"></canvas>
   <button onclick="saveCanvas();">Save as PNG</button>
   <div id="link"></div>
 </body>
</html>
```

The saveImage.php code:

```php
<?php
if(isset($GLOBALS["HTTP_RAW_POST_DATA"])){
        $imageData=$GLOBALS['HTTP_RAW_POST_DATA'];
        $filteredData=substr($imageData,strpos($imageData,",")+1);
        $unencodedData=base64_decode($filteredData);
        $fp=fopen('canvas.png','wb');
        if(fwrite($fp,$unencodedData)){
                fclose($fp);
                echo 'ok';
        }
}
?>
```

The download.php code:

```php
<?php
$fsize=filesize('canvas.png');
header('Content-Disposition:attachment;filename="canvas.png"');
header('Content-type:application/force-download');
header('Content-type:image/png');
header('Content-length:'.$fsize.'');
readfile('canvas.png');
?>
```

Summary

As you can see, the HTML5 canvas drawing API provides a wide range of possibilities that allow you to draw directly inside your web pages and applications. You can draw basic or complex shapes with paths, use colors and gradients, and draw text. Combining all this functionality lets you create great web content without the use of any third-party plug-in.

In the next chapter, you will see how to go further with the HTML5 canvas drawing API. You will be able to manipulate elements inside your canvas context to create powerful web content and add interactivity and animation to it directly with HTML5.

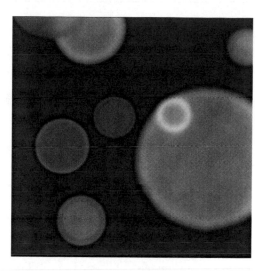

Chapter 7

HTML5 Canvas

We saw in the previous chapter how to use the HTML5 canvas drawing API. We will now manipulate canvas a bit more deeply and see how it can be used for rendering graphs, game graphics, or other visual images on the fly. As you learned previously, canvas is a rectangular area that you can add to your HTML5 page and that you can use to render and manipulate graphics through several available methods. In this chapter, you will see what you can do with canvas and its other APIs.

Apple initially created the canvas element to make dashboard widgets in its Safari browser with the use of the Mac OSX WebKit. Later it was adopted by other browsers and eventually became a standard accepted by the WHATWG (Web Hypertext Application Technology Working Group, http://whatwg.org/html).

In Chapter 6, we covered how you can draw shapes and text using the canvas element. However, you can do much more than just drawing static bitmaps with canvas. The canvas element opens a wide range of possibilities for HTML—you can render graphics and make them interactive, manipulate images, make animations, build games, and more.

Prior to the advent of the canvas element, whenever you wanted to do this in HTML4, you had to rely on a third-party proprietary plug-in like Flash, Silverlight, and others. Now all these capabilities are available to you in your HTML5 document through the canvas element.

There are a lot of things that you can achieve through the canvas element, and we won't be able to cover them all in a single chapter. Nonetheless, in this chapter, you will see how you can use the canvas element to add rich graphics easily inside your browser. We cover the following aspects of the canvas element:

- An overview of the canvas APIs

- How to detect the canvas element and canvas text support

- The standard screen-based coordinate system and transformations

- How you can manipulate pixels inside a canvas

- How to apply shadows and blurring to graphic elements

- How to build animations with the canvas element

Solution 7-1: Understanding the canvas APIs

As seen in the previous chapter, the canvas element is a rectangular area that allows you to render graphics and bitmap images dynamically inside web browsers. As such, it offers a wide range of graphic possibilities to allow you to control all the pixels of its content and manipulate them in many ways. When we talk about rendering graphics, we first have to point out that the canvas has no drawing or rendering capabilities of its own and that everything you'll render within it will be through the use of JavaScript code.

What's involved

You can declare a <canvas> element in your HTML5 page as seen in Chapter 6, and shown here:

```
<canvas id="aCanvas" width="640", height="480">
Your browser doesn't support the canvas element!
</canvas>
```

This will declare a <canvas> element of 640 pixels in width, 480 pixels in height, and the ID "aCanvas." Any child element of your canvas will be considered by your browser as fallback content, and it will show only if your browser isn't canvas-compliant. The HTML5 specification suggests that your fallback content match your canvas content as much as possible.

To do anything on the canvas, you first need to access the <canvas> element, and from there access its drawing context object where the actual drawing and pixel handling takes place. As previous mentioned, you'll do all this with JavaScript code. As the canvas element is available through the DOM, just like any other element, you'll access your canvas through its "id" attribute:

```
var  canvas=document.GetElementbyId('aCanvas');
```

You can also add a canvas programmatically by inserting it into the DOM directly with JavaScript and adding it to the page:

```
<head>
<script type="text/Javascript" language="javascript">
var canvas=document.createElement("canvas");
canvas.setAttribute('width', 640');
canvas.setAttribute('height','480');
canvas.setAttribute('id', 'aCanvas');
document.body.appendChild(canvas);
</script>
</head>
```

This will have exactly the same result: a canvas of 640 pixels by 480 pixels and an ID of 'aCanvas'.

> *Tip: Setting the width and height of a canvas will automatically reset the whole canvas element. If in the course of running an application you need to empty your canvas, just resetting its height and width will easily do the trick.*

At the time of this writing, only the 2D context is supported in the HTML5 specifications, so we will only discuss this context. It's worth noting, however, that wide progress has been made in the use of a 3D context through WebGL support, which shows great promise for handling 3D graphics in the canvas element. We expect that fairly soon it will be available as well, opening new and amazing HTML5 possibilities.

Get a reference to your 2D context by using the getContext() method of the canvas object you retrieved from the DOM, as follows:

```
var context=canvas.getContext('2d');
```

Then, through its context, you can use the set of tools available in its drawing API, such as:

- Transformations (including scale and rotate)

- Shadows

- Complex shapes, including Bezier curves and arcs (see Chapter 6)

For a complete list and overview of the available 2D context API methods, refer to this useful canvas 2D context cheat sheet: http://www.nihilogic.dk/labs/canvas_sheet/HTML5_Canvas_Cheat_Sheet.pdf

One important point to understand is that the Canvas uses an immediate mode renderer. This means that when you call a method to draw in the Canvas, the browser will immediately render that change before moving on to the next line of code. Therefore, whenever you want to change anything in your canvas, you'll have to re-issue all the drawing commands used on that canvas, even if the change affected only one element. That being said, the canvas element provides two methods to let you store and reset the state of your canvas at any point. (The canvas drawing state is a snapshot of all the styles, clipping, and transformation values that have been applied.)

- *save():* This will save the current style, clipping, and transformation values.

- *restore():* This will reset the style and transformation values to what they were when you last called the save() method on your context. If you haven't saved anything, then this method will do nothing.

For example, let's say you draw a circle on your canvas context with its strokeStyle set to be grey, then you call the save() method on your context and draw another circle with a white strokeStyle. If you then call restore(), both circles will have a grey stroke and all the style properties that were defined when you last saved your canvas state will now be restored. Remember that we are in an immediate rendering mode, and that the browser renders changes as it proceeds through the code. We will see more clearly how we can use this information when dealing with canvas transformations methods.

How to build it

1. Create a canvas in a regular HTML5 page:

```
<!DOCTYPE HTML>
<html>
<head>
<meta http-equiv="Content-Type" content="text/html; charset=utf-8">
<title>Canvas</title>
<script type="text/Javascript" language="Javascript">
var canvas;
var context;
window.onload=init;

function init(){
        canvas=document.createElement("canvas");
        canvas.setAttribute('width', '500');
        canvas.setAttribute('height','500');
        canvas.setAttribute('id', 'canvasId');
        canvas.style.border="solid 1px #ccc";
        document.body.appendChild(canvas);
}
</script>
</head>
<body>
</body>
</html>
```

Here you are creating a function called init(), which will create your canvas from scratch using JavaScript. The canvas is 500 by 500, and has a grey border of 1 pixel. With window.onLoad=init;, you are telling the page to run the init function when the page finishes loading and to add the canvas. Why use this global event handler instead of just adding the code into the body tag with onLoad? It will work either way, but if you want to re-use the same JavaScript code (by calling it from a separate source) for several pages, window.onLoad=init; will be more adaptable.

You can also achieve the same result with the following code (we use this in this solution code):

```
<!DOCTYPE HTML>
<html>
<head>
<meta http-equiv="Content-Type" content="text/html; charset=utf-8">
<title>solution 7-1</title>
<script type="text/Javascript" language="Javascript">

window.onload=init;
function init(){
        var canvas=document.getElementById('canvas');
}
</script>
</head>
<body>
<canvas id="canvas" width="500" height="500" style="border:solid 1px #ccc"></canvas>
</body>
</html>
```

Depending on your needs, you can use either possibility, the latter being easier and more than enough for simple canvases.

> **2.** Retrieve the canvas context, and get the access to the API set of tools by adding the following in your init() function after having defined or retrieved your canvas object:

```
var context=canvas.getContext('2d');
```

From now on, you have access to all the methods available to the canvas context API.

> **3.** With a new draw()function, draw three differently-sized rectangles and use the save() and restore() methods to set their respective styles:

```
function draw(){
        context.fillStyle='#000099';
        context.fillRect(0,0,200,155);
        context.save();

        context.fillStyle=#FF66FF';
        context.globalAlpha=.6;
        ccontext.fillRect(15,15,120,120);
        context.save();
        context.fillStyle='#993333';
        context.globalAlpha=1;
        context.fillRect(30,30,90,90);

}
```

This code draws three simple rectangles, a blue one and a smaller pink one with alpha values of 0.6 (as you saw in Solution 6-4, the colors blend, making them appear more violet) and a maroon one with an alpha value of 1. After drawing the first two shapes, you respectively saved the canvas context states, storing them one after another for further usage if desired.

> **4.** Add two other simple rectangles, and set their styles by restoring the states you previously saved.

```
        context.restore();
        context.fillRect(145,15,40,120);

        context.restore();
        context.fillRect(55,55,40,40);
}
```

This first restores the previous state that was saved, then it draws a rectangle. The settings that apply to that shape are those defined in the state you just restored: an alpha of 0.6 and a pink fillStyle color.

Then call the restore() method again, and it will restore the state previous to the one that you just applied; that is, the original state values (the first one you saved), rendering another blue shape.

> **5.** Close your draw() function, and call it in the init() function.

```
function init(){
        var canvas=document.getElementById('canvas');
        draw();
}
```

Loading your page will produce the result shown in Figure 7-1.

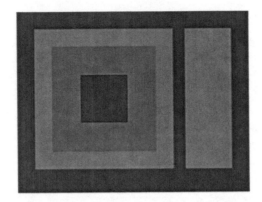

Figure 7-1. Shapes drawn using save() and restore() methods

Using the save() and restore() methods in this manner, while not practical, provides a simple understanding of their results. Their utility is much more obvious when you have to deal with pixel transformations and interactivity, as you will see later in this chapter. This also shows clearly how the canvas is dealing with graphic rendering by handling commands sequentially.

The complete code for this example is shown here:

```
<!DOCTYPE HTML>
<html>
<head>
<meta http-equiv="Content-Type" content="text/html; charset=utf-8">
<title>solution 7-1</title>
<script type="text/Javascript" language="javascript">
var context;
window.onload=init;

function init(){
        var canvas=document.getElementById('canvas');
        context=canvas.getContext('2d');
        draw();
}
function draw(){
        context.fillStyle='#000099';
        context.fillRect(0,0,200,155);
        context.save();
        context.fillStyle='#FF66FF';
        context.globalAlpha=.6;
        context.fillRect(15,15,120,120);
        context.save();
        context.fillStyle='#993333';
        context.globalAlpha=1;
        context.fillRect(30,30,90,90);
        context.restore();
```

```
        context.fillRect(145,15,40,120);
        context.restore();
        context.fillRect(55,55,40,40);
}
</script>
</head>
<body>
<canvas id="canvas" width="500" height="500" style="border:solid 1px #ccc"></canvas>
</body>
</html>
```

Expert tips

You can have only one context per canvas. This means that once you have drawn something on it, if you were to make any changes, even to a single element among many, the entire scene will have to be redrawn. Sometimes, it can be interesting to use several canvases as layers, one on top of another, to redraw only what you need for specific events.

You can see this concept in action in a small example, where you draw two basic overlapping graphs and change each graph's values without having to redraw the other one by using separate layers. (Here we won't bother with drawing the scale values, but will only use a plain graph.)

1. Create two canvases with the same heights and widths in a regular <div> element.

```
<!DOCTYPE HTML>
<html>
<head>
<meta http-equiv="Content-Type" content="text/html; charset=utf-8">
<title>solution 7-1-2</title>

</head>
<body>
<div id="graphs">
<canvas id="first_layer" width="500" height="200" ></canvas>
<canvas id="second_layer" width="500" height="200" ></canvas>
</div>
</body>
</html>
```

2. The two canvases are here, but right now they are just next to another like any regular HTML element. To make them overlap each other, you'll use CSS to position them and set their z-index. You can either put this directly in your HTML5 page inside a <style></style> tag, or in an external CSS file. In this example, let's just have everything on the same page for code readability.

```
#graphs{
        position:relative;
        width:500px;
        height:220px;
}
#first_layer{
        z-index: 1;
```

```
        position:absolute;
        left:20px;
        top:0px;
}

#second_layer{
        z-index: 2;
        position:absolute;
        left:20px;
        top:0px;
}
```

To modify your 2 canvases separately, add some buttons below the canvas to call out different values:

```
<button id="graph1" onClick="drawGraph(context,data,'#ccc')">graph1 -  2001</button>
<button id="graph2" onClick="drawGraph(context,data2,'#ccc')">graph1 - 2005</button>
<button id="graph3" onClick="drawGraph(context2,data3,'red')">graph2 -  2001</button>
<button id="graph4 onClick="drawGraph(context2,data4,'red')">graph2 - 2005</button>
```

Now add your JavaScript code to define your drawGraph() function. First retrieve the two canvases and their respective context area, and then define the variables you will need:

```
<script type="application/javascript" language="javascript">

window.onload=init;

var context;
var context2;

var data=[30,50,90,50]; // values for the first graph for 2001
var data2=[80,40,75,110]; // values for the first graph for 2005

var data3=[20,60,140,80]; // values for the second graph for 2001
var data4=[40,80,75,130]; // values for the second graph for 2005
var barswidth=40; // width of the bars for your graphs

function init(){

        var c=document.getElementById('first_layer');
        var c2=document.getElementById('second_layer');

        context=c.getContext('2d');
        context2=c2.getContext('2d');

}
```

You can now code the functions necessary to render a simple graph. The following function will create a rectangular shape in the context specified, within the parameters of the size and width also defined in the parameters.

```
function drawBars(ctx,sx,sy,w,h,color){

        ctx.beginPath();
        ctx.rect(sx,sy, w, h);
```

```
        ctx.closePath();
        ctx.fillStyle=color;
        ctx.strokeStyle="#333";
        ctx.lineWidth=.2;
        ctx.globalAlpha=.7;
        ctx.fill();
        ctx.stroke();

}
```

Now let's work with the function that will actually draw the graph you want on the context. You can see that it takes three parameters: the context on which you want to render this graph, the values you want to use, and the color you want to use for your graph. As this is the last function you'll need, you can now close your script:

```
function drawGraph(ctx,values,style){

        ctx.clearRect(0,0,500,500);

        for(var i=0;i<values.length;i++){
                drawBars(ctx,i*(barswidth+5),200-values[i],barswidth,values[i],style);
        }
}
</script>
```

First this function will clear the context to start on a blank canvas using the clearRect() method, and then it will draw the graph with the desired values. As a result, each time you click on a button, it will redraw only the selected graph with the values you want, as shown in Figure 7-2. You can achieve the same visual result in a single layer, of course, but it would mean redrawing everything on each event, even the other graph with the same values. Depending on your needs, you can use either method. The use of multiple canvases as layers can enhance the performance of animations and games, which can help improve your applications' performance on mobile browsers.

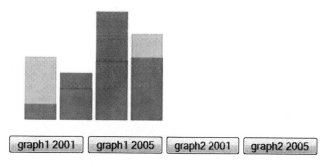

Figure 7-2. Graphs using multiple canvases as layers

Solution 7-2: Detecting the canvas and canvas text support

Whenever you want to deliver web content, insuring compatibility is a major priority. Even as HTML5 gains further support from the leading browsers, all of them (especially older versions) will not support the canvas element. Also, some support canvas but still not support the canvas text API.

The basic way to deal with situations where the browser does not support canvas is to add fallback content inside your <canvas></canvas> tag, as you saw in Chapter 6, matching your canvas content as much as possible. However, this might not always be as accurate, and you can be limited as the fallback content won't be able to provide everything your canvas does, such as interactive content. Thus, you might want to check browser support dynamically when loading your page, and supply other content that better fits your needs than relying on the fallback content of your canvas tag. You might even choose to adapt your whole page accordingly, and create an appropriate alternative to ensure a better user experience. For example, you could code an alternate content in JavaScript that would match your canvas content better than a simple image or plain text.

What's involved

A simple way to check if your browser supports the canvas element occurs when retrieving the canvas object and its context. If the browser doesn't support the canvas element, then when retrieving the canvas object through the DOM you'll just have a basic object without anything canvas-specific. So if you try to call the getContext() method, it won't return any function. You can write a small block of code to achieve this:

```
        var canvas=document.getElementById('canvas');
if(!!canvas.getContext){

}
```

As such, if the browser doesn't support the canvas element, you can add any alternative you wish. Otherwise, just proceed as usual to retrieve the canvas context.

```
else{
        var context=canvas.getContext('2d');
}
```

If your browser supports the canvas element, it doesn't necessarily mean that it supports the canvas text API. Thus you need to check that as well, in case you want to draw any text on your canvas. Follow the same procedure: calling a method specific to the canvas text API and seeing what it returns. If it doesn't return any function, then it is not supported.

```
if(!!context.fillText){
        //the Canvas text API is supported and you can proceed with your code
}
else{
        // you can add an alternative text, or add any other element to replace it through➥
  the DOM.
}
```

How to build it

1. Create two simple functions that will check canvas and canvas text support. First, code a canvasSupport function. The principle is to create a canvas to access its context object through the DOM. As seen previously, if the canvas element isn't supported, the canvas object won't be able to call the getContext() method and it will return an undefined value. Then you can use the JavaScript double-negative trick to coerce the returned value into a Boolean (true or false): if it's true, it means that the context is defined and that the canvas is supported; otherwise, it isn't.

```
function canvasSupport(){
        return !!document.createElement("canvas").getContext;
}
```

2. Create a function to check the canvas text support by calling the fillText() method from a canvas context. If your browser doesn't support it, it will return an undefined value and not a function. Again, you coerce the returned value into a Boolean.

```
function canvasTextSupport(){
        var context=document.createElement("canvas").getContext('2d');
        return !!context.fillText;
}
```

3. Call your functions on the load page event:

```
window.onload=init;

function init(){

        if(canvasSupport){

                // proceed with the use of the canvas APIs

                If(canvasTextSupport){
                        //proceed with your code using the Canvas text API
                }
        }

        else{
                //add any alternative you wish in complement of the fallback content if you→
    wish.
        }
}
```

4. Now take a look at the previous example, where you used several canvases as layers to show graphs in an interactive way. You would still want users who don't have HTML5-compatible browsers to be able to see your graphs, so you'll just code a small alternative for them to be able to see pictures of your different graphs. Here they won't see the super-imposition of graphs as done in HTML5, but they will still have classical buttons and images. This code will load only for non-compliant browsers, and would be as follows:

```
<!DOCTYPE HTML>
<html>
<head>
<meta http-equiv="Content-Type" content="text/html; charset=utf-8">
<title>solution 7-2</title>
<script language="Javascript" language="Javascript">

var context;
var context2;

var data=[30,50,90,50];// values for the first graph for 2001
var data2=[80,40,75,110];// values for the first graph for 2005

var data3=[20,60,140,80];//values for the second graph for 2001
var data4=[40,80,75,130];//values for the second graph for 2005

var barswidth=40;// width of the bars for your graphs

window.onload=init;

function canvasSupport(){

        return !!document.createElement("canvas").getContext;
}

function canvasTextSupport(){
        var context=document.createElement("canvas").getContext('2d');
        return !!context.fillText;
}

function init(){

        if(canvasSupport()){
                // proceed with the use of the canvas APIs
                var c=document.getElementById('first_layer');
                var c2=document.getElementById('second_layer');
                context=c.getContext('2d');
                context2=c2.getContext('2d');

                if(canvasTextSupport){
                        context.font="bold 15px arial";
                        context.fillText("Click on the buttons to see the corresponding➥
  graphs",10,20);
                }
        }
        else{
                //add your alternative for older browsers versions
                alternative_HTML5();
        }
}


function drawBars(ctx,sx,sy,w,h,color){

        ctx.beginPath();
```

```
        ctx.rect(sx,sy, w, h);
        ctx.closePath();
        ctx.fillStyle=color;
        ctx.strokeStyle="#333";
        ctx.lineWidth=.2;
        ctx.globalAlpha=.7;
        ctx.fill();
        ctx.stroke();


}


function drawGraph(ctx,values,style,txt){

        ctx.clearRect(0,0,500,500);

        for(var i=0;i<values.length;i++){
                drawBars(ctx,i*(barswidth+5),200-values[i],barswidth,values[1],style);
        }

}


function alternative_HTML5() {

        document.getElementById('nav').style.visibility="hidden";
        document.getElementById('graphs').style.height="0";
        var alt_canvas=document.createElement("div");
        alt_canvas.setAttribute('width', '500');
        alt_canvas.setAttribute('height','500');
        alt_canvas.setAttribute('id', 'alt_canvas');
        document.body.appendChild(alt_canvas);


        var legend=document.createElement("div");
        legend.setAttribute('id', 'legend');
        document.getElementById('alt_canvas').appendChild(legend);
        document.getElementById("legend").innerHTML="Click on the buttons to see the⇥
corresponding graphs<br />";


        var img_container=document.createElement("img");
        img_container.id="alt_graphs";
        document.getElementById('alt_canvas').appendChild(img_container);

        img_container.src="graph1.jpg";

        var buttons=document.createElement("div");
        buttons.setAttribute('width', '500');
        buttons.setAttribute('height','50');
        buttons.setAttribute('id', 'buttons');
        document.getElementById('alt_canvas').appendChild(buttons);

        add('graph1','graph1.jpg');
        add('graph2','graph2.jpg');
```

187

```
            add('graph3','graph3.jpg');
            add('graph4','graph4.jpg');
}

function add(val,img) {
            var element=document.createElement("input");
            element.setAttribute("type", 'button');
            element.setAttribute("value", val);
            element.setAttribute("name", img);

            document.getElementById("buttons").appendChild(element);
            if(element.addEventListener){
                    element.addEventListener('click',function(){swapImage(img,val)},false);
            }
            //for older versions of IE.
            else if (element.attachEvent){
                    element.attachEvent('onclick', function(){return swapImage(img,val);});
            }
}

function swapImage(im,val){
            document.getElementById("legend").innerHTML=val;
            document.images['alt_graphs'].src=im;

}
</script>
<style>
#graphs{
position:relative;
width:500px;
height:220px;
}
#first_layer{
z-index: 2;
position:absolute;
left:20px;
top:0px;
}

#second_layer{
z-index: 1;
position:absolute;
left:20px;
top:0px;
}
</style>
</head>

<body>
<div id="graphs" >
    <canvas id="first_layer" width="500" height="200" ></canvas>
    <canvas id="second_layer" width="500" height="200"></canvas>
</div>
<div id="nav">
<button id="graph1" onClick="drawGraph(context,data,'#ccc','graph1')">graph1 2001</button>
```

```
<button id="graph2" onClick="drawGraph(context,data2,'#ccc','graph2')">graph1 2005</button>
<button id="graph3" onClick="drawGraph(context2,data3,'red','graph3')">graph2 2001</button>
<button id="graph4" onClick="drawGraph(context2,data4,'red','graph4')">graph2 2005</button>
</div>
</body>
</html>
```

Expert tips

If you don't want to write your own function to check for browser support, you can use Modernizr. It is an open-source JavaScript library that detects support for many HTML5 features (like geolocation, video, local storage, and so forth), as well as CSS3. As there is a good chance that there will more elements on your page than canvases, you can use it to handle all kinds of support detection that you may require.

As for canvas and canvas text, it's really easy. You first include the library (we used the latest version available at the time of this writing):

```
<script src="modernizr-1.7.min.js"></script>

if (Modernizr.canvas) {

    var c=document.createElement('canvas');
    c.setAttribute('width', '500');
    c.setAttribute('height','500');
    c.setAttribute('id', 'canvas');    var context=c.getContext('2d');


}

else{

        //no canvas support
        var alt_canvas=document.createElement("div");
        alt_canvas.setAttribute('width', '500');
        alt_canvas.setAttribute('height','500');
        alt_canvas.setAttribute('id', 'alt_canvas');
        document.body.appendChild(alt_canvas);

}
```

...and for canvas text support:

```
if (Modernizr.canvastext) {
// draw your text
        context.fillStyle="#000";
        context.font="bold 15px Arial";
        context.fillText("Some text drawn in your canvas.",20,40);
} else {
//no canvas text support
        var alt_canvas_text=document.createElement("div");
        alt_canvas_text.setAttribute('width', '500');
        alt_canvas_text.setAttribute('height','40');
```

```
    alt_canvas_text.setAttribute('id', 'alt_canvas_text');
    document.body.appendChild(alt_canvas);
    document.getElementById('alt_canvas_text').innerHTML="Some alternative text."
}
```

You can download the latest version of Modernizr along with the user documentation at this address: http://www.modernizr.com/.

Solution 7-3: Understanding the standard screen-based coordinate system and canvas transformations

The HTML5 canvas also provides methods that allow you transform operations, like scaling, rotating, translating, and even transformation-matrix operations, and they are all about the canvas coordinate system. As a matter of fact, when you perform a transformation on the canvas context, you are transforming the entire context's coordinate system according to your goal (rescaling, moving a shape, and so on), not what is drawn on it. In this solution, you will see how to manipulate the coordinate system to achieve just that.

What's involved

You can perform several transformation operations on your canvas context. Each of them requires modifying the coordinates of the context. The process is first to modify the coordinate system, and then to draw on it as usual. In short, you don't modify the content of the context, but the context itself.

- *Scaling canvas objects:* You achieve this by using the scale() method, which scales the canvas context itself; that is, the x and y-axis coordinates. This method takes two parameters: the scale factor in the horizontal direction, and the scale factor in the vertical direction. Those scale values are based on the unit size of 1: scale(1,1) will keep the same scale as the original, values larger than 1 will increase it, and values smaller than 1 will decrease it. The values must always be positive.

```
context.scale(scaleX,scaleY);
```

> Note: To have a proportional scaling value, you must give equal scaleX and scaleY values.

- *Translating canvas objects:* If you want to move a shape or anything drawn on the canvas, first use the translate() method. It will move the canvas and its origin to a different point in the grid that you define through two parameters. The first parameter is the amount (in pixels) the canvas is moved on the horizontal axis. The second parameter is the amount it's moved up or down on the vertical axis. This point is then the new origin (0,0), and whatever you draw will have it as origin.

```
context.translate(x,y);
```

- *Rotating canvas objects:* The rotate() method will rotate the context to the angle given as its parameter. The angle value is in radians.

```
context.rotate(angle);
```

- *Using transformation matrix:* The transform() method will change the transformation matrix to apply the matrix given by its parameters, as shown here:

```
context.transform(a,b,c,d,e,f);
```

The parameters correspond to the matrix-transforming values shown in Figure 7-3.

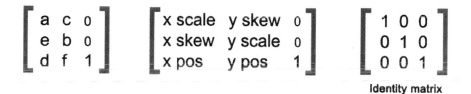

Identity matrix

Figure 7-3. Matrix transforming values

> *Note: Only the values corresponding to a, b, c, d, e, and f are accessible for modification. When a matrix causes no transformations, you have what is known as an "identity matrix."*

You can also use the setTransform(a,b,c,d,e,f) method. It resets the current transform to the identity matrix (refer to Figure 7-3), and then calls the transform() method with its parameters.

You can also perform rotation, scaling, and translation through the transformation matrix. The advantage is that you can perform them all at once. On the other hand, if you are unfamiliar with 2D matrix systems, it might be safer for you to use the other specific methods one after another.

After applying any transformation, you may want to go back to the original coordinate system for your next drawing or operation (unless you just really like mind exercises!).That's where the save() and restore() methods of the canvas will prove to be most useful. (See Solution 7-1 to learn about the save() and restore() methods). Before using any transform method, you can preserve the original coordinate system by saving the canvas state through the save() method. Then, after finishing your transformation, you simply restore the canvas state from pre-transformation stage, and then perform any new operation with the original regular coordinate system. We advise that you use this process for each transformation you want to perform. Otherwise, it could very quickly become complicated as the coordinates are redefined for each transformation.

How to build it

To see how to use the transformations with the coordinate system, let's create some drawings using all the transform methods. This example is designed to show how this works rather than creating a usable drawing.

1. Start by creating a basic HTML5 page, with a canvas and an onload event function to retrieve the canvas and its context.

```
<!DOCTYPE HTML>
<html>
<head>
<meta http-equiv="Content-Type" content="text/html; charset=utf-8"><title>solution 7-3/title>
<script type="application/Javascript" language="Javascript">
var context;
window.onload=init;
function init(){
if(document.getElementById('canvas').getContext){
        context=document.getElementById('canvas').getContext('2d');
        draw();
}
else{
        //add anything you want for non-compliant browsers
}
}
</head>

<body>
<canvas id='canvas' width= "500" height= "500">
</body>
```

2. Code your draw() function, which contains the commands to draw shapes with transformations. Start to draw a couple of round shapes and position them in a circular way using the rotate() method.

```
function draw(){

        context.save();
        context.translate(250,250);

        for (var i=0;i<8;i++){
          context.rotate(Math.PI*2/(8));
                        context.fillStyle = 'rgb('+(30*i)+','+(10*i)+','+(200-3*i)+')';
          context.beginPath();
          context.arc(0,12.5,4,0,Math.PI*2,true);
          context.fill();
        }

        context.restore();
```

First you start to save your original context. Then with a translation, you set that you want your drawing to start at the point (250,250) of the original canvas and the origin will be translated to that point from now on. You draw eight circles using a loop, and in your drawing you rotate the canvas eight times with a value of 360 degrees (Math.Pi × 2 in radians) divided by 8 to place them in circular arrangement and equidistant from each other.

Now you draw other shapes on your canvas, but you don't want the current transformations (the canvas has been rotated 8 times and translated) to apply, so you call restore() and bring back the last saved drawing state, or the original state in this case.

3. Draw another set of shapes using a loop—this time, squares. Again, start by saving the current canvas state. First you set a new translation value, and the origin is now at the new point (258,250).

```
context.translate(258,250);
for (var j=0;j<70;j++){
        var sin=Math.sin(Math.PI/6);
        var cos=Math.cos(Math.PI/6);
        color=Math.floor(255 / 120 * j);
        context.fillStyle="rgb(" + color + "," + color + "," + color + ")";
        context.transform(cos,sin,-sin,cos,j*2,j/2);
        context.globalAlpha=.8;
        context.lineWidth=.2;
        context.strokeStyle="#333";
        context.fillRect(20,20,25,25);
        context.strokeRect(20,20,25,25)
    }
}
```

Here you are drawing squares, and on each of them you apply a matrix transformation that will rotate and translate them, creating the drawing below (see Figure 7-4). At the end of this loop, the canvas context will have been transformed 70 times. As you are not drawing anything more, there is no need to save and restore the canvas context.

Figure 7-4. Drawing with shapes and colors transformations

The complete code for this example is shown here:

```
<!DOCTYPE HTML>
<html>
<head>
<meta http-equiv="Content-Type" content="text/html; charset=utf-8">
<title>solution 7-3</title>
<script>
var context;
window.onload=init;
function init(){
        if(!!document.createElement('canvas').getContext){
                context=document.getElementById("canvas").getContext("2d");
                draw();
```

```
                }
        else{
                //add anything you want for non-compliant browsers
        }
}

function draw(){
        context.save();
        context.translate(250,250);

        for (var i=0;i<8;i++){
                context.rotate(Math.PI*2/8);
                context.fillStyle = 'rgb('+(30*i)+','+(10*i)+','+(200-3*i)+')'
                context.beginPath();
                context.arc(0,12.5,4,0,Math.PI*2,true);
                context.fill();
        }
        context.restore();

        context.translate(258,250);
        for (var j=0;j<70;j++){
                var sin=Math.sin(Math.PI/6);
                var cos=Math.cos(Math.PI/6);
                c=Math.floor(255/120*j);
                context.fillStyle = "rgb("+c+","+c+","+c+")";
                context.transform(cos,sin,-sin,cos,j*2,j/2);
                context.globalAlpha=.8;
                context.lineWidth=.2;
                context.strokeStyle="#333";
                context.fillRect(20,20,25,25);
                context.strokeRect(20,20,25,25);
        }
        context.restore();
}
</script>
</head>
<body>
<canvas id="canvas" width="500" height="500"></canvas>
</body>
</html>
```

Expert tips

If you want to rotate an image from its center, you first need to translate the context in order to move the origin. Then apply your rotation and draw your image accordingly, as follows:

```
var img=new Image();
img.src='yourImagePath.jpg';

img.onload=function(){
        context.translate(img.width/2, img.height/2);
        context.rotate(90*Math.PI/180); // here we apply a 90 degrees rotation
        context.drawImage(img,-img.width/2,-img.height/2,img.width, img.height);
}
```

Solution 7-4: Pixel manipulations

As you learned earlier, the canvas APIs provide ways that let you manipulate any pixel inside the canvas. You saw that you can draw shapes and apply transformations to them, but there are also methods that allow you to draw or apply changes literally pixel-by-pixel on the canvas.

What's involved

You achieve manipulation of pixels on a canvas by using the ImageData object. It represents the pixel data of the current state of the canvas context area that you selected. It has these properties: width and height in pixels, and "data"—a canvasPixelArray element containing the color components of each pixel of the image data; that is, red, green, blue, and alpha (each with a value from 0 to 255). Pixels are ordered from left to right and from top to bottom. It's through this image object data that you will be able to perform pixel-by-pixel operations on your canvas.

When it comes to pixel manipulations, the canvas API provides three methods to perform the following operations:

- *Creating image data:* Call the createImageData() method, which takes 2 parameters: width, and height of your image data in pixels. It will create a set of transparent black pixels that you can then manipulate by assigning values to the data canvasPixelArray.

If we were to make a representation of the pixels array, it would look like something like the image shown in Figure 7-5.

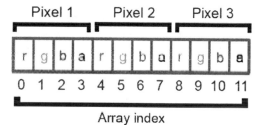

Figure 7-5. A pixels array

```
var canvas=document.getElementById('canvas');
var context=canvas.getContext('2d');
var imagedata=context.createImageData(canvas.width,canvas.height);
```

This will create an imagedata object containing the pixel data for the whole canvas context.

> *Note: You can specify coordinates when creating your image data to select a specific area of the canvas context. By default, they are set to 0,0, so if you only give the width and height of the canvas as parameters, your image data will cover the whole canvas.*

```
var canvasPixelArray=imagedata.data;
```

Now that you have access to every pixel through canvasPixelArray, you can start manipulating it however you like. As each pixel has four color values (red, green, blue, and alpha), scroll through the array and set colors values for each pixel.

The following code will assign the following RGBA values to each pixel of the imagedata object: 255,200,125, and 150.

```
for (var i=0;i< canvasPixelArray.length;i+=4) {

    canvasPixelArray [i]=255            // red channel
    canvasPixelArray [i+1]=200;         // green channel
    canvasPixelArray [i+2]=125;         // blue channel
    canvasPixelArray [i+3]=150;   // alpha channel

}
```

- *Retrieving a pixel array* : You can also retrieve the pixel array from an existing canvas through the getImageData() method.

It takes four parameters—the x and y positions and width and height in pixels of the area you want to retrieve.

```
context.getImageData(x,y,width,height);
```

With this method you can access the array of pixels of the shapes you drew on the canvas, or of images that you added on your canvas context, through the drawImage() method. Then you can do any kind of pixel manipulation to create things like filters, for example.

- *Painting image data on the context:* Once you have created an imageData object and have done any kind of pixel manipulation on it, you can paint your imagedata on the context by calling the putImageData() method. It has three parameters: the imagedata object and its x and y coordinates.

```
Context.putImageData(imagedata,0,0);
```

How to build it

To see a practical example of pixel manipulation, we will take a photo and apply basic color filters to it and show the resulting manipulated version next to the original photo on the canvas, as shown in Figure 7-6. (This example is meant for readability, and is not particularly optimized.)

Figure 7-6. A photo with different colors filters applied through pixel manipulation

To achieve this, follow these steps:

1. Create a basic HTML5 page with a canvas.

```
<!DOCTYPE HTML>
<html>
<head>
<meta http-equiv="Content-Type" content="text/html; charset=utf-8">
<title>solution 7-4/title>
</head>
<body>
<canvas id="canvas" width="500" height="500"></canvas>
</body>
</html>
```

2. Then, inside your <head></head> tag, check the canvas support, and load an image upon loading of the page.

```
<script type="text/Javascript" language="Javascript">

var context;
window.onload=init;

function init(){

if(!!document.getElementById('canvas').getContext){

        var photo=new Image();
        photo.onload=imageLoaded;
        photo.src="pic.jpg";

}

else{
        //add anything you want for non-compliant browsers

}

}
```

3. When the image has finished loading, access your canvas context and add the photo on the canvas in the upper-left corner (at the origin). Then get the imagedata object of your photo by calling the getImageData() method and passing the photo coordinates on the canvas and its width and height. By doing so, the imagedata object will get the pixel data of this area of the canvas only.

```
function imageLoaded(evt){

        context=document.getElementById('canvas').getContext('2d');
        originalPic=evt.target;
        context.drawImage(originalPic,0,0);
        var imgd=context.getImageData(0,0, originalPic.width,originalPic.height);

        applyBluefilters(imgd);
        applyRedfilters(imgd);
        applyGreenfilters(imgd);


}
```

4. Now that you have your photo's pixel data available, create some custom methods to apply basic color filters to them.

```
function applyBluefilters(img){

        var pixelsArray=img.data;
        for(var i=0;i<pixelsArray.length;i+=4){

                img.data[i]=img.data[i]/2;
                img.data[i+1]=img.data[i+1]/2;
                img.data[i+2]=img.data[i+2]*2.5;
                img.data[i+3]=img.data[i+3];

}

        context.putImageData(img,170,0);
}
```

Here you first retrieve the array containing the pixels data. For each pixel, first get its red, green, blue, and alpha values and reassign new values according to your needs. To achieve this blue filter effect, reduce the red and green values and put in a little more blue. When it's done, paint your new imagedata on the context.

5. Create methods to apply the red and green filter by playing with the RGB values of each pixel according to the effect you want to achieve.

```
function applyRedfilters(img){

        var pixelsArray=img.data;

        for(var i=0;i<pixelsArray.length;i+=4){
```

```
        }

        context.putImageData(img,0,170);

}

function applyGreenfilters(img){

        var pixelsArray=img.data;

        for(var i=0;i<pixelsArray.length;i+=4){


        r=img.data[i]*3;
        g=img.data[i+1]/2;
        b=img.data[i+2]/2;
        a=img.data[i+3];
        img.data[i]=r;
        img.data[i+2]=b;
        img.data[i+3]=a;
        r=img.data[i]/2;
        g=img.data[i+1]*4;
        b=img.data[i+2]/2.5;
        a=img.data[i+3];

        img.data[i]=r;
        img.data[i+1]=g;
        img.data[i+2]=b;
        img.data[i+3]=a;

        }

        context.putImageData(img,170,170);
}
</script>
```

6. Call your custom methods on your image loadEvent().

```
function imageLoaded(evt){

        context=document.getElementById('canvas').getContext('2d');
        originalPic=evt.target;
        context.drawImage(originalPic,0,0);
        var imgd=context.getImageData(0,0, originalPic.width,originalPic.height);

        applyBluefilters(imgd);
        applyRedfilters(imgd);
        applyGreenfilters(imgd);

}
```

The complete code for this example is shown here. (You need to have your image, "pic.jpg," in the same folder.)

```
<!DOCTYPE HTML>
<html>
<head>
<meta http-equiv="Content-Type" content="text/html; charset=utf-8">
<title>solution 7-4</title>
<script type="text/Javascript" language="Javascript">
var context;
window.onload=init;

function init(){
        if(!!document.getElementById('canvas').getContext){
        var photo=new Image();
        photo.onload=imageLoaded;
        photo.src="photo_01.jpg";
        }
        else{
        //add anything you want for non-compliant browsers
        }
}

function imageLoaded(evt){
        context=document.getElementById('canvas').getContext('2d');
        originalPic=evt.target;
        context.drawImage(originalPic,0,0);
        var imgd=context.getImageData(0,0,originalPic.width,originalPic.height);
        applyBluefilters(imgd);
        applyRedfilters(imgd);
        applyGreenfilters(imgd);
}

function applyBluefilters(img){
var pixelsArray=img.data;
for(var i=0;i<pixelsArray.length;i+=4){
        r=img.data[i]/2;
        g=img.data[i+1]/2;
        b=img.data[i+2]*2.5;
        a=img.data[i+3];
        img.data[i]=r;
        img.data[i+1]=g;
        img.data[i+2]=b;
        img.data[i+3]=a;}
context.putImageData(img,170,0);
}

function applyRedfilters(img){
var pixelsArray=img.data;
for(var i=0;i<pixelsArray.length;i+=4){
        r=img.data[i]*3;
        g=img.data[i+1]/2;
        b=img.data[i+2]/2;
        a=img.data[i+3];
        img.data[i]=r;
        img.data[i+2]=b;
        img.data[i+3]=a;
}
}
```

```
context.putImageData(img,0,130);
}

function applyGreenfilters(img){
var pixelsArray=img.data;
for(var i=0;i<pixelsArray.length;i+=4){
        r=img.data[i]/2;
        g=img.data[i+1]*4;
        b=img.data[i+2]/2.5;
        a=img.data[i+3];
        img.data[i]=r;
        img.data[i+1]=g;
        img.data[i+2]=b;
        img.data[i+3]=a;
}

context.putImageData(img,170,130);
}
</script>
</head>
<body>
<canvas id="canvas" width="500" height="500"></canvas>
</body>
</html>
```

Expert tips

Manipulating pixels can reduce performance. If you are using the same imagedata of your canvas context several times and you need to restore it (on a frame event, mouse event, or in a loop, and so forth), you can use the toDataUrl method instead of putImageData() (See Chapter 6, Solution 6-8 for more details about this method).

```
savedImagedata=new Image()
savedImagedata.src=canvas.toDataURL("image/png");
```

Whenever you need to restore it, use this code:

```
context.drawImage(savedImagedata,x,y) ;
```

Solution 7-5: Applying shadows and blurring

The canvas API also provides methods to create nice blurred shadow effects on anything that you draw on the canvas (shapes, paths, text, images, and so forth).

What's involved

As with much of what you have learned thus far about the canvas API, adding shadows to elements you draw means applying those effects on the canvas context itself at the time of drawing, and thereby applying it to what you are drawing. The canvas API provides the context properties related to shadows that will let you define its color, position and blur level. (If you are familiar with applying shadow effects with CSS, you will find yourself in very familiar territory here.):

- *shadowColor:* This property sets the context shadow color. When the context is created, it's transparent black.

```
context.shadowColor="#333";
```

- *shadowOffsetX:* This property returns and sets the horizontal shadow offset in pixels.
  ```
  context.shadowOffsetX=5;
  ```

- *shadowOffsetY:* This property returns and sets the vertical shadow offset in pixels.

```
context.shadowOffsetY=5;
```

- *shadowBlur:* This property returns and sets the blur level. Its values must be greater than 0.

```
context.shadowBlur=10;
```

After setting the context shadow properties, they will be applied on anything that you draw on the canvas until you reset them.

How to build it

To see how to apply blurred shadows on your context, let's draw simple shapes, rounded rectangles, and apply different shadows to them inside the canvas. It should give the result shown in Figure 7-7:

Using shadows

Figure 7-7. Using shadows

1. Create a basic HTML5 page with a canvas. First check for canvas support upon load, then access the canvas context.

```
<!DOCTYPE HTML>
<html>
<head>
<meta http-equiv="Content-Type" content="text/html; charset=utf-8">
```

```
<title>solution 7-5/title>

<script type="text/Javascript" language="Javascript">
var context;
window.onload=init;

function init(){
        if(!!document.getElementById('canvas').getContext){

                context=document.getElementById('canvas').getContext('2d');


        }
else{
        // add anything you wish for non-compliant browsers
        }
}
</script>
</head>
<body>
<canvas id="canvas" width="300" height="340">
Your browser doesn't support HTML5 Canvas !
</canvas>
</body>
</html>
```

2. Now create a custom method to draw rounded squares using paths.

```
function drawRoundRect(x,y,width,height,radius){

  context.beginPath();
  context.moveTo(x +radius, y);
  context.lineTo(x+width-radius, y);
  context.quadraticCurveTo(x+width, y, x + width,y+radius);
  context.lineTo(x+ width, y+height-radius);
  context.quadraticCurveTo(x+width,y+height, x+width-radius, y+height);
  context.lineTo(x+radius, y+height);
  context.quadraticCurveTo(x,y+height, x, y+height-radius);
  context.lineTo(x,y+radius);
  context.quadraticCurveTo(x, y,x+radius,y);
  context.closePath();

  //defining the gradient fill
  gradient=context.createLinearGradient(x+width/2, y,x+width/2, y+height);
  gradient.addColorStop(0., "rgb(218, 51, 163)");
  gradient.addColorStop(0.5, "rgb(167, 0, 118)");
  gradient.addColorStop(0.5, "rgb(192, 69, 160)");
  gradient.addColorStop(1.0, "rgb(192, 64, 163)");
  context.fillStyle=gradient;


  //defining the stroke color
    context.strokeStyle="#B3B3B3";

  //rendering the shape on the context
```

```
context.stroke();
context.fill();
```

}

The function takes these parameters: x and y position of your square on the canvas grid, its width and height, and the radius of the rounded corners you want to apply. It uses quadratic curved paths to create the round corners. You also fill your shape with a "web 2.0-like" gradient.

3. Create a custom method to apply blurred shadows to your context. By doing this, you can re-use it several times.

```
function applyShadow(r,g,b,a,posX,posY,blur){

        context.shadowColor='rgba('+r+','+g+','+b+','+a+')';
        context.shadowOffsetX=posX;
        context.shadowOffsetY=posY;
        context.shadowBlur=blur;
```

}

The parameters are the red, green, blue, and alpha values of the shadow color, its horizontal and vertical position from the element drawn on the context, and the Gaussian blur level.

4. When you apply shadow properties to your context, they will then apply to anything you draw on it. Thus you will make a small custom method to reset those values to default in case you want to draw anything without a shadow.

```
function resetShadow(){

  context.shadowColor='rgba(0,0,0,0)';
  context.shadowOffsetX=0;
  context.shadowOffsetY=0;
  context.shadowBlur=0;
```

}

The default context shadow color is transparent black, so you're just resetting it to that.

5. Now use those methods to draw your shapes with different shadow parameters by changing the context shadow properties as you go. Then, draw some text without any shadow.

```
function init(){

        if(!!document.getElementById('canvas').getContext){

                context=document.getElementById('canvas').getContext('2d');

                applyShadow(102,102,102,.8,-2,-2,5);
                drawRoundRect(30,30,100,100,10);

                applyShadow(102,102,102,.8,2,-2,10);
                drawRoundRect(140,30,100,100,10);
```

```
                applyShadow(102,102,102,.8,2,2,10);
                drawRoundRect(140,140,100,100,10);

                resetShadow();

                context.fillStyle='#333';
                context.font='Bold 22px Arial';
        context.fillText('Using shadows',60, 275);

        }

}
```

As this is a simple example, just draw your shapes when calling the init() function.

Start by defining the context shadow properties so that your first shape is dark gray, with an alpha value of 0.8, a position of –2, and a blur level of 5. Then draw your first rounded square. As you want a different shadow for your next square, you again call the custom applyShadow() method, set a new value for the context shadow, and draw your second square. Use the same procedure for your last square.

As you want your text to not have any shadow, call the resetShadow() method, and it will reset all the values to 0. You can then draw your text using shadows.

The complete code for this example is shown here:

```
<!DOCTYPE HTML>
<html>
<head>
<meta http-equiv="Content-Type" content="text/html; charset=utf-8">
<title>solution 7-5</title>
<script type="text/Javascript" language="Javascript">
var context;
window.onload=init;
        function init(){
        if(!!document.getElementById('canvas').getContext){
                context=document.getElementById('canvas').getContext('2d');
                applyShadow(102,102,102,.8,-2,-2,5);
                drawRoundRect(30,30,100,100,10);
                applyShadow(102,102,102,.8,2,-2,10);
                drawRoundRect(140,30,100,100,10);
                applyShadow(102,102,102,.8,2,2,10);
                drawRoundRect(140,140,100,100,10);
                resetShadow();
                context.fillStyle='#333';
                context.font='Bold 22px Arial';
                context.fillText('Using shadows',60, 275);
        }
        else{
        //add anything you want for non-compliant browsers
        }
}

function drawRoundRect(x,y,width,height,radius){
        context.beginPath();
```

```
            context.moveTo(x +radius, y);
            context.lineTo(x + width-radius, y);
            context.quadraticCurveTo(x + width, y, x + width, y+radius);
            context.lineTo(x + width, y + height - radius);
            context.quadraticCurveTo(x + width, y + height, x + width - radius, y + height);
            context.lineTo(x + radius, y + height);
            context.quadraticCurveTo(x, y + height, x, y + height - radius);
            context.lineTo(x, y + radius);
            context.quadraticCurveTo(x, y, x + radius, y);
            context.closePath();
            //defining the gradient fill
            gradient = context.createLinearGradient(x+width/2, y,x+width/2, y+height);
            gradient.addColorStop(0., "rgb(218, 51, 163)");
            gradient.addColorStop(0.5, "rgb(167, 0, 118)");
            gradient.addColorStop(0.5, "rgb(192, 69, 160)");
            gradient.addColorStop(1.0, "rgb(192, 64, 163)");
            context.fillStyle=gradient;
            //defining the stroke color
            context.strokeStyle="#B3B3B3";
            //rendering the shape on the context
            context.stroke();
            context.fill();
    }

    function applyShadow(r,g,b,a,posX,posY,blur){
            context.shadowColor='rgba('+r+','+g+','+b+','+a+')';
            context.shadowOffsetX=posX;
            context.shadowOffsetY=posY;
            context.shadowBlur=blur;
    }

    function resetShadow(){
            context.shadowColor='rgba(0,0,0,0)';
            context.shadowOffsetX=0;
            context.shadowOffsetY=0;
            context.shadowBlur=0;
    }
</script>
</head>
<body>
<canvas id="canvas" width="300" height="340">
Your browser doesn't support HTML5 Canvas !
</canvas>
</body>
</html>
```

Expert tips

Drawing shadows really consumes processing power. Therefore, we advise that you don't use it a lot in animations if you want to achieve a smooth result.

Solution 7-6: Animating canvas

One really exciting feature of canvas is the ability to create animations inside the canvas itself to make your drawings move. The great advantage is that it lets you create animations directly in your HTML pages without relying on third party plug-ins. Is this completely new? Not exactly. It was already possible to create animations using CSS and/or SVG combined with JavaScript, in HTML4. You can find some amazing examples of this on the Web. However, with the drawing API of the canvas, it becomes much easier to achieve this, and it has some very exciting possibilities.

What does animation in the canvas element imply? If you like animations, you most probably have heard of flip books. If not, they're a pad of drawings representing the different states of an animation (a man walking, for example) that you hold in on hand and, as you rapidly flip through the pages, the flip book makes its content move by creating the illusion of continuous action. This is exactly how you are going to create animations with the canvas element; that is, by repeatedly redrawing the canvas with different content (shapes, images, or whatever you can draw on the canvas context) over a span of time.

What's involved

Let's go through the steps to animating on the canvas:

1. Set a loop that will repeat at a defined interval.

2. At each interval:

   - Draw on your canvas with new positions, shapes, and so on—whatever you need to animate.

   - Render the drawing on the canvas.

   - Clear the canvas. (Obviously, if you don't clear your canvas, each new drawing will superimpose itself on another at each interval.)

   - Repeat the loop.

3. If you want your animation to stop, just clear the interval. (You can have an infinite loop, as well.)

As you have probably guessed, handling timing and redrawing of the canvas means using JavaScript. The principle is rather simple: you create a looped interval, and redraw your canvas at the specified time interval.

To carry out the above procedure, you can use JavaScript timing events—the following methods, specifically:

   - *The setInterval(callback, time) method:* `setInterval` calls a function at regular intervals, defined in milliseconds, as the second parameter. This can be used to periodically update the position, color, and/or style of what is drawn on the canvas element.

   - *The clearInterval(callback, time) method:* `clearInterval()` clears the interval.

Here is an example:

```
var context;
var canvas;
var posX=0;
var posY=0;
window.onload=init;

function init(){
        canvas=document.getElementById('canvas')
        context=canvas.getContext('2d');
        setInterval(drawShape,20); // calls the drawShape() function every 20 milliseconds.

}

function drawShape(){

        if(posX<=canvas.width-30){
                clearContext();
                ctx.fillRect(posX++,posY,30,30);
        }
        else{
                clearInterval(drawShape,20);
        }
}

function clearContext(){
        context.clearRect(0,0,canvas.width,canvas.height);
}
```

In this small example, we are redrawing a square every 20 milliseconds with a new x position by increasing it at each new interval and clearing the context, thus giving the illusion that it moves toward the right. As we want our square to stop moving when it reaches the right side of the canvas, we check its position at each loop interval, and when it reaches the edge, we clear the interval.

- *setTimeout(callback, time) and clearTimeout(callback, time) methods:* These methods are used to call a function after a given amount of time. The following code will have the same visual result as the previous example, but it uses a different approach:

```
function init(){
        canvas=document.getElementById('canvas')
        context=canvas.getContext('2d');
        drawShape();

}

function drawShape(){

        if(posX<=canvas.width-30){
                clearContext();
                context.fillRect(posX++,posY,30,30);
                setTimeout(drawShape,20); // will call the drawShape function in 20↦
  millisecond
```

```
        }
}
function clearContext(){
        context.clearRect(0,0,canvas.width,canvas.height);
}
```

- *SetTimeOut() method:* This can be used if you want to set several timings in your animation, as you can check how much time has passed once the function is called. This lets you to plan your animation based on time rather than on positions if needed. To clear the delay set by setTimeOut(), use the clearTimeOut() method.

> *Note: On all methods, the time is defined in milliseconds (1,000 milliseconds=1 second).*

Updating the canvas context rendering is what you need to do to build an animation in HTML5. After that, it's more about how you manage it with your code and the different API graphic tools that we covered.

How to build it

To build a simple animation where a ball moves on the canvas and detects wall collisions, follow these steps.

1. Create a basic HTML5 page with a canvas.

```
<!DOCTYPE HTML>
<html>
<head>
<meta http-equiv="Content-Type" content="text/html; charset=utf-8">
<title>solution 7-6</title>

<body>
<canvas width="500" height="250" id="canvas">
Your browser doesn't support the HTML5 Canvas element !
</canvas>
</body>
</html>
```

2. Check the canvas support, and access the canvas and its context through the DOM on the page load. You also define the variables that you will need for your code animation.

```
<script type="text/Javascript' language="Javascript">

var canvas;
var context;
var xpos=50; //initial x position of the ball
var ypos=50;//initial y position of the ball
var speed=3; //speed of the ball
var dirX=1; //initial x direction of the ball
var dirY=-1; //initial y direction of the ball
```

```
window.onload=init;

function init(){

        if(!!document.getElementById('canvas').getContext){

          canvas=document.getElementById('canvas');
          context=canvas.getContext('2d');

        }
        else{
          //add anything you want for non-compliant browsers
        }
}
```

3. Write the function to draw your ball. As you want to make it move on the canvas, its coordinates are set as parameters:

```
function drawBall(x,y){

            context.beginPath();
            context.arc(x,y,20, 0, Math.PI*2, true);
            context.fillStyle="red";
            context.fill();


}
```

4. Write a function to clear the context. As the animation in the canvas is redrawing the context with each new step, you need to reset your canvas to a blank area each time:

```
function clearContext(){

        context.clearRect(0,0,canvas.width,canvas.height);
    }
```

To clear the context, use the clearRect() method on all of the canvas area. (Remember that clearRect clears the specified area of all pixels.)

5. Now you are ready to bring in some animation. For this, use the setInterval method to call an animate() function containing the new position of your ball on each new frame. As you want your animation to start when the page loads, add it in your init() function.

```
function init(){

        if(!!document.getElementById('canvas').getContext){

          canvas=document.getElementById('canvas');
          context=canvas.getContext('2d');
    setInterval(animate,20);

    }
}
```

This will call the animate() function every 20 milliseconds.

6. Now let's see the different variables that you need to change to make sure that your ball moves on the canvas. First, set xpos and ypos variables that will define the ball coordinates at each new interval. Also define a speed variable, a dirX variable, to set the ball direction on the x-axis, and a dirY to set the ball direction on the y-axis.

```
var xpos=50;
var ypos=50;
var speed=3;
var dirX=1;
var dirY=1;
```

At the start, your ball will be placed on the (50,50) point, and it will have a speed of 3 pixels per frame and go down from there.

You now have all the elements to code your animate() function to make your ball move:

```
function animate(){

        clearContext();

        xpos+-speed;
        ypos+=speed;
        drawBall(xpos,ypos);
}
```

The first thing you do is to clear your canvas by calling the small function you coded for that purpose. You can now set the new x and y positions of your ball by adding the speed values to its last position. Redraw your ball with these new values using the drawBall() function. Now, at each interval, the x and y coordinates of the ball will increase by 3 pixels and, if you load the page, the ball will start from the upper-left corner of your canvas and fall down diagonally indefinitely. When it reaches the edge of the canvas, it will just disappear.

Now we want the ball to bounce off the canvas edges. To do this, add a simple collision test in your animate() function. It's pretty simple, you just check the last position of your ball and see if it reaches the canvas area coordinates (minus the radius of the ball). If it does, change the direction by multiplying your direction variable by -1.

```
if (xpos>=canvas.width-20 || xpos<=20){
        dirX*=-1;
}
 if(ypos>=canvas.height-20 || ypos<20){
        dirY*=-1;
}
```

You can now set the direction of the ball by multiplying the speed by the direction variables. Your animate() function will do these tasks: clearing the context, checking for collisions, changing the x and/or y direction if necessary, setting the new coordinates for your ball on the canvas area, and finally drawing the ball on the canvas using the new coordinates.

```
function animate(){

        clearContext();

        if (xpos>=canvas.width-20 || xpos<=20){
         dirX*=-1;
        }
        if(ypos>=canvas.height-20 || ypos<20){
         dirY*=-1;
        }

        xpos+=speed*dirX;
        ypos+=speed*dirY;
        drawBall(xpos,ypos);
}
```

Don't forget to close your script tag.

```
</script>
</head>
```

The complete code for this example is shown here:

```
<!DOCTYPE HTML>
<html>
<head>
<meta http-equiv="Content-Type" content="text/html; charset=utf-8">
<title>solution 7-6</title>
<script type="text/Javascript" language="Javascript">

var canvas;
var context;
var xpos=50;//initial x position of the ball
var ypos=50;//initial y position of the ball
var speed=3;//speed of the ball
var dirX=1;//initial x direction of the ball
var dirY=1;//initial y direction of the ball

window.onload=init;

function init(){
        if(!!document.getElementById('canvas').getContext){
        canvas=document.getElementById('canvas');
        context=canvas.getContext('2d');
        setInterval(animate,20); // setting the interval
        }
        else{
        //add anything you want for non-compliant browsers
        }
}

function drawBall(x,y){
        context.beginPath();
        context.arc(x,y,20, 0, Math.PI*2, true);
        context.fillStyle="red";
```

```
        context.fill();
}

function animate(){

        clearContext();
        if(xpos>=canvas.width-20||xpos<=20){
        dirX*=-1;
        }
        if(ypos>=canvas.height-20||ypos<20){
        dirY*=-1;
        }
        xpos+=speed*dirX;
        ypos+=speed*dirY;
        drawBall(xpos,ypos);
}

function clearContext(){
        context.clearRect(0,0,canvas.width,canvas.height);
}
</script>
</head>

<body>
<canvas width="500" height="250" id="canvas">
Your browser doesn't support the HTML5 Canvas element !
</canvas>
</body>
</html>
```

Expert tips

Animation in canvas is a very broad subject, and there is much to learn. Here are few tips, however, that could be very useful to you if you want to start animating with canvas.

Redrawing the canvas can consume a lot of CPU cycles, so you have to take this into consideration when it comes to mobile browsers. Here are a few things you can do to optimize your animations (or your games).

In Solution 7-1, you saw that it is possible to use several canvases as layers. Well, it's even more useful for animations. If your animation has only one drawn element that is changing, for example, then it can be very beneficial to redraw this one only and save the drawing API from executing unnecessary tasks. This is also relevant for games.

To clear the context, there is a simple trick that saves another drawing operation: if you reset the canvas width and height, it instantly clears it.

You can, in some cases, use a buffering technique to avoid flickering canvas, for example, by creating two canvases at the same screen location and using the visibility property to show the buffer when your drawing is done.

213

Summary

As you can see, the HTML5 canvas and its APIs provide a new and powerful way to new create engaging web content and applications, while natively increasing the user experience. Indeed, you can now use and manipulate images and gradients; draw, transform, and animate content directly in your HTML page, and update it at any time, giving you boundless possibilities to code, from simple applications to games.

In the next chapter, you will learn about using HTML5 communication APIs.

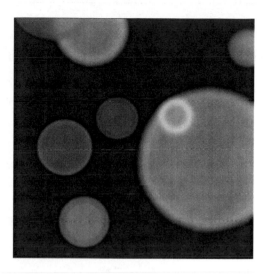

Chapter 8

HTML5 Communication APIs

At this point in the book, it is already clear that HTML5 offers many new tools to create applications that interact in a more native manner with the server.

In this chapter, we look at the techniques and solutions for avoiding browser sandbox security limitations, and we use a new technique to create documents that communicate from different domains (cross-document messaging), which involves the use of the postMessage API. You will learn what Cross-Origin Resource Sharing (CORS) means and how to use it. Quite simply, CORS is a browser technology specification that defines ways for a web service to provide interfaces for sandboxed scripts coming from different domains under the same origin policy.

Next, we explore new ways of real-time communication between the client and the server that allow you to find out where the server begins to interact with the client. This is due to the Server-Sent Events specification, which instructs an API to open an HTTP connection to receive push notifications from a server.

Finally, we will talk about the latest features in XMLHttpRequest Level 2.

> Note: XMLHttpRequest (XHR) is an API available in web browser scripting languages such as JavaScript. It is used to send HTTP or HTTPS requests directly to a web server and load the server response data directly back into the script. The data might be received from the server as XML text, or as plain text (from Wikipedia http://en.wikipedia.org/wiki/XMLHttpRequest).

Understanding the postMessage API

All web applications loaded in a browser are affected by the browser's sandbox security, which is a security mechanism used to run applications in a restricted environment.

This means that if someone tries to exploit the browser to execute malicious code, the browser sandbox prevents this code from causing damage to the host machine.

This is why web applications aren't able, for example, to create, modify, or read files or any information on the host file system. Also, they cannot load and access scripts on pages in different locations that do not use the same protocol, port number, and host domain.

Of course, you can overcome this limitation with various techniques. One is the use of a web server proxy — instead of making your XMLHttpRequest calls directly to the web service, you make your calls to your web server proxy. The proxy then passes the request to the web service, and passes the response data back to the client application.

However, with HTML5 and the new postMessage API, you can now enable cross-origin communication so that your web application uses a controlled mechanism to enable cross-site scripting without needing to use any kind of workaround.

The postMessage syntax, according to http://dev.w3.org/html5/postmsg/, is as follows:

```
window.postMessage(message, targetOrigin [, ports ])
```

The message parameter contains the message to be posted, the targetOrigin indicates what the origin of otherWindow has to be in order for the event to be dispatched, and the ports attribute can optionally contain an array of ports to the given window.

If the origin of the target window doesn't match the given origin, the message is discarded. This prevents information leakage.

To send the message to the target, regardless of origin, set the target origin to "*". To restrict the message to same-origin targets only, without needing to state the origin explicitly, set the target origin to "/".

Here is a practical example to explain this mechanism: Imagine a scenario in which the hostPage.htm web page contains an iframe element containing the embeddedPage.htm page. A script in the hostPage.htm page calls postMessage() on the Window object of the embeddedPage.htm page, then a message event executes on that object and is marked as originating from the Window of page hostPage.htm.

This would be the code written in the hostPage.htm page:

```
var element = document.getElementsByTagName('iframe')[0];
element.contentWindow.postMessage('Hello postMessage API', 'http://www.mydomain.com/');
```

When the postMessage() is called, a message event is dispatched to the target window. This interface has a type message event that exposes the data property, which returns the data of the message.

You can use addEventListener() to register an event handler for the message event:

```
window.addEventListener('message', messageHandler);
function messageHandler(e)
{
    alert(e.data);
}
```

In the `messageHandler` event handler, we only show an alert window with the text contained in the data property. However, it is a best practice to check if the message that you are receiving is from the expected domain. To do this, you can use the origin property, which returns the origin of the message:

```
if (e.origin == 'http://www.mydomain.com/') {
```

Then we can check what the message text:

```
if (e.data == 'Hello postMessage API') {
```

Finally, you can decide whether or not to send a message back to the HTML page that you sent the message to in the first place by using the source property, which returns the `WindowProxy` of the source window:

```
    e.source.postMessage('Hello', e.origin);
  } else {
    alert(e.data);
  }
}
```

Securing the postMessage communication

This new approach to cross-site scripting is very powerful and useful, but it could expose the server to attacks. This is why it is very important to use the postMessage API carefully with some precautions:

Do not use the * in the `targetOrigin` argument in messages that contain any confidential information:

```
window.postMessage('I'm sending confidential information', '*');
```

Instead, specify a domain, as otherwise there is no way to guarantee that the message is only delivered to the recipient for whom it was intended:

```
window.postMessage('I'm sending confidential information', 'http://www.mydomain.com/');
```

Always check the origin attribute to ensure that messages are only accepted from trusted domains from which they expect to receive messages:

```
if (e.origin == 'http://www.mydomain.com/')
{
// whatever
 }
```

Or even:

```
if (e.origin !== 'http://www.mydomain.com/')
    return;
```

This way, you avoid other pages from being bound to spoof this event for malicious purposes.

For additional safety, check that the received data is in the expected format:

```
if (e.origin == 'http://www.mydomain.com/')
{
if (e.data == 'Hello postMessage API')
  {

  }
}
```

Try avoiding the use of innerHTML or outerHTML to inject the received data message, as the message could contain a script tag and execute it immediately. Instead, use the textContent property to write the message string.

Solution 8-1: Checking for postMessage API browser support

The postMessage API allows you to find a way of communicating text-based messages across browser windows. The communication can happen between iframes, windows, and pop-ups. The postMessage APIs are supported by the following browsers:

1. Internet Explorer 8.0+

2. Firefox 3.0+

3. Safari 4.0+

4. Google Chrome 1.0+

5. Opera 9.5+

Regardless of support, it is still a best practice to check API compatibility of the browser you are loading the page on, especially because the application could expose serious problems if the postMessage API isn't supported.

What's involved

To be able to execute the support check, use the JavaScript typeof operator, which allows you to check the data type of its operand. Table 8-1 shows a list of possible values returned by the type of operator.

Table 8-1. JavaScript Data typeof Operators

Data Type	Description
number	Indicates a number
string	Indicates a string
boolean	Indicates a Boolean
object	Indicates an object
null	Indicates a null
undefined	Indicates not defined
Function	Indicates a function

It is quite simple to use the typeof operator; all you need to do is place the command before the variable you want to check, and it will automatically return its data type:

```
var num = 1;
var str = "Hello HTML5";
alert( typeof num );   // it returns number
alert( typeof str );   // it returns string
```

To check for browser support of the postMessage API, let's create a condition that will make sure the typeof of the postMessage doesn't return an undefined value.

How to build it

To check for browser support for the postMessage API, all you have to do is insert the following JavaScript condition in the script block before writing the functions that use the new API:

```
if (typeof window.postMessage != 'undefined')
{
alert ('The postMessage API is supported');
}
```

This code has to be between the script block of the page, as shown in the following example:

```
<!DOCTYPE HTML>
<html>
    <head>
    <title>Solution 8-1: Checking for postMessagi API browser support  </title>
      <script type='text/javascript'>
function postMessageSupport(){
if (typeof window.postMessage != 'undefined')
{
alert ('The postMessage API is supported');
}
}
</script>

    </head>
    <body>
```

```
    <h2>Solution 8-1: Checking for postMessageAPI browser support </h2>
<p>
<input type="button" value="Check for postMessage support!" onclick="postMessageSupport()" />
</p>
  </body>
</html>
```

In order to check for support of the postMessage API, you can simply click on the button input type and the JavaScript function will be executed.

Cross-documents messaging and CORS

In the previous paragraphs, we talked about how all web applications loaded into a browser are affected by its sandbox security. This means that the browser doesn't allow access to resources that are outside the host server. If a company has a large website including several sub-domains to run specific activities, such as hosting applications, databases, or department data, that might be a problem.

This is why developers tried to find approaches to overcome this limitation. One of the most popular approaches is to create server-side proxies, but the developer community asked for a native cross-domain requests approach.

This led to the W3C introducing a new approach in many browsers to overcome the problem. It is commonly known as CORS, or Cross Origin Resource Sharing.

CORS is a browser technology specification that defines ways for a web service to provide interfaces for sandboxed scripts coming from different domains under the same origin policy.

This approach provides for the use of custom HTTP headers, which tell the browser how to communicate with the server. By doing so, the browser and server have enough information about each other to determine whether or not the request or response should fail.

Imagine the following scenario: A resource has a simple text resource residing at www.domainA.com, which contains the string "Hello CORS!", and you would like www.domainB.com to be able to access it. If the server decides that the request should be allowed, the server returns a response combined with an Access-Control-Allow-Origin header to www.domainA.com.

Basically, the Access-Control-Allow-Origin header returns the same origin. (If it's a public resource, it'll return the wildcard *.)

This cross-origin sharing standard is used to enable cross-site HTTP requests for:

1. Invocations of the XMLHttpRequest API in a cross-site approach

2. Web Fonts (for cross-domain font usage in @font-face within CSS) so that servers can deploy TrueType fonts that can only be cross-site loaded and used by websites that are permitted to do so

In this chapter, you will use CORS to create cross-document messaging (Solution 8-2) and a cross-origin XMLHttpRequest (Solution 8-6).

Solution 8-2: Sending messages between windows and iframes

In the previous section, we talked about cross-document messaging and postMessage APIs and how they allow us to enable cross-origin communication across different resources.

In this solution, we will show how to make an iframe communicate with its host web page, which will be published on a different domain on purpose.

What's Involved

The object you will use to create the communication between the parent page and the iframe published on a different domain is the postMessage() method.

The syntax of the method has three parameters: the message, the URL of the targetOrigin, and the port.

```
window.postMessage('Hello postMessage API', 'http://www.mydomain.com/');
```

When the postMessage() method is called, a message event is dispatched in the target window. This interface has an event type message that exposes the data property, which returns the data of the message.

You can use addEventListener() to register an event handler for the message event:

```
window.addEventListener('message', messageHandler);
function messageHandler(e)
{
    alert('This is the origin of the message received: ' + e.origin + ' /n And this is the
message: ' + e.data);
}
```

In the messageHandler event handler, we simply show an alert window with the text contained in the data property. However, it is a best practice to check if the message you are receiving comes from the expected domain by using the origin property, which returns the origin of the message:

```
if (e.origin == 'http://www.mydomain.com/')
{
alert('This is the origin of the message received: ' + e.origin + ' /n And this is the
message: ' + e.data);
} else {
  // prevent from receiving this message as the target origin does not match !
}
```

Let's proceed to the solution with an example.

How to build it

First of all, you need to provide a good description of the application context. To start, download the Solution_8_2.html file published on the following domain: http://casario.blogs.com, in the files folder (http://casario.blogs.com/files/Solution_8_2.html).

This file, saved as chatIframe.html, acts as a container for an iframe. This file is published on the domain http://www.comtaste.com in the demo folder: http://www.comtaste.com/demo/chatIframe.html.

The example you will create allows the two files published on different domains to communicate.

Let's work on the first file—the one that acts as a container for the iframe. Start with the few user interface elements declared in the body:

```
<body>
  <h2>Solution 8-2</h2>
```

Insert a message, and click on the button to send a message to the iframe below:

```
      <p>
      <input type="text" id="message" value="This message is contained within the main
window" style="width: 350px" /> <button id="sendBtn"> Send Message </button>
      </p>
   <br />
  <p>
<iframe id="chatFrame" src="http://www.comtaste.com/demo/chatIframe.html" style=
"height:640px; width:480px" />
      </p>
  </body>
```

You declared a text input and a button that will allow the user to send a message to the iframe on the page.

The iframe is then loaded from the following URL: www.comtaste.com/demo/chatIframe.html.

You have to make it so that the message contained in the text input message is sent when the user clicks on the sendBtn button, so insert a script block and declare the first two event handlers:

```
<script type='text/javascript'>
window.addEventListener("load", init, true);
window.addEventListener("message", msgHandler, true);
```

The second event listener is registered on the message event. This event is executed by the window object when it receives any message. This is the event handler that will receive the message from the iframe and display it in the text input.

Next, add a global variable that contains the targetOrigin, meaning the domain that will accept the message (in our case, the domain www.comtaste.com where the page loaded by the iframe is located):

```
var targetURL = 'http://www.comtaste.com';
```

Register the event handler on the button click on the init() event listener, which will invoke the postMessage() method:

```
function init()
{
        document.getElementById('sendBtn').addEventListener("click", sendMsg, true);
}
function sendMsg()
```

```
{
document.getElementById('chatFrame').contentWindow.postMessage(document.getElementById('messag
e').value, targetURL);
}
```

The contentWindow property returns the Window object generated by the iframe element chatFrame. The postMessage() is called, and it contains the following parameters:

1. *message*: document.getElementById('message'). A value that is the text contained in the text input control.

2. *targetOrigin*: it contains the value that indicates what the origin of contentWindow is for the event to be dispatched (http://www.comtaste.com). To indicate no preference the * wildcard is used (although it's not a best practice).

Complete the script block with the event listener of the event message:

```
function msgHandler(e)
{
        if (e.origin == targetURL)
        {

                document.getElementById('message').value = e.data;

        } else {
                alert('This message has been sent from an unknown domain: ' + e.origin);
        }

}
```

In this event listener, check if the message is coming from the trusted domain (www.comtaste.com) to insert it in the text input message:

```
document.getElementById('message').value = e.data;
```

We use the data property of the event object, transported by the message event, which contains the message inserted in the iframe.

Here is the complete code for the Solution_8.2.html file published on the domain http://casario.blogs.com:

```
<!DOCTYPE HTML>
<html>
   <head>
   <title>Solution 8-2 </title>
     <script type='text/javascript'>
window.addEventListener("load", init, true);
window.addEventListener("message", msgHandler, true);

var output = document.getElementById("result");

var targetURL = 'http://www.comtaste.com';

function init()
```

```
{
        document.getElementById('sendBtn').addEventListener("click", sendMsg, true);

}

function sendMsg()
{
        document.getElementById('chatFrame').contentWindow.postMessage(document.↪
getElementById('message').value, targetURL);
}

function msgHandler(e)
{
        if (e.origin == targetURL)
        {

                document.getElementById('message').value = e.data;

        } else {
                alert('This message has been sent from an unknown domain: ' + e.origin);
        }

}

</script>

  </head>
  <body>
    <h2>Solution 8-2</h2>
        Click on the button to send a message to the iFrame below:
        <button id="sendBtn"> Send Message </button>

        <p>This is the message:
        <input type="text" id="message" value="This message is contained within the main↪
 window" style="width: 350px" />
        </p>
    <br />
    <p>        <iframe id="chatFrame" src="http://www.comtaste.com/demo/chatIframe.html"↪
style="height:480px; width:640px" />
    </p>
  </body>
</html>
```

Now we can move onto the code for the file loaded in the iframe: chatIframe.html.

The code is almost identical. The only real difference is in the global variable targetURL, which this time will have to contain the URL on which the Solution_8_2.html page part is published as a value:

```
var targetURL = 'http://casario.blogs.com';
```

The rest of the code remains unchanged because the communication we have created is bidirectional, from the parent (Solution_8_2.html) to the child (chatIframe.html).

Here is the complete code for the `chatIframe.html` file published on the domain www.comtaste.com:

```html
<!DOCTYPE HTML>
<html>
    <head>
    <title>Solution 8-2 </title>
      <script type='text/javascript'>

window.addEventListener("load", init, true);
window.addEventListener("message", msgHandler, true);

var targetURL = 'http://casario.blogs.com';

function init()
{

        document.getElementById('sendStatus').addEventListener("click", sendMsg, true);

        sendMsg(document.getElementById('message').value);
}

function sendMsg()
{
        messageTxt = document.getElementById('message').value;

        window.top.postMessage(messageTxt, targetURL);
}

function msgHandler(e)
{
        if (e.origin == targetURL)
        {

                document.getElementById('message').value = e.data;
        } else {
                alert('This message has been sent from an unknown origin domain:' + e.origin);
        }

}



</script>

    </head>
    <body>
      <h2>Solution 8-2: This is the IFrame</h2>

        Click on the button to send a message to the iFrame below:
          <input type="text" id="message" value="This message is sent from the chatIFrame
file" width="300px" />
          <button id="sendStatus">Send Message </button>
```

```
    </body>
</html>
```

To test the solution, you can publish these two files on different domains. The only thing you need to remember to do is change the value in the `targetURL` global variables of the two files by specifying your domain.

Figure 8-1 shows the final result with the messages exchanged between the two web pages.

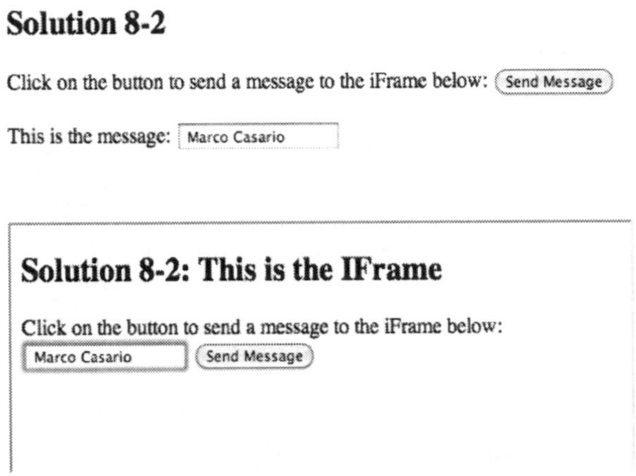

Solution 8-2

Click on the button to send a message to the iFrame below: (Send Message)

This is the message: | Marco Casario |

Solution 8-2: This is the IFrame

Click on the button to send a message to the iFrame below:

| Marco Casario | (Send Message)

Figure 8-1. Messages exchanged between two web pages

Solution 8-3: Using Server-Event technologies to write real-time web applications

Communication between client and server using the HTTP protocol implements a request-response model. This model allows you to send messages from the client, an HTTP request to the server, and wait for an HTTP response from the server. In this communication, it isn't possible to know where the server initiates interaction with the client.

With HTML5, the communication model has additional new and powerful functions to create real-time web applications.

What's involved

The Server-Sent Events specification defines an API for opening an HTTP connection for receiving push notifications from a server. The new EventSource interface was introduced to implement the specification to enable servers to push data to web pages over HTTP or using dedicated server-push protocols.

Using the `EventSource(url)` constructor is really simple. It only takes one argument, the URL parameter, which specifies the URL to which to connect:

```
var sourceURL = new EventSource('yourServerSideScript');
```

Now it's possible to register an event listener on the onmessage event:

```
sourceURL.onmessage = function (event) {
  // whatever you want
};
```

The message on the server side is sent using the text/event-stream MIME type:

```
data: This is the first message.
data: This is the second message
data: it has two lines.
```

Using this new approach for client/server communication instead of approaches that use iframe or the XMLHttpRequest object (on which AJAX is based) helps conserve battery use on portable devices. You can find more information at www.w3.org/TR/eventsource/#eventsource-push section.

CONNECTIONLESS PUSH AND OTHER FEATURES

User agents running in controlled environments, for example browsers on mobile handsets tied to specific carriers, may offload the management of the connection to a proxy on the network. In such a situation, the user agent is considered to include both the handset software and the network proxy for the purposes of conformance.

After having established a connection, a browser on a mobile device might detect that it is on a supporting network and request that a proxy server on the network takes over the management of the connection. The timeline for such a situation might be as follows:

- The browser connects to a remote HTTP server and requests the resource specified by the author in the EventSource constructor.

- The server sends occasional messages.

- In between two messages, the browser detects that it is idle except for the network activity involved in keeping the TCP connection alive, and it decides to switch to sleep mode to save power.

- The browser disconnects from the server.

- The browser contacts a service on the network and requests that the service, a "push proxy," maintain the connection instead.

- The "push proxy" service contacts the remote HTTP server and requests the resource specified by the author in the EventSource constructor (possibly including a Last-Event-ID HTTP header, and so on).

- The browser allows the mobile device to go to sleep.

- The server sends another message.

- The "push proxy" service uses a technology such as OMA push to convey the event to the mobile device, which wakes only long enough to process the event and then returns to sleep.

This can reduce the total data usage, and can therefore result in considerable power savings.

How to build it

To be able to see the EventSource() constructor in action, you have to create a server side file by using any server-side language: you can use Java, Python, PHP, or any other web programming language. In this solution, we have invoked a PHP file that reads a text file containing some information. This information, once the server side script has read it, is sent to the client through the EventSource() and is inserted in the web page in some list items.

Start creating the HTML page by adding elements in the body:

```
<body>
    <h2>Messages sent from the Server</h2>
        <ul id="responseMessages">

        </ul>
  </body>
```

You only have one header and an unordered list, which will be populated by our event source. Now you can insert the script block that will have an event listener on the load event of the window:

```
window.addEventListener("load", init, false);
```

In the init() event handler, we start by creating a reference to the list element by using the getElementById() method and create a function that will insert the text in the HTML list:

```
function init() {

var myList = document.getElementById ('msgList');

function msgHandler (message)
{
var elementLI = document.createElement ('li');

elementLI.innerHTML = message;

if (myList.children.length)
{
myList.insertBefore (elementLI, myList.firstChild);
}
else
{
myList.appendChild (elementLI);
}

for (var i = 10, j = myList.children.length; i < j; i++)
{
myList.removeChild (myList.children [i]);
}
}
```

You can begin creating the EventSource object.

If the browser supports the EventSource, the constructor is invoked:

```
if (typeof (window.EventSource) !== 'undefined')
{
var source = new EventSource ('sse.php');
```

At this stage, the browser resolves the URL specified in the url property that points to the PHP file sse.php.

All you need to do is manage the onmessage event of the EventSource object that is invoked every time the server returns a message to the client:

```
source.onmessage = function (event)
{
                    var msgSplit = event.data.split ('\n');
                    if (msgSplit.length == 2) {
                        msgHandler ('<a target="_blank" href="mailto:' + msgSplit [1] +↪
 '/">' + msgSplit [0] + '</a>');
                        return ;
                    }
                    else if (msgSplit.length == 3) {
                        msgHandler ('<a target="_blank" href="mailto:' + msgSplit [1] +↪
 '" title="' + msgSplit [2] + '"/">' + msgSplit [0] + '</a>');
                        return ;
                    }

                    msgHandler (event.data);
                };
        }
        else
        {
            msgHandler ('Your browser does not support the EventSource Interface');
        }
```

Here is the complete code of the HTML page:

```
<!DOCTYPE HTML>
<html>
    <head>
      <script type='text/javascript'>

            window.addEventListener("load", init, false);

        function init() {

var myList = document.getElementById ('msgList');

function msgHandler (message)
{
var elementLI = document.createElement ('li');

elementLI.innerHTML = message;

if (myList.children.length)
{
```

```
myList.insertBefore (elementLI, myList.firstChild);
}
else
{
myList.appendChild (elementLI);
}

for (var i = 10, j = myList.children.length; i < j; i++)
{
myList.removeChild (myList.children [i]);
}
}


if (typeof (window.EventSource) !== 'undefined')
var source = new EventSource ('sse.php');

source.onmessage = function (event)
{
                        var msgSplit = event.data.split ('\n');
                        if (msgSplit.length == 2) {
                            msgHandler ('<a target="_blank" href="mailto:' + msgSplit [1] +
'/">' + msgSplit [0] + '</a>');
                            return ;
                        }
                        else if (msgSplit.length == 3) {
                            msgHandler ('<a target="_blank" href="mailto:' + msgSplit [1] + '"
title="' + msgSplit [2] + '"/">' + msgSplit [0] + '</a>');
                            return ;
                        }

                        msgHandler (event.data);
                    };
                }
                else
                {
                    msgHandler ('Your browser does not support the EventSource Interface');
                }

};
            </script>

    </head>
    <body>
      <h2>Messages sent from the Server</h2>
            <ul id="msgList">

            </ul>
    </body>
</html>
```

Expert tips

The Opera browser uses the Event Source interface as an HTML Element:

```
<event-source id="es" src="youServerSideScript" />
```

This element is added between the header tags of the web page. Once you have created the HTML element, you can access it using the getElementBy:

```
document.getElementById("es")
```

and register the event listeners in it with the addEventListener method.

Solution 8-4: Running code in different browsing contexts using message channels

With the introduction of the new HTML5 cross-document messaging specifications, it's now possible to enable independent pieces of code running in different browsing contexts to communicate directly. This is possible thanks to channel messaging.

This technique means that the channels are implemented as two-way pipes with a port at each end. Messages that are asynchronous are sent in one port are delivered at the other port and vice-versa. Messages are delivered as DOM events.

What's involved

It is simple to create a channel message. First of all, you need to use the MessageChannel() constructor which, once instantiated, returns a new MessageChannel object with two new MessagePort objects. In fact, each channel has two message ports:

```
channel = new MessageChannel()
channel.port1
channel.port2
```

Port1 and port2 return the first and second MessagePort objects. Data sent through one port is received by the other port, and vice versa.

> *Tip: To learn more about MessagePort, visit twww.whatwg.org/specs/web-apps/ current-work/multipage/comms.html#messageport.*
>
> *Each MessagePort object can be entangled with another (a symmetric relationship). Each MessagePort object also has a task source called the port message queue that is initially empty. A port message queue can be enabled or disabled, but it is initially disabled. Once enabled, a port can never be disabled again (though messages in the queue can get moved to another queue or removed altogether, which has much the same effect).*
>
> *When the user agent creates a new MessagePort object owned by a script's global object owner, it must instantiate a new MessagePort object and let its owner be owner.*

When the MessageChannel() constructor is called, it must run the following algorithm:

- Create a new MessagePort object owned by a Window object (in JavaScript, it corresponds to the global object), and let port1 be that object.

- Create a new MessagePort object owned by a Window object (in JavaScript, it corresponds to the global object), and let port2 be that object.

- Entangle the port1 and port2 objects.

- Instantiate a new MessageChannel object, and let the channel be that object.

- Let the port1 and port2 attributes of the channel object be port1 and port2.

- Return the channel.

How to build it

In this brief example, you will see how to create a message channel to use with the postMessage API.

1. Instantiate the MessageChannel() constructor:

```
var myChannel = new MessageChannel();
```

2. Use the postMessage() method to send a message to the second port, port2, while port1 is kept as the local port:

```
window.postMessage('This is my blog !', 'http://casario.blogs.com', [myChannel.port2]);
```

3. To receive messages, one listens to message events:

```
channel.port1.onmessage = handleMessage;
function handleMessage(event) {
  if (event.origin !== "http://casario.blogs.com")
    return;
// event.data returns "This is my blog !"
}
```

Essentially, in message channels, you have to handle two onmessage events—one for each port:

1. MessageChannel.port1.postMessage will invoke MessageChannel.port2.onmessage

2. MessageChannel.port2.postMessage will invoke MessageChannel.port1.onmessage

Solution 8-5: Uploading files using the XMLHttpRequest Level 2

The XMLHttpRequest object was definitely one of those that began the Web 2.0 revolution. Actually, it is the object upon which the applications that use AJAX as client server communication technology are based.

Microsoft introduced XMLHttpRequest in 1999 to provide a highly-interactive user interface for the Microsoft Outlook Google adopted program, but as a web application.

It was only after the object to create services, such as Gmail and Google Maps, that it went on to become very popular, and we began to witness an actual web application revolution.

Why is this object so special? Because it brought about the possibility of carrying out the request on the HTTP and HTTPS protocols of a resource to a web server independently from the browser. In this request, it is possible to send information in the form of GET or POST variables, much like sending data in a form.

The request between the client and server is asynchronous, which means that there is no need to wait for it to finish in order to carry out other operations, which mix up the typical data flow of a web page in several ways.

In fact, the flow is normally contained in two steps at a time—user request (link, form, or refresh) and server response, which then leads to a new user request.

In 2006, the W3C finally recognized the importance of XMLHttpRequest and formed a workgroup to standardize the API provided by this browser object.

XMLHttpRequest Level 2 is a new effort to define an improved specification of XMLHttpRequest objects. Among the new features supported by the object's specifications is the possibility of uploading files, since the send function of the XMLHttpRequest Level 2 object can take a file or a BLOB object as a parameter.

> A blob (that stands for binary large object or basic large) is a collection of binary data stored as a single entity in a database management system. Blobs are typically images, audio or other multimedia objects.

It also created the possibility of sending or retrieving data to URI s that are not in the same domain as the browser document in which the XMLHttpRequest was created (the CORS, approach already discussed at the beginning of this chapter).

What's involved

Using the XMLHttpRequest Level 2 object is similar to the previous version of the same object.

In fact, all you have to do is call the XMLHttpRequest() constructor:

```
var req = new XMLHttpRequest();
```

At this point, it is possible to open the request with the object's -Open() method, or send the request with the send() method:

```
req.open('GET', 'http://www.comtaste.com/', true);
```

The third parameter of the open() method specifies that the request is handled asynchronously (when set to true).

To check to see if the transaction is successful, you create an event handler function object and assign it to the request's onreadystatechange attribute. If everything goes well and the request contains no errors, the HTTP status returns 200. If an error occurs, an error message is displayed:

```
req.onreadystatechange = function (e) {
  if (req.readyState == 4) {
    if(req.status == 200)
     alert(req.responseText);
    else
     alert ("Error loading page.");
  }
};
req.send(null);
```

Here are the main properties of the XMLHttpRequest object:

- readyState: Verifies the status of an object and can have a value from 0 to 4:

  - 0 = Uninitialized: The object exists but has not been instantiated.

  - 1 = Open: The object is open.

  - 2 = Sent: The request has been sent.

  - 3 = Receiving: The data is reaching the destination.

  - 4 = Loaded: The operation is completed.

- responseText: Returns the result of an HTTP request in text format.

- responseXML: Returns the result of an HTTP request in XML format.

- Status: Returns the state of a transaction; contains several success and error message numbers that are similar to those of a web server, such as 404 (File Not Found), 500 (Internal Server Error), and so on.

Here are the main methods:

- abort: Preventatively terminates the HTTP request.

- getResponseHeaders: Returns the headers of the request.

- open: Opens the request.

- send: Sends the request.

- setRequestHeader: Sets the headers of the request.

How to build it

The XMLHttpRequest Level 2 specification provides the send() method with the ability to accept a File object argument. This allows you to stream binary data to the server asynchronously.

Using the HTML5 FormData, you can select the file to be sent to the server. The formData object creates a set of key/value pairs that can be used with the send() method of the XMLHttpRequest object.

Although the FormData is intended to send form data, it can be used independently from forms in order to transmit data:

```
var formElement = document.getElementById("fileInput");
var formData = new FormData(formElement);
var xhr = new XMLHttpRequest();
xhr.send(formData);
```

In the example above, we created a formData object that contains the value inserted in the form element with an id equal to fileInput (in our case, an input file). This formData object is then passed to the send() method of the XMLHttpRequest object.

The transmitted data is in the same format that the form's submit() method would use to send the data if the form's encoding type were set to "multipart/form-data":

```
<form enctype="multipart/form-data">
```

For this solution, you will create a simple form that uses the post method to send data with only one input file element:

```
<form enctype="multipart/form-data" method="post">
<label>Select a file to upload:</label>
<input type="file" name="myFile" id="myFile" required>
</form>
```

The file selected by the user and added to the form will be passed onto a formData object, so insert a script block and create a JavaScript function that will be executed at the click of a button:

```
<script>

function sendForm()
{
}
```

Create two variables in this function, one that contains the reference to the file input type and another that points to an output element (that you will create later):

```
var output = document.getElementById("result");
var data = new FormData(document.getElementById("myFile"));
```

Now you can call the XMLHttpRequest constructor and send the file selected by the user in the form to a PHP file (you can use any server-side language) that will save it onto the server's file system:

```
var xhr = new XMLHttpRequest();
xhr.open("POST", "uploadImage.php", false)
xhr.send(data);
```

Finally, you can provide the user with feedback if the data transmission is successful or if there are problems:

```
if (xhr.status == 200) {
    output.innerHTML += "Uploaded!";
  } else {
```

```
    output.innerHTML += "The following error has occurred: " + xhr.status;
  }
}
</script>
```

Make the last finishing touches to the file by adding the `<output>` element, which we have already discussed in the chapter on Forms, and a link that invokes the `sendForm()` JavaScript function. Here is the complete code of the web page:

```
<!DOCTYPE HTML>
<html>
   <head>
   <title>Solution 8-5: Using XMLHttpRequest Level 2  </title>
     <script>

function sendForm() {
  var output = document.getElementById("result");

  var data = new FormData(document.getElementById("fileinfo"))

  var xhr = new XMLHttpRequest();
  xhr.open("POST", "uploadImage.php", false)
  xhr.send(data);
  if (xhr.status == 200) {
    output.innerHTML += "Uploaded!";
  } else {
    output.innerHTML += "Error " + xhr.status + " occurred uploading your file.<br />";
  }
}

</script>

   </head>
   <body>

    <form enctype="multipart/form-data" method="post">

    <label>Select a file to upload:</label>
    <input type="file" name="myFile" id="myFile" required>
</form>

<output name="result" id="result" />

<a href="javascript:sendForm()">Upload File</a>

   </body>
</html>
```

Expert tips

With the `formData` object, it is possible to add data at runtime and also to send normal, non-file, multipart/form-data values. In fact, by using the `append()` method, you can inject fields into the `formData` object by calling this method:

```
var myData = new FormData();
myData.append("firstName", "Marco");
myData.append("lastName", "Casario");
myData.append("file", myFile.files[0]);
var xhr = new XMLHttpRequest();
xhr.open("POST", "submitForm.php");
xhr.send(myData);
```

We have created a formData object in this piece of code containing three values: fields named "firstName" and "lastName", plus a file data grabbed from the file input type (myFile.files[0]).

Solution 8-6: Checking for XMLHttpRequest level 2 cross-origin browser support

Among the most important new developments introduced by XMLHttpRequest Level 2 is the possibility of overcoming the limitation of the previous version of this object: communication to the same origin server only.

The new XMLHttpRequest Level 2 object, on the other hand, supports CORS, which we have covered in this chapter, and it allows your web page to communicate with services on different origins. Therefore, this feature becomes crucial in many application contexts, but you have to be sure that it is supported by the browser.

XMLHttpRequest Level 2 is already support by some browsers, but it is still far from being universally adopted. Table 8-2 details browser support for XMLHttpRequest Level 2.

Table 8-2. XMLHttpRequest Level 2 Browser Support

Browser	Version
Internet Explorer	Not yet supported (It supports the XDomainRequest object.)
Firefox	03.05.00
Google Chrome	02.00.00
Opera	Not yet supported
Safari	04.00.00

As you can see from this table, you have to be sure the browser on which the web page is loaded supports this object before using XMLHttpRequest Level 2. This will allow you to make the application more robust and to avoid strange browser behavior.

What's involved

In order to be able to check if a browser supports cross-origin communication, you will use the withCredentials attribute. This property controls the credentials flag, which contains a Boolean value. This value returns true when user credentials are to be included in a cross-origin request. It returns false when they are to be excluded from a cross-origin request and when cookies are to be ignored in its response. The default value for the attribute is false.

As in Solution 8-1, in this case you will also create a condition that checks if the withCredentials property of XMLHttpRequest returns the undefined value:

```
if (typeof xhr.withCredentials != 'undefined') {}
```

If this condition returns false, and the withCredentials property is therefore not supported by the browser, our application will behave accordingly.

How to build it

In order to create this solution, you will add an event listener that, upon the load event of the web page, will check to see if the browser supports the cross-origin feature. The result of the control will write text on an output element.

Therefore, insert the addEventListener method, which will register the load event on the init function that you write next:

```
window.addEventListener("load", init, false);
```

The init() event handler starts by instancing the XMLHttpRequest object and creates a reference to the output element with the id result:

```
var output = document.getElementById("result");
var xhr = new XMLHttpRequest();
```

At this point, it will check the withCredentials attribute of the XMLHttpRequest object to see if the value returned by the property is undefined:

```
if (typeof xhr.withCredentials != 'undefined')
{
}
```

Now you can write the result of the condition in the output element. Here is the complete code for this solution:

```
<!DOCTYPE HTML>
<html>
    <head>
    <title>Solution 8-6: Checking for the XMLHttpRequest Level 2 cross-origin browser support
</title>
        <script type='text/javascript'>
         function init()
            {
            var output = document.getElementById("result");
            var xhr = new XMLHttpRequest();

if (typeof xhr.withCredentials != 'undefined')
{
 output.value += " Your browser supports the XMLHttpRequest Level 2 and its cross-origin
feature!";
```

```
    } else {
      output.value += " Cross-origin XMLHttpRequest not supported by your browser.";
    }
            }

            window.addEventListener("load", init, false);
</script>

    </head>
    <body>
      <h2>Solution 8-6: Checking for the XMLHttpRequest Level 2 cross-origin browser support
</h2>

      <output name="result" id="result"> This is the output: </output>

    </body>
</html>
```

You can see the result in Figure 8-2. The web page has been loaded in Google Chrome 9.0.

Solution 8-6: Checking for the XMLHttpRequest Level 2 cross-origin browser support

This is the output: Your browser supports the XMLHttpRequest Level 2 and its cross-origin feature !

Figure 8-2. Chrome 9.0 supports the cross-origin XMLHttpRequest attribute.

Expert tips

To be sure that all browsers are able to use the cross-origin feature, you can add an else if condition to the solution's code that will use the XdomainRequest object (supported by Internet Explorer) if it is not supported in another browser.

From the MSDN documentation (http://msdn.microsoft.com/en-us/library/cc288060(v-vs.85).aspx): The XDomainRequest object is a safe, reliable, and lightweight data service that allows scripts on any page to connect anonymously to any server and exchange data. Developers can use the XDomainRequest object when cross-site security is not an issue.

You can change the previous statement as follows:

```
if ("withCredentials" in xhr)
{
output.value += " Your browser supports the XMLHttpRequest Level 2 and its cross-origin➥
  feature !";
xhr.open(method, url, true);
} else if (typeof XDomainRequest != 'undefined')
{
output.value += " Your browser supports the XDomainRequest and its cross-origin feature !";
  xhr = new XdomainRequest();
xhr.open(method, url);
  } else {
```

```
    output.value += " Cross-origin XMLHttpRequest not supported by your browser.";
xhr = null;
  }
        }
```

Summary

The new HTML5 Communication API is an important step in providing robust approaches to developers who want to create collaborative and data-intensive applications.

In this chapter, you've learned some techniques and solutions for avoiding browser sandbox security limitations by creating documents that communicate from different domains (cross-document messaging). You've used the postMessage API and the Cross-Origin Resource Sharing (CORS) approach to provide interfaces for sandboxed scripts coming from a different domain under same origin policy.

You've also learned how to create real-time communication between the client and the server to find out where the server begins to interact with the client using the Server-Sent Events specification, which instructs an API to open an HTTP connection to receive push notifications from a server. You also read an overview of the XMLHttpRequest Level 2.

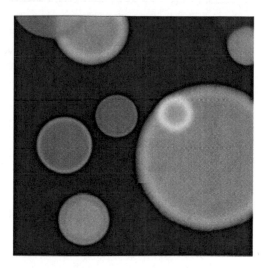

Chapter 9

HTML5 WebSocket

WebSocket is a technology that provides bi-directional, full-duplex communications channels over a single Transmission Control Protocol (TCP) socket. It is designed to be implemented in web browsers and web servers, but it can be used by any client or server application. The WebSocket application programming interface (API) is being standardized by the W3C (http://dev.w3.org/html5/websockets/), and the WebSocket protocol is being standardized by the IETF (www.ietf.org/). Since ordinary TCP connections to ports other than 80 are frequently blocked by administrators outside of home environments, it can be used as a way to overcome these restrictions and provide similar functionality (with some additional protocol overhead) while multiplexing several WebSocket services over a single TCP port.

With WebSocket, you'll have the ability to create a bi-directional, permanent, and real-time connection between the server and the client through the browser. In this chapter, you'll learn how to establish a WebSocket connection with the server and how to push data to the client immediately. By doing that you'll definitively solve the low-latency issue with real-time web applications that need to push data to the client, when compared to approaches that use XMLHttpRequest-based AJAX requests, for example.

Solution 9-1: Checking for WebSocket browser support

WebSocket is one of the novelties that may actually lead to a revolution in the development of web applications. The old approaches that simulate real-time client-server communications and their related HTTP protocol overheads would slowly cease to exist.

As usual, because it is a new feature, you have to be sure that your browser supports this API before you create complex applications. At the moment, the browsers that have been tested to support WebSocket are as follows:

- Chrome 4.0
- Firefox 4.0 beta
- Opera 10.7 +
- Safari 5.0.2
- iOS 4.2 (Mobile Safari)
- Android 2.3 (codenamed Gingerbread)

Because you can't neglect users with other browsers or older versions of these browsers, you need to equip WebSocket applications with a sniffer to check for support.

See how to do this in the following solution.

What's involved

Just as with Solution 9-1, use the typeof JavaScript operator to check for support. This operator checks for the data type of its operand.

Table 9-1 shows a list of possible values returned by the typeof operator.

Table 9-1. Possible Data Types Returned by the typeof Operator

Data Type	Description
number	Indicates a number
string	Indicates a string
boolean	Indicates a Boolean (usually denoted true and false, or 1 and 0)
object	Indicates an object
null	Indicates null
undefined	Indicates not defined
Function	Indicates a function

It's very simple to use the typeof operator: all you have to do is put the command before the variable you want to check, and it returns the data type automatically:

```
var num = 1;
var str = "Hello HTML5";
alert( typeof num );    // it returns number
alert( typeof str );    // it returns string
```

To check for browser support, create a condition to make sure the WebSocket's typeof doesn't return an undefined value.

How to build it

To check if the browser supports `postMessage`, all you have to do is insert the following JavaScript condition into the script block before writing the functions that use the new APIs:

```
if (window.WebSocket) {
  alert("WebSockets is supported in your browser.");
}
```

You can also use the JavaScript operator to get the same result:

```
if ("WebSocket" in window) {
  alert("WebSockets is supported in your browser.");
}
```

This code has to be surrounded by the page script block, as shown in the following example:

```
<!DOCTYPE HTML>
<html>
    <head>
    <title>Solution 9-1: Checking for WebSocket  browser support  </title>
      <script type='text/javascript'>

if (window.WebSocket)
{
alert ('The WebSocket is supported');
} else {
  alert("WebSocket is NOT supported in your browser.");
}
</script>

    </head>
    <body>
      <h2>Solution 9-1: Checking for WebSocket browser support </h2>

    </body>
</html>
```

Expert tips

Here are two web services you can use to check if your browser supports WebSocket:

```
http://jsconsole.com/?WebSocket
http://websockets.org/
```

These links will report WebSocket support, as shown in Figure 9-1.

 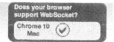

Figure 9-1. WebSocket support report

Solution 9-2: Establishing a WebSocket connection

WebSocket allows you to establish an open connection between the client and the server.

To create this type of client-server communication, all you have to do is use the methods of the WebSocket object and its API so that, as soon as the data changes on the web server, it can send a request to the client without having to poll.

What's involved

The WebSocket object is used to establish a socket server connection. The constructor of the object takes two parameters, url and protocols:

- *url* specifies the URL to access. It accepts URL with the protocols ws: or wss:. The ws: is the protocol for WebSocket connections. The wss: is for a secure WebSocket connection.

- *protocols* is optional, and it contains a string or an array of strings.

Here is an example of how to set up a WebSocket connection:

```
var myWS = new WebSocket("ws://www.comtaste.com/socket");
```

Once the WebSocket constructor is created, you can access the readyState attribute to obtain the state of the connection. The values for the readyState attribute are shown in Table 9-2.

Table 9-2. The readyState Values

Value	Numeric Value	Description
CONNECTING	0	The connection has not yet been established.
OPEN	1	The WebSocket connection is established and communication is possible.
CLOSING	2	The connection is going through the closing handshake.
CLOSED	3	The connection has been closed or could not be opened.

WebSocket, only has two methods, send() and close():

- *send(data)* transmits data using the connection.

- *close()* closes the connection between the client and the server.

If no error has occurred during the connection, it executes the open event, upon which your application is ready to send data to the server using this syntax:

```
myWS.send("Hello WebSocket connection !");
```

The server is able to send back messages at any time using the same procedure.

To intercept the messages received by the server, use the message event transporting an event object with the data property containing the message.

Let's see how to create a complete example.

How to build it

The web page for this solution will have only one button, which will launch a JavaScript method to check to see if the browser supports the WebSocket API. Here is the declaration of the button element:

```
<body>
 <h2>Solution 9-1: Checking for WebSocket browser support </h2>

 <p><button id="socketBtn"> Create a WebSocket Connection </button></p>
```

Open a script block and attach an event handler to the load event of the page:

```
<script type="text/javascript">
window.addEventListener("load", init, false);
```

The init() event handler will only be responsible to register an event listener on the click of the button element you created previously:

```
function init()
{
document.getElementById ('socketBtn').addEventListener('click', establishSocket,true);
}
```

It all happens in the establishSocket() function, which checks for browser support for the WebSocket API:

```
function establishSocket()
{
   if ("WebSocket" in window)
{
```

If there is support for the creation of the WebSocket constructor, the connection will be created. We show how to use the event handlers to check to see if the socket connection has been established in the next solution:

```
var ws = new WebSocket("ws://localhost/echo");
```

Here is the complete code for this solution:

```
<!DOCTYPE HTML>
<html>
   <head>
     <title>Solution 9-2: Establishing a WebSocket connection</title>
     <script type="text/javascript">

        window.addEventListener("load", init, false);

        function init()
        {

                document.getElementById ('socketBtn').addEventListener('click',➥
establishSocket,true);

        }
```

```
        function establishSocket()
        {
                if ("WebSocket" in window)
        {
          alert("WebSocket is supported by your Browser!");

          var ws = new WebSocket("ws://localhost/echo");


        } else {

    alert("WebSocket is not supported by your browser!");
 }

        }
 </script>
</head>
<body>
 <h2>Solution 9-1: Checking for WebSocket browser support </h2>

 <p> <button id="socketBtn"> Create a WebSocket Connection </button></p>

</div>
</body>
</html>
```

By clicking on the socketBtn button, the application will try to create a socket connection with the local server, but only after it has checked that the browser supports the WebSocket API, as shown in Figure 9-2.

Solution 9-2: Establishing a websocket connection

Figure 9-2. Browser WebSocket API support message

Expert Tips

To test the example you have just created, you will have to have an in-socket server-side component on your server. There are many that can be found on the Web, and we provide step-by-step instructions on how to install one in Solution 9-4.

However, in the meantime, you can use pywebsocket, which you can download from these addresses:

- http://code.google.com/p/pywebsocket/

- http://chemicaloliver.net/internet/getting-started-web-sockets-using-pywebsocket-mod_python-and-apache-in-ubuntu/

- www.travisglines.com/web-coding/how-to-set-up-apache-to-serve-html5-websocket-applications-with-pywebsocket

This is an open source socket server created in Python that aims to provide a WebSocket extension for Apache HTTP Server, mod_pywebsocket.

Start by downloading the mod_pywebsocket-x.x.x.tar.gz file from the pywebSocket project page.

Follow these instructions to install and use the socket server:

Unzip the mod_pywebsocket-x.x.x.tar.gz file, and point to the /src directory (pywebsocket-x.x.x/src/)

From a Terminal shell, run:

sudo python setup.py build

Then type:

sudo python setup.py install

Then, read document by:

sudo mod_pyWebSocket

This will install it into your Python environment.

The pyWebSocket comes with example code you can find in the /src/example folder. You can test the server by running this example.

In order to start the server, go to the pyWebSocket-x.x.x/src/mod_pyWebSocket folder and run the following command:

sudo python standalone.py -p 8000 -w /example/

This will start the server listening at port 8000 and use the handlers directory specified by the -w option where your echo_wsh.py resides.

Solution 9-3: Handling WebSocket events

Once the WebSocket constructor has been created, the application will try to make the socket connection between the server and the client. However, it is necessary to check if the connection has been established successfully if you want the operation to run smoothly. Also, once the socket connection has been established, you will need to receive notification any time a message is sent or received by the remote server.

This is why it is necessary to create event handlers to meet these kinds of needs.

In this solution, you will see which events are provided by the WebSocket and how to use them in your applications.

What's involved

In the previous solution, you saw how to establish a socket server connection by creating the WebSocket constructor:

```
var ws = new WebSocket("ws://localhost/echo");
```

But in doing so, you had no idea whether or not the connection had been successfully opened between the client and the server, nor were you able to react to any errors that might occur.

This is why you have to create event handlers for the socket connection as soon as the constructor is created: to help you see if any errors have occurred, if the connection has been correctly established, or to receive messages sent by the server.

A list of events you can use, and their descriptions, are provided in Table 9-3:

Table 9-3. WebSocket Events

Event	Description
Open	This event occurs when socket connection is established.
Message	This event occurs when client receives data from server.
error	This event occurs when there is any error in communication.
close	This event occurs when connection is closed.

Let's see how a web application that uses a socket connection manages these events.

How to build it

Begin with the code from the previous solution, which included a button that launches a JavaScript method to check to see if the browser supports the WebSocket API. If the browser supports this feature, a WebSocket connection will be created using the send() method:

```
function establishSocket()
{
    if ("WebSocket" in window)
{
var ws = new WebSocket("ws://localhost/echo");
```

Here, insert the new code to manage the first event that is executed when the connection between the client and the server has been opened correctly and if no errors have occurred:

```
ws.onopen = function()
    {
        ws.send("Message to send");
        alert("Socket connection established. The Message is being  sent...");
    };
```

Now that you are sure the connection has been opened successfully, you can use the send() method of the WebSocket to send a message to the server.

Then add three event handlers: one for message events to manage the reception of messages from the server, a second for the close event, and a third for handling the error event in order to provide an error mechanism.

```
ws.onmessage = function (evt)
    {
        var received_msg = evt.data;
        alert("Message is received...");
    };
    ws.onclose = function()
    {

        alert("Socket connection is being closed...");
    };
```

The error event, which executes if any kind of error occurs during the connection, deserves separate treatment. In this event handler, you can check to see if the readyState attribute's value is (1) OPEN or (2) CLOSING and, if so, execute a simple event named error at the WebSocket object.

```
        ws.onerror = function(evt)
        {
                alert ('The following error occurred: ' + error);
        }
```

Here is the complete code for the web page:

```
<!DOCTYPE HTML>
<html>
    <head>
        <title>Solution 9-3: Handling WebSocket events</title>
        <script type="text/javascript">

            window.addEventListener("load", init, false);

            function init()
            {

                    document.getElementById ('socketBtn').addEventListener('click',↪
        establishSocket,true);

            }

            function establishSocket()
            {

                    if ("WebSocket" in window)
                {
                    alert("WebSocket is supported by your Browser!");

                    var ws = new WebSocket("ws://localhost/echo");
```

```
                            ws.onopen = function()
        {
            ws.send("Message to send");
            alert("Socket connection established. The Message is being  sent...");
        };

        ws.onmessage = function (evt)
        {
            var received_msg = evt.data;
            alert("Message is received...");
        };
        ws.onclose = function()
        {
            alert("Socket connection is being closed...");
        };

            ws.onerror = function(evt)
            {
                    // check to see if the readyState attribute's value is (1) OPEN or➥
    (2)CLOSING, and if so, fire a simple event named error at the WebSocket object.
                    alert ('The following error occurred: ' + error);
            }

            } else {

        alert("WebSocket is not supported by your browser!");
      }

            }

  </script>
  </head>
  <body>
   <h2>Solution 9-3: Handling WebSocket events    </h2>

  <p>  <button id="socketBtn"> Create a WebSocket Connection </button></p>

  </div>
  </body>
  </html>
```

Solution 9-4: Using a WebSocket server with the WebSocket API

To be able to create a socket connection, you need a few elements installed on your server. What you need is a socket server that can establish a connection with the client and wait for messages from that client and those that will be sent by the server.

In this solution, we will go through the necessary steps to set up a local server and a socket server in PHP to test a real socket connection with the WebSocket API.

What's involved

To create a complete example, you have to have a PHP socket server on the machine. Thus you need to install it on your remote server, or set up a local server where you install all the necessary modules.

You can use some web tools to help with this task. One such tool is XAMPP (http://www.apachefriends.org/en/xampp.html).

XAMPP (see Figure 9-3) is a free, easy-to-install Apache distribution containing MySQL, PHP, and Perl. XAMPP is very easy to use—just download, extract, and start.

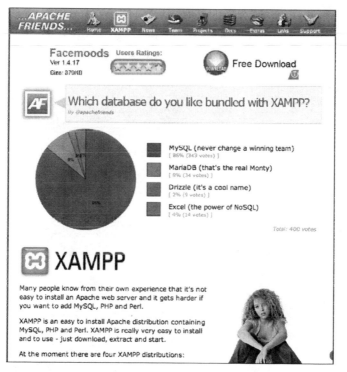

Figure 9-3. The XAMPP home page

At the moment, there are four XAMPP distributions:

- XAMPP for Linux

- XAMPP for Windows

- XAMPP for Mac OS X

- XAMPP for Solaris

The installation phase is going to differ slightly according to the server version you choose. In any case, it is still very simple to install XAMPP on your machine.

For Mac, the installation is done by opening the DMG-Image named XAMPP Mac OS X 1.7.3.dmg. All you need to do is drag and drop the XAMPP folder into your Applications folder to install the software and all its modules, as shown in Figure 9-4.

Figure 9-4. Just drag the XAMPP DMG file to the Applications folder on your Mac to install the server.

You need about 320 MB of disk space to install it. Once installed, you start XAMPP by opening the Applications folder and then opening the XAMPP Control, as shown in Figure 9-5.

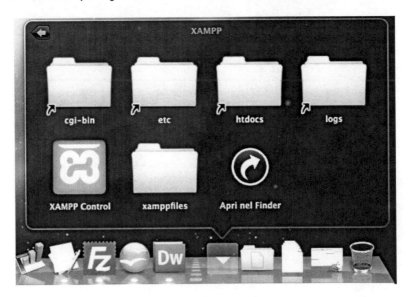

Figure 9-5. The XAMPP Control

You have to start up the services that you'll need. In this case, you only need to start Apache (you could also start MySQL and ProFTPD), as shown in Figure 9-6.

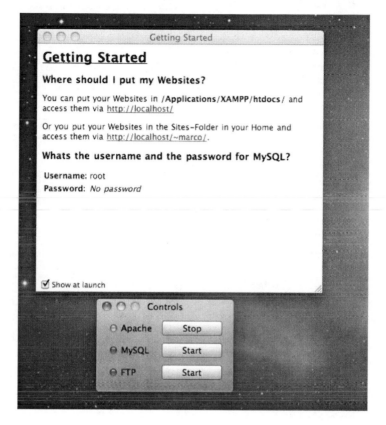

Figure 9-6. Starting Apache

To check if your local web server is up and running, open the browser and type in the following URL: `http://localhost`. The start page will appear with a welcome message:

```
Welcome to XAMPP for Mac OS X 1.7.3!
Congratulations:
You successfully installed XAMPP on this system!
```

The opening screen for XAMPP for Mac OS X is shown in Figure 9-7.

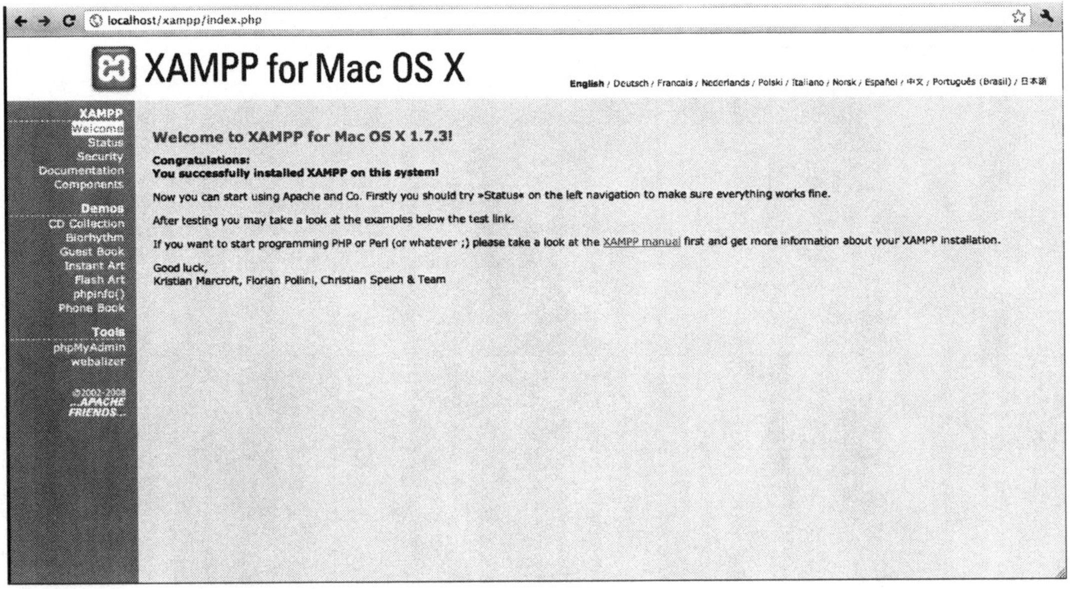

Figure 9-7. The XAMPP for Mac OS X start page

The start page of XAMPP features links to check the status of the installed software and some small programming examples.

As for the socket server, you can install phpwebsocket, which is an open source project you can download from the following address: http://code.google.com/p/phpwebwocket/. You'll need three files from this project when you go to the source of the project, http://code.google.com/p/phpwebsocket/source/browse/#svn/trunk/%20phpWebSocket, and you can copy them to the web server as shown in Figure 9-8.

- server.php

- websocket.class.php

- websocket.demo.php

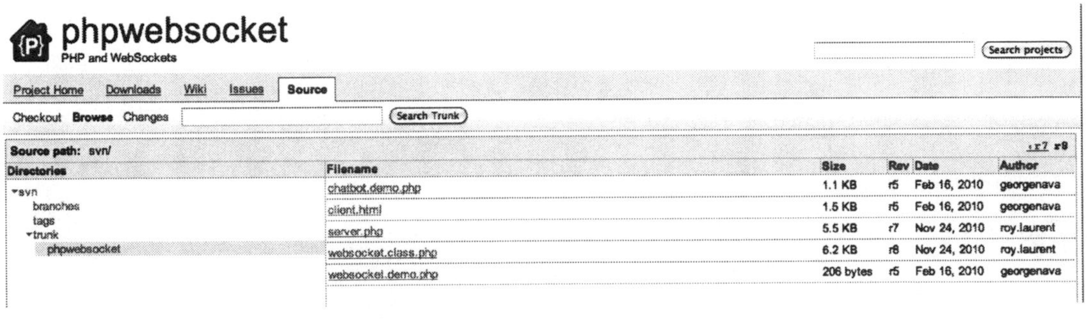

Figure 9-8. Copying phpwebsocket files to the web server

Other than phpwebsocket, you can also decide to install:

- jWebSocket (Java)

- web-socket-ruby (ruby)

- Socket IO-node (node.js)

- NodeJS (server-side JavaScript framework used by multiple WebSocket servers)

- Kaazing WebSocket Gateway (Java-based WebSocket Gateway)

- mod_pyWebSocket (Python-based extension for the Apache HTTP Server)

- Netty (Java network framework which includes WebSocket support)

- wsproxy (WebSockets to generic TCP socket proxy)

- websocket (Python)

If necessary, you can change the address of your local host and the port to use by opening the server.php file and changing the value in the $master variable:

```
$master = WebSocket("localhost",12345);
```

By following these few simple steps, you will be able to create a real connection to a socket server using the WebSocket API.

How to build it

Once the server has been set up with the socket server in PHP, there is very little change from the client's perspective compared to the example created in Solution 9-3.

In fact, you can start with that code and make a few small additions. In particular, insert two new user interface elements: a button and a text input, which will allow the user of the web page to send a message to the server:

```
<body>
<h2>Solution 9-4: Using a WebSocket server with the WebSocket API    </h2>
<p>
<input type="text" value="Insert a message to send" id="message" />
<button id="messaggeBtn"> Send message! </button>
 </p>

</body>
```

In the script block, on the other hand, change the connection string to the socket server:

```
ws = new WebSocket("ws://localhost:8000/socket/server.php");
```

Then add a function that deals with sending the message that the user inserts in the input text with an id equal to message. This method is invoked by clicking the button with an event listener that is attached to the button in the init() function:

```
function init()
        {
                establishSocket();

                document.getElementById ('messageBtn').addEventListener('click',↪
 sendMsg,true);

        }
function sendMsg()
{
    var text = document.getElementById('message').value;
    if(text=="")
{
        alert('Please enter a message');
        return ;
    }
    try{
        ws.send(text);

    } catch(exception){
        alert('Error:' + exception);
    }

}
```

We call the establishSocket() function, which will make the socket connection, in the init() function.

The sendMsg() method, on the other hand, takes the value of the text inserted in the text input and, if it's empty, it will produce an alert. It will use the send() method of the WebSocket to send the message to the server. The send() is invoked by inserting a try()...catch() in a JavaScript statement, which will allow us to manage any errors that may occur:

```
try{
        ws.send(text);

    } catch(exception){
        alert('Error:' + exception);
    }
```

With these few lines of code, we have sent a message to the open socket server. Before concluding the solution, you also have to manage the closure of the socket connection.

This is why we use the close() method of the WebSocket API, which will be invoked upon the click of a simple button:

```
function closeConnection()
        {
        ws.close();
    }
```

Add the last part to your code, which consists of the link that invokes the closeConnection() method to close the connection. Insert an <a> element in the body that recalls the JavaScript function:

```
<p><a href="javascript:closeConnection()">Close socket connection</a></p>
```

You're done. To test the code and see it in action, remember that you have to activate the phpwebsocket socket server with a command line. From the XAMPP Control, you can access the shell by clicking the "Shell" button if you are using the Windows version. For Mac, you open a Terminal shell window and type:

```
sudo su
```

With this command, you have logged in as root.

If XAMPP doesn't start, invoke this command:

```
/Applications/XAMPP/xamppfiles/xampp start
```

The Terminal shell window of Mac OS X is shown in Figure 9-9.

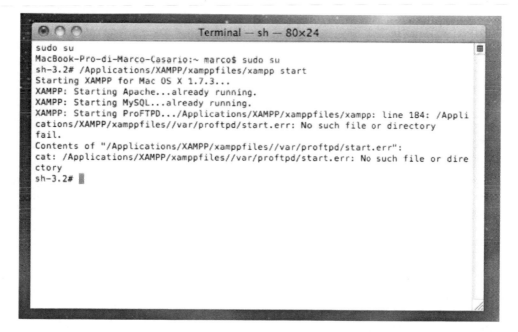

Figure 9-9. The Terminal shell window of Mac OS X

At this point, for both Windows and for Mac, the procedure doesn't change. Here is the command to start the socket server:

```
php -q yourPath\server.php
```

The WebSocket server has now started.

You can execute the example code for this solution from http://localhost.

Here is the complete code for the solution:

```html
<!DOCTYPE HTML>
<html>
    <head>
      <title>Solution 9-4: Handling WebSocket events</title>

     <script type="text/javascript">

        var ws;

        window.addEventListener("load", init, false);

        function init()
        {
                establishSocket();

                document.getElementById ('messageBtn').addEventListener('click',↪
    sendMsg,true);

        }

        function establishSocket()
        {

                if ("WebSocket" in window)
        {
          alert("WebSocket is supported by your Browser!");

            ws = new WebSocket("ws://localhost:8000/socket/server.php");

                    ws.onopen = function()
     {

     ws.send("Message to send");
     alert("Socket connection established. Connection status: " + this.readyState);
     };

     ws.onmessage = function (evt)
     {
       var received_msg = evt.data;
       alert("Message is received...");
     };
     ws.onclose = function()
     {

       alert("Socket connection is now closed ! ");
     };

         ws.onerror = function(evt)
         {
                 //  check to see if the readyState attribute's value is OPEN (1) or↪
    CLOSING (2), and if so, fire a simple event named error at the WebSocket object.
                 alert ('The following error occurred: ' + error);
```

```
                    }

                } else {

            alert("WebSocket is not supported by your browser!");
        }

                    }

                function sendMsg()
                {

        var text = document.getElementById('message').value;
        if(text=="")
{
            alert('Please enter a message');
            return ;
        }
        try{
            ws.send(text);

        } catch(exception){
            alert('Error:' + exception);
        }
                    }

                function closeConnection()
                {

        ws.close();

            }

                function onkey(event)
                {
                if(event.keyCode==13)
                { sendMsg();
                }
                }
    </script>
</head>
<body>
<h2>Solution 9-4: Using a WebSocket server with the WebSocket API    </h2>

<input type="text" value="Insert a message to send" id="message" /> <button id=↪
"messaggeBtn"> Send message! </button>
<p> </p>
<p><a href="javascript:closeConnection()">Close socket connection</a></p>
</body>
</html>
```

Expert tips

To add a user-friendly touch to this simple application, you could make sure that the message is sent to the socket server not only by clicking a button, but also if the Return or Enter key is pressed.

This result is easy to obtain. Simply manage the onkeypress event of the input element and associate it with an event handler that will only have to check whether or not the user has pressed Return or Enter with an if condition using a numeric value contained in the keycode property (which corresponds to the value 13).

Insert these little changes in the code, starting from the input text:

```
<input type="text" value="Insert a message to send" id="message" onkeypress=➥
"onkey(event)" /> <button id="messaggeBtn"> Send message ! </button>
```

Now insert the onkey() function in the script block of your file:

```
function onkey(event)
        {
        if(event.keyCode==13)
        { sendMsg();
        }
        }
```

Save and load the completed file.

Another quick way of checking if your browser supports WebSocket is to type this JavaScript command in your browser's address bar, instead of a URL:

```
javascript:alert("This browser does " + (window.WebSocket ? "" : "not ") + "support➥
 WebSocket API");
```

By executing the command, we will immediately know if WebSocket is supported, as shown in Figure 9.10.

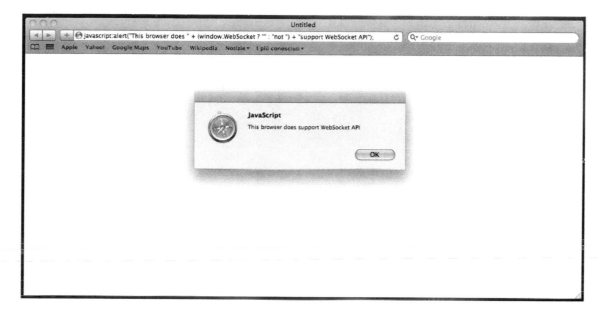

Figure 9-10. The Safari web browser supports the WebSocket API.

Summary

WebSocket is one of the most important new APIs introduced in HTML5. More and more, the Web is providing applications that allow us to collaborate in real time with people across the world.

With WebSocket, you'll have the ability to create a bi-directional, permanent, and real-time connection between the server and the client through the browser. Once a WebSocket connection has been established, the server can immediately push data out to the client. That's why WebSocket solves the problem of the low-latency issue when compared with an XMLHttpRequest-based AJAX request, for example.

In this chapter, you've learned the basics of working with WebSocket. There is a lot more you can do. Enjoy playing with it!

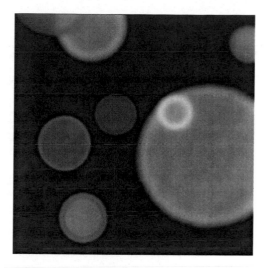

Chapter 10

HTML5 Geolocation API

Wouldn't it be great if a web application just knew where you are located? Imagine being able to search information specific to your current location—where are the closest restaurants, which of your friends are nearby, what is the traffic situation like for your town...

This is all possible and a relatively straightforward feature to add using the HTML5 Geolocation API. Location-aware applications are a popular topic, and in the not-too-distant future they will bring an end to your having to specify your current location manually.

One issue that always comes up when you think about this feature is privacy. You might not always want applications to know your location and potentially share it with the general public. Luckily, the way that the feature is implemented, users need to allow their location to be shared explicitly on a per domain and per session basis. The user also has the option to always allow or to always deny the location to be shared.

Keeping this in mind, geolocation is usually going to be an optional feature in your HTML5 projects, and you will need to perform error handling in case users don't allow you to get their location.

There is relatively good support for the Geolocation API on desktop and mobile devices, as you can see in Table 10-1. As with everything technology-related, this will only get better.

Table 10-1. Support for the Geolocation API

Firefox	IE	Chrome	Safari	Opera	iPhone	Android	BlackBerry
3.5+	9.0+	5+	5+	10.63+	3.2+	2.1+	OS 6.0

Understanding the Geolocation API

The ability for the browser to find out your approximate location seems almost like magic, but there are a few secret ingredients that make this possible.

First of all, there is the user's IP address. This indicates in what country and region a user is connected to the Internet through his or her service provider. This all happens behind the scenes through the browser, but it might be interesting to know how this works technically.

Each country, region, and city is assigned a certain IP range. Whenever users connect to the Internet, they are given an IP address that matches their location. There are services that maintain regularly-updated databases of IP ranges at the country, region, and city levels.

To be a little more precise, browsers gather information about the Wi-Fi signals in your neighborhood. This includes both private and public networks. These Wi-Fi signals get indexed and geo-referenced by companies that offer this service.

The Wi-Fi signal information that gets sent to the service includes the MAC address (a unique identifier for the wireless router), the signal strength, the SSID (name of the wireless network), and milliseconds since it was last detected. It does this for each of the wireless signals it detects for the user.

If the service used has indexed this particular location, it can give a much more accurate location, up to the block and street at which you're located.

This Wi-Fi signal geolocation also happens behind the scenes, and it is entirely dependent on how well your area has been covered. If you're in the middle of a major city like San Francisco or New York, you'll generally have a better approximation of your location than when you're traveling in the middle of nowhere.

The IP-based geolocation is a solution that always works but does not give the best possible result. It might also give a wrong result if the user is connected to a corporate VPN or is on a proxy server.

A combination of these two methods is used by all browsers to give the most accurate location they can gather.

Mobile devices and smartphones, as opposed to working in browser on desktop and laptop computers, are a different story. Mobile devices and smartphones often have a dedicated GPS built-in and, as we cover later in this chapter, it is possible to use this GPS to request a very accurate location of the user.

In the following solutions, we show just what you can do with the HTML5 Geolocation API.

Solution 10-1: Using the navigator object

In this solution, we look at the navigator object and how it's involved in determining Geolocation API support in the user's browser.

What's involved

If you've used JavaScript, you probably know that the navigator object is not exactly new; you can use it to look up the browser language, user agent, installed plug-ins, and so on. What is new is the geolocation object that it now holds, and that it allows you to use the Geolocation API to get the user's location.

How to build it

Naturally, the first thing you want to do when working with the Geolocation API is to detect if it is supported by the user's browser. Luckily, this is not difficult.

```
<!DOCTYPE html>
<html>
<head></head>
<body>
  <script type="text/javascript">
    if(navigator.geolocation) {
      alert('browser supports geolocation :)');
    } else {
      alert('browser does not support geolocation :(');
    }
  </script>
</body>
</html>
```

You really can't get more basic detection than this. The code is checking whether the navigator object has geolocation defined or not. Later in this chapter, you'll see other ways of detecting if the Geolocation API is supported in a particular browser.

If you're using a current browser (which you probably are, reading a book on developing HTML5), you'll see an alert box saying "browser supports geolocation :)," as shown in Figure 10-1. If you're testing this in a browser that does not have geolocation support, you'll see the alert box pop-up saying "browser does not support geolocation :(" (see Figure 10-2).

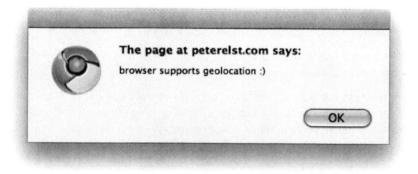

The page at peterelst.com says:

browser supports geolocation :)

OK

Figure 10-1. Alert box showing the Geolocation API is supported in the browser

Figure 10-2. Alert box showing the Geolocation API is not supported in the browser

In a real-world situation where the Geolocation API is not supported, you will likely prompt the user to specify their location or fall back to display non-location-specific information.

Inside of the navigator.geolocation object there are the following three methods:

- getCurrentPosition() attempts to get the current location of the user asynchronously.

- watchPosition() starts monitoring the location of a user at an interval.

- clearWatch() stops monitoring the location of a user.

We get into a lot more detail about these methods in Solution 10-2. For now, you've taken the first step by having detection in place to see if the browser supports the Geolocation API.

Solution 10-2: Getting the current position

In this solution, you will get access to the user's geolocation position using API calls, result, and fault handlers.

What's involved

Once you've determined that the user's browser supports the Geolocation API, you can attempt to get the current position. It is important to remember that it is not enough simply for the browser to support geolocation; the user also has to explicitly allow this information to be made available.

As soon as you request the user's location, a notice will appear and, unless the user has already specified always to allow geolocation detection for your site, the user will need to click an allow button.

Because the user needs to interact with the browser, and determining location might take a few seconds, the method call to get the current position is done asynchronously. When the user's location is successfully obtained, a given function will be called, passing in the coordinates. When getting the user's location fails, a given function will be called passing in the error details.

How to build it

You saw how to do basic detection of geolocation capability in the user's browser in Solution 10-1. Now that you know if it's supported, you can trigger the method to get the current location. It really couldn't be easier:

```
<!DOCTYPE html>
<html>
<head></head>
<body>
  <script type="text/javascript">
    if(navigator.geolocation) {
      navigator.geolocation.getCurrentPosition(function(){}, function(){});
    } else {
      alert('browser does not support geolocation :(');
    }
  </script>
</body>
</html>
```

> Note: To test geolocation features reliably across browsers, you might be required to upload your files to an online resource or to test them on a local server. Security restrictions do not always allow access to the Geolocation API when viewing your page locally.

Running this code in a modern browser will prompt users to choose whether to share or deny access to their location to that particular site (see Figure 10-3).

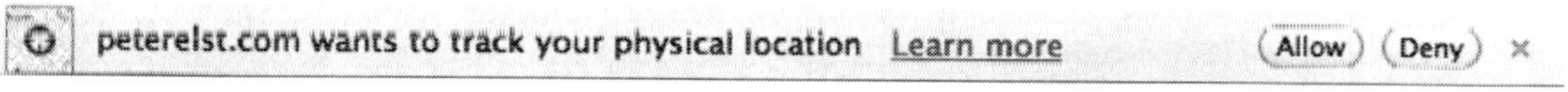

Figure 10-3. Google Chrome browser prompting for geolocation access

If the users agree to share their location, the browser will do its magic and call the first function specified as an argument calling getCurrentPosition, in our case the function called "successGeo". If users do not permit their location to be shared, or an error occurred trying to get their location, the second function will get called, in our case called "failGeo".

Let's implement these functions now.

```
<!DOCTYPE html>
<html>
<head></head>
<body>
  <script type="text/javascript">
    function successGeo(position) {
      alert('We found the treasure: '+position);
    }
    function failGeo(error) {
      alert('Houston, we have a problem: '+error);
```

267

```
      }
    if(navigator.geolocation) {
      navigator.geolocation.getCurrentPosition(successGeo, failGeo);
    } else {
      alert('browser does not support geolocation :(');
    }
  </script>
</body>
</html>
```

When you run this code on a browser that supports geolocation, it will prompt you to share your location or deny access. When you agree to share your location, you will normally see (unless there was an error finding your location) an alert box saying "We found the treasure" and showing the Position object instance (see Figure 10-4).

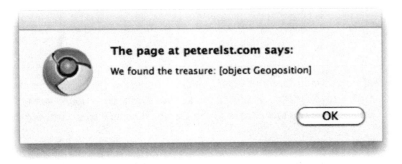

Figure 10-4. Alert box showing the Position object instance after getting geolocation access

If you deny access to geolocation, you will see an alert box saying "Houston, we have a problem" and the PositionError instance (see Figure 10-5).

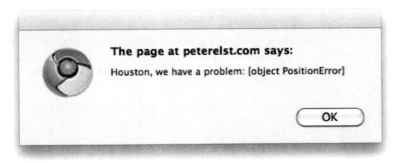

Figure 10-5. Alert box showing the PositionError instance after being denied geolocation access

In Solutions 10-3 and 10-4, you will learn more about this Position object and what you can do with it. You will also study the PositionError object and the information it contains.

Expert tips

The getCurrentPosition method we've been using has a third optional argument allows you to set a few extra options. The three options that are available are:

- enableHighAccuracy is a Boolean setting that allows you to use accurate GPS detection (when available).

- maximumAge specifies how recently (in milliseconds) location detection needs to have occurred.

- timeout specifies when (in milliseconds) an attempt to get a user location needs to time out.

Smartphones and tablet computers in particular now have access to GPS hardware that can provide very accurate location information. If you are targeting your site for one of these devices, you can try enabling high accuracy by specifying this in the third argument object:

```
navigator.geolocation.getCurrentPosition(successGeo, failGeo, {enableHighAccuracy: true});
```

It's important to note that setting enableHighAccuracy to true will not automatically fall back to less accuracy if it's not available. This means it might trigger the error function, and you can then try again with enableHighAccuracy set to false.

Mobile devices with GPS hardware will let the user specify whether or not to use high accuracy location detection. Even when the GPS is turned off, most of these devices are still able to use other mechanisms to get the most accurate location possible.

Getting the geolocation of a user can take a few seconds (especially with high accuracy enabled), so browsers will typically cache the results. You can use the maximumAge property to make sure the detected location is fresh and not older than X amount of milliseconds:

```
navigator.geolocation.getCurrentPosition(successGeo, failGeo, {maximumAge: 60000});
```

The above code uses the maximumAge property in the third argument to ensure the user's location is detected after no longer than 60 seconds.

To ensure users have a good experience on your site or application, you will want to make sure that they're not stuck waiting for the location to be determined. With high accuracy enabled, it can sometimes take a little while (GPS trying to get a lock on satellites, and so forth). In that situation, it's good practice to use the timeout property.

```
navigator.geolocation.getCurrentPosition(successGeo, failGeo, {enableHighAccuracy: true,↪
  timeout: 5000});
```

The line of code above will attempt to get high accuracy location information and set the timeout to 5 seconds. If it takes the network longer than 5 seconds to give back a location, it will trigger the error function and you can handle it differently, either by trying to get a location without high accuracy or falling back to user input.

Solution 10-3: Using the position object

In this solution, we will look at the position object that is returned when the user has allowed geolocation access, and how it can be used to get location information.

What's involved

At this point, we've detected that the user has geolocation support, we've triggered the getCurrentPosition method, and the user has agreed to share his or her location. What happens next is that, behind the scenes, the browser (or in some cases, the GPS hardware) detects the user's location and returns this back as an argument to the success function specified.

In this solution, you'll be looking at the information you get back in this Position object.

How to build it

Here we're looking at what information we get back when the user has agreed to share the location information, and the browser has succeeded in retrieving the geolocation.

In Solution 10-2, you saw a very simple success function that would be triggered and shows an alert box. It's now time to do something more meaningful with the position data that is determined.

First of all, you'll need to know which of the following properties are inside this position argument:

- timestamp returns the time when the location was detected.

- coords.latitude returns the latitude of the detected location, in degrees.

- coords.longitude returns the longitude of the detected location, in degrees.

- coords.accuracy returns how accurate the location is, in meters.

- coords.altitude returns the altitude, when available.

- coords.altitudeAccuracy returns the altitude accuracy, in meters, when available.

- coords.speed returns speed (based on previous detected position), in meters/second.

- coords.heading returns the angle, in degrees clockwise from true north.

Here is where things get a bit tricky. Only three of these eight properties are guaranteed to be specified on all browsers and devices implementing the Geolocation API: coords.latitude, coords.longitude, and coords.accuracy. Any of the other properties can be unsupported and report null. Let's give this a try in our code and see what location is returned.

```
<!DOCTYPE html>
<html>
<head></head>
<body>
  <script type="text/javascript">
    function successGeo(position) {
      alert('latitude: '+position.coords.latitude);
```

```
      alert('longitude: '+position.coords.longitude);
      alert('accuracy: '+position.coords.accuracy);
    }
    function failGeo(error) {
      alert('Houston, we have a problem: '+error);
    }

    if(navigator.geolocation) {
      navigator.geolocation.getCurrentPosition(successGeo, failGeo);
    } else {
      alert('browser does not support geolocation :(');
    }
  </script>
</body>
</html>
```

Running this code and allowing the browser to get your position will trigger three alerts: one showing the latitude, one showing the longitude, and one showing the accuracy in meters (see Figure 10-6). These three properties should in no case be undefined when the success function is triggered.

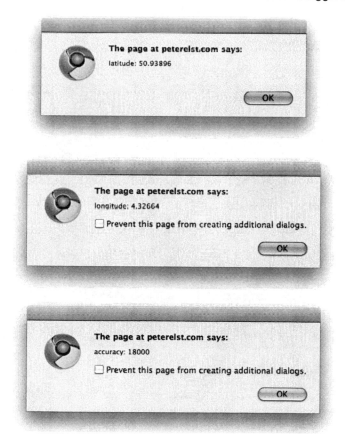

Figure 10-6. Alert boxes showing latitude, longitude, and accuracy values

In later solutions, you'll be looking at more advanced uses of this position information. For now, however, you've learned how to get the user's position in latitude and longitude as well as how accurate this information is in meters.

Expert tips

If you're working on your website or application and want to visualize what a latitude and longitude corresponds to quickly, you can simply pass this data to a query string for Google maps:

```
function successGeo(position) {
document.location = 'http://maps.google.com/maps?q='+position.coords.latitude+','
+position.coords.longitude;
}
```

When used for a getCurrentPosition call, the above function would redirect the browser to Google Maps, with the detected latitude and longitude displayed on a map (see Figure 10-7).

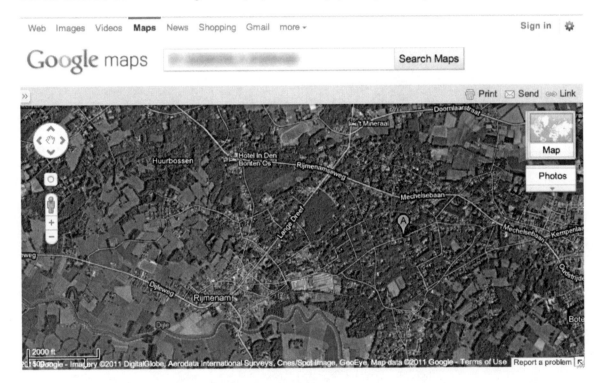

Figure 10-7. Google Maps showing detected geolocation position

While this is useful for simple testing, you will typically want to use the Google Maps API and get a token for your site to get a clean implementation of a location map.

Solution 10-4: Handling position errors

In this solution, we look at position errors when using the Geolocation API, what error information you'll get back, and how to address it.

What's involved

Unfortunately, you can't always rely on things going perfectly. There will be situations when using the Geolocation API where the user either doesn't allow location sharing or there's a technical glitch that prevents detection from working. This could be GPS hardware not being enabled when you request high-accuracy location data, a problem with the location database the browser is using, a slow network connection, or another problem.

It's important that you catch errors like this and transparently handle them so that the user doesn't have a broken Web experience. In this solution, we look at the information we get when errors occur.

How to build it

If an error occurs while getting the user's position, we know that it's not because the browser doesn't support the Geolocation API (see Solution 10-1), but rather because the user didn't allow sharing or there was a technical problem.

Let's first look at what information is available in the PositionError instance that is returned to the error handling function code, which is a number representing the specific error that occurred.

message A text message specifying the error.

For practical reasons, you will always just want to check the code property of the PositionError instance. The error message string could differ among browsers.

The following error codes can get returned:

- *0:* an unknown error, something went wrong getting the location.

- *1:* the user disallowed sharing his or her location.

- *2:* the position can't be found, the network is down, or GPS is unavailable.

- *3:* timeout occurred, as it took too long to get the user's location.

Now that you know about these error codes, you can use them in the code example:

```
<!DOCTYPE html>
<html>
<head></head>
<body>
  <script type="text/javascript">
    function successGeo(position) {
      alert('latitude: '+position.coords.latitude);
      alert('longitude: '+position.coords.longitude);
      alert('accuracy: '+position.coords.accuracy);
```

```
    }
    function failGeo(error) {
      if(error.code == 1) {
        alert('You did not let me see your location, are we no longer friends?');
      }
    }

    if(navigator.geolocation) {
      navigator.geolocation.getCurrentPosition(successGeo, failGeo);
    } else {
      alert('browser does not support geolocation :(');
    }
  </script>
</body>
</html>
```

Running the above code in a browser supporting geolocation will prompt users whether or not they want to share their position. In this case, click "deny," which will trigger the `failGeo` function and pass in an instance of the `PositionError` object with an error code of 1. You should see an alert box come up saying "You did not let me see your location, are we no longer friends?" (See Figure 10-8.)

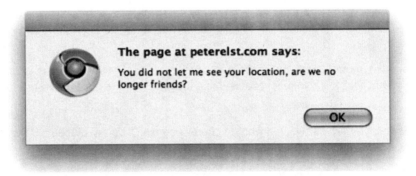

Figure 10-8. Alert box showing message after the user denies geolocation access

In a practical implementation, when the user does not allow sharing their location, you might show a message onscreen explaining why your site would like to use it, allowing them to change their mind and/or fall back to a version that does not rely on location-specific data.

If you get error code 2 while `enableHighAccuracy` is set to true, you might want to change it to false and try again to get position information back. In case you get this error and high accuracy was not requested, it is likely the network is down and you might want to try calling `getCurrentPosition` again after X amount of seconds.

If you get a timeout with error code 3 when using high accuracy, you can set that to false and try again or fall back to having the user specify their location.

Having good error handling is essential for a good user experience when implementing geolocation in your site or application.

Solution 10-5: Tracking the user's position

In this solution, we look at monitoring the user's position over time and how to implement that in projects.

What's involved

It's great being able to find out the current positions of users, but what if they're moving around? This situation applies mostly to mobile sites or applications using the Geolocation API.

Rather than having to poll constantly for changes, you can use a method called `watchPosition` that works pretty much in the same way as the `getCurrentPosition` method we discussed earlier.

In this Solution, we look at how to start and stop monitoring position changes.

How to build it

When thinking about tracking the location of a user who is moving around, you probably anticipate having to set up a function call at an interval to periodically check the `currentPosition` and compare it against the previous one. It is actually easier than that. The `watchPosition` method in the Geolocation API will take care of this for you. Using this method, the device will figure out what the optimal polling time is and pass on the location every time to the success function.

Just tweak the code you already have to start monitoring the user's position rather than just getting it once:

```
<!DOCTYPE html>
<html>
<head></head>
<body>
  <script type="text/javascript">

    function successGeo(position) {
      alert('Target is moving at '+position.coords.speed+' meters per second');
    }
    function failGeo(error) {
      alert('Houston, we have a problem: '+error);
    }

    if(navigator.geolocation) {
      var watchID = navigator.geolocation.watchPosition(successGeo, failGeo);
    } else {
      alert('browser does not support geolocation :(');
    }
  </script>
</body>
</html>
```

You see above that not a whole lot has changed here; the `watchPosition` method has the same implementation as `getCurrentPosition`. The first argument is required and calls the function with the position information when it is successfully retrieved, the second argument is called when an error occurs and passes in information about the error, and the third argument lets you specify options such as high accuracy, timeout, and maximum cache of the location in milliseconds.

One thing that is different is that calling the watchPosition method returns a number; in this case, we're storing it in a variable called watchID. When you want to stop monitoring the user's position you can call the clearWatch method and pass in that number:

```
navigator.geolocation.clearWatch(watchID);
```

Testing this example is a little more difficult. One way to do it is to put this page up online, load it up on your smartphone, and jump on your bicycle or into your car. At an interval determined by the device and when it has found that your position has changed, it will call the function and pass in the data.

When you're monitoring the user's position, the device will have a reference to the previous timestamp and position and can determine the approximate speed at which you are traveling. Obviously, this works best when using high accuracy GPS positioning or you're somewhere with particularly good location database accuracy.

Running our example code above, you'll see alert boxes come up telling you the speed at which you're moving (see Figure 10-9).

Figure 10-9. The alert box on an iPhone, showing travel speed

With examples like this you really start to see the power of geolocation in the browser, especially if you consider bringing in other people's positions. Being able to see which friends in your social network are close by, or track your walking route through a city, are features that are now relatively easy to implement in any site or application.

Expert tips

When testing geolocation position monitoring, you'll probably find that some devices are polling a bit too fast for your particular use case. In that instance, you can put in a conditional statement and a threshold for when to run your code.

Using what is called the haversine formula, you can calculate the distance between two given latitude and longitude pairs:

```html
<!DOCTYPE html>
<html>
<head></head>
<body>
  <script type="text/javascript">

    var lastLat = 0;
    var lastLon = 0;

    function toRad(value) {
      return value * Math.PI / 180;
    }
    function distanceCoords(lat1,lon1,lat2,lon2) {
      var R = 6371;
      var dLat = toRad(lat2-lat1);
      var dLon = toRad(lon2-lon1);
      var a = Math.sin(dLat/2) * Math.sin(dLat/2) + Math.cos(toRad(lat1)) *
              Math.cos(toRad(lat2)) * Math.sin(dLon/2) * Math.sin(dLon/2);
      var c = 2 * Math.atan2(Math.sqrt(a), Math.sqrt(1-a));
      return R * c;
    }

    function successGeo(position) {
      var currentLat = position.coords.latitude;
      var currentLon = position.coords.longitude;
      if(distanceCoords(lastLat, lastLon, currentLat, currentLon) > 1) {
        lastLat = currentLat;
        lastLon = currentLon;
        alert('The user has moved at least 1 kilometer');
      }
    }

    if(navigator.geolocation) {
      var watchID = navigator.geolocation.watchPosition(successGeo);
    } else {
      alert('browser does not support geolocation :(');
    }

  </script>
</body>
</html>
```

The above code uses a formula to check that the distance between the last recorded position and the current position is above a given value, in this case 1 kilometer. If the function gets called and the user has not moved sufficiently, whatever code is inside the conditional statement just gets skipped.

This code snippet is especially useful when plotting positions on a map when you want to have a minimum distance between waypoints.

Solution 10-6: Using the geo.js open source library

In this solution we look at the open source geo.js library, how it can be used for geolocation support on devices using non-standard APIs, and how you can simulate position monitoring over time.

What's involved

Up until now, we've just been focusing on modern browsers implementing the W3C Geolocation API. Before this was widely available (or with manufacturers who like to do it their own way), there were and still are other APIs in use.

The open source geo.js framework (http://code.google.com/p/geo-location-javascript) is an easy way to abstract all of these APIs; it also lets you add support for older BlackBerry, Nokia, webOS, and other mobile devices.

How to build it

The first thing you need to do to use the geo.js library is to download it. You can find the code at the following URL: http://code.google.com/p/geo-location-javascript. Apart from linking in this external geo.js file, you'll notice that everything looks very similar to the standard HTML5 Geolocation API.

```
<!DOCTYPE html>
<html>
<head>
<script src="geo.js" type="text/javascript"></script>
</head>
<body>
  <script type="text/javascript">
    function successGeo(position) {
      alert('Latitude: '+position.coords.latitude);
      alert('Longitude: '+position.coords.longitude);
    }
    function failGeo(error) {
      alert('Error: '+error.code);
    }

    if(geo_position_js.init()) {
      geo_position_js.getCurrentPosition(successGeo, failGeo);
    } else {
      alert('browser does not support geolocation :(');
    }
  </script>
```

```
</body>
</html>
```

Did you spot the difference? It's not so easy to spot because it's essentially the exact same implementation we've been using all this time, except that geo.js takes care of all the platform-specific code behind the scenes.

Where you previously used references to navigator.geolocation, you can now write geo position_js. The only thing needed to start is a call to the init method of geo.js. This will also let you know whether or not geolocation is available for that particular browser and platform.

When running this code on a geolocation-capable device and platform, the successGeo function will be called and you'll see the alert boxes showing the user's latitude and longitude (see Figure 10-10).

Figure 10-10. Showing latitude and longitude alert boxes on iPhone using geo.js

Expert tips

Apart from support for additional browsers and platforms, geo.js is also a very useful feature for testing code that tracks a user whose position is moving. We talked about tracking a user's position over time in Solution 10-5, though there must be easier ways than driving around to test your application. (Not to mention the risk of coding while your hands should be on the wheel!)

In geo.js, you can use geo_position_js_simulator and pass an array of positions and durations to its init method.

```
var locations = new Array();
locations.push({ coords:{latitude:41.399856290690956,longitude:2.1961069107055664}, ↪
duration:5000 });
locations.push({ coords:{latitude:41.400634242252046,longitude:2.1971797943115234}, ↪
duration:5000 });
locations.push({ coords:{latitude:41.40124586762545,longitude:2.197995185852051}, ↪
duration:5000 });
locations.push({ coords:{latitude:41.401921867919995,longitude:2.1977806091308594}, ↪
duration:2000 });
locations.push({ coords:{latitude:41.402533481174856,longitude:2.197566032409668}, ↪
duration:5000 });

geo_position_js_simulator.init(locations);
```

You can see that instead of calling geo_position_js, we use geo_position_js_simulator to call the init method. Each of the entries in the array is an object containing coordinates with latitude and longitude as well as a duration for the position.

The geo_position_js_ simulator will then use this mock position and timing information to play back and simulate the user moving. Once you're done testing your application, you can just switch back to using the regular code and actual location data coming from the browser. Isn't that great?

Summary

In this chapter, you looked at the HTML5 Geolocation API—how it works technically and the end user experience. You've experienced solutions on detecting support for the API, getting the current position, and dealing with coordinates. Of course, we also covered dealing with errors you might experience; both when a user decides not to share position information and when there are network or other technical issues.

Moving on from that, you have seen how to implement position tracking for a user and how you can calculate a minimum threshold. Finally, we discussed how the geo.js library is used to give additional support for doing geolocation on devices that use non-standard implementations.

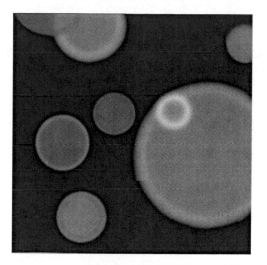

Chapter 11

HTML5 Local Storage

Within the past ten years, we have experienced a Web revolution: everyone wanted to have an Internet presence, and the majority of our existing applications moved from the desktop to the Web. While it sounds great, we are now in the mobile era, where we are not only working at the workplace on our desktop computers; we're also working on the train with laptops, in a plane with tablet computers, or just about any other place with smartphones.

Of course, you can't rely on a 24/7 uninterrupted connection: not all flights have Wi-Fi on board yet, you might lose your 4G connection while travelling through a tunnel, and there are spots where you won't have Wi-Fi access or where you'll get a choppy connection at best. Reading static web pages offline is pretty easy, but what about web applications like Gmail, your favorite RSS reader, or any other crucial application for your work?

Historically, all existing attempts to put web applications offline were either specific to a browser or they relied on a third-party plug-in (Adobe Flash, Adobe AIR, Google Gears, and so on). This is what HTML5 is trying to solve.

In this chapter, you will learn how to create and serve a manifest file to enable HTML5 offline storage support and understand the ApplicationCache object and event flow.

Solution 11-1: Understanding Occasionally-Connected Applications

An Occasionally-Connected Application is based on the idea that a user must be able to continue working with an Internet application even when temporarily disconnected from the network or when remote resources are not available. To do this, the application must be cached on your device, either in entirety or in part. Also, if needed, any user data saved locally while offline must be synchronized when the connection becomes available again.

> Note: Using the HTML5 caching mechanism when online will also benefit your application. It will load faster because most of the resources will be local.

To illustrate the above description, imagine a sales person working with a CRM (Customer Relationship Management) application: while visiting a client on site, he wants to be able to gather their requirements by using part of the existing CRM application on his tablet, much lighter than a traditional laptop, without the need to have an internet connection. When he will be back to his office, he wants the data to automatically synchronize over the network so that he could continue the business process on his desktop computer.

This is a simple example but you can now easily imagine how important Occasionally-Connected Applications will be in a near future.

What's involved

To use the two offline capabilities in HTML5, you need to do the following:

- Work with a browser that supports the HTML5 Offline Application Cache and Local Storage
- Declare a manifest file to tell which files should be cached
- Manage connection changes (eventually)

Let's first have a look at browser support for the Application Cache and Local Storage, shown in Table 11-1 and Table 11-2, respectively. It's difficult to get a definitive list of what features are supported by which browser as they are updated regularly. You can get this kind of information from websites such as http://caniuse.com or, better yet, check it out yourself using websites that detect the features that your current browser supports such as http://html5test.com/ or http://www.modernizr.com/.

Table 11-1. Browsers Supporting Application Cache

Firefox	IE	Chrome	Safari	Opera	iPhone	Android
3.0+	-	7.0+	4.0+	10.6+	3.2+	2.1+

Table 11-2. Browsers Supporting Local Storage

Firefox	IE	Chrome	Safari	Opera	iPhone	Android
3.5+	8.0+	7.0+	4.0+	10.5+	3.2+	2.1+

You see that both features work with the current version of most browsers with one important exception—Internet Explorer (even version 9) still doesn't support Application Cache.

You will see in Solution 11-3 exactly what a manifest file does, so the only thing left is how to detect network status. Before storing data, you may want to know whether or not the user is online. This can be useful, for example, to decide whether to store a value locally (client side) or to send it to the server. To do so, you can use the HTML5 API's navigator.onLine property. This is a property that maintains a true/false value (true for online; false for offline) and will execute online and offline events. You can register listeners for these events by doing the following:

- Use addEventListener on the window, document, or document.body

- Set the .ononline or .onoffline properties on document or document.body to a JavaScript Function object

- Specify ononline="..." or onoffline="..." attributes on the <body> tag

Here again, behavior and support depend on the browser: most support the switch to the "Work in Offline Mode" via the browser's menu, while some fail to detect a physical network status change. Chrome supports none.

Let's look do a simple example.

How to build it

Start by creating a new HTML5 page to test the online property of the navigator object.

1. Create the following HTML5 page:

```
<!DOCTYPE HTML>

<html>

<head>
        <meta http-equiv="Content-Type" content="text/html; charset=utf-8">
        <title>Understanding the Occasionally Connected Applications - Testing Network➥
 Status</title>
    <script type="text/javascript" language="javascript">
function update() {
        elt = document.getElementById("status");
        elt.innerHTML = (navigator.onLine ? "Online" : "Offline");
}
function init() {
        setInterval("update()", 500);
}
</script>
</head>

<body onload="init();">
<div>Network Status: <span id="status"></span></div>

</body>
</html>
```

When this page is launched from a remote web server and you have network access, the network status should read "Online." Then switch to "Work offline" using your browser's menu, and the status will change to "Offline."

    2.   Test which element the event is sent back to. After the first <div> tag, add the following code:

```
<div>Received by the body: <span id="bodyStatus"></span></div>
<div>Received by the window: <span id="windowStatus"></span></div>
```

Then, add in the JavaScript section after setInterval:

```
bdy = document.getElementById("bodyStatus");
document.body.setAttribute("ononline",  "bdy.innerHTML = \"online\"");
document.body.setAttribute("onoffline", "bdy.innerHTML = \"offline\"");

win = document.getElementById("windowStatus");
window.addEventListener("online", function(){win.innerHTML="online"},  false);
window.addEventListener("offline",function(){win.innerHTML="offline"}, false);
```

You can now test with different browsers such as Internet Explorer, Firefox or Opera by switching to the Work offline mode. Note how their behavior differs.

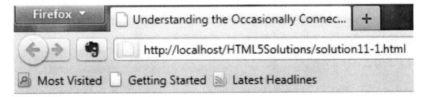

Figure 11-1. testing the online property of the navigator object

> Note: At the moment, I don't recommend to rely on the navigator.onLine property as it's
> badly implemented in the different browsers: you don't want to know if the user manually
> switch to offline mode via the menu but you want to know when his internet connection
> will drop. Then it's better to use the existing fallback mechanism in the manifest (see
> solution 1-3) or implement your own using JavaScript for example.

Solution 11-2: Checking for HTML5 storage support

As previously mentioned, a lot of offline storage capabilities already exist. The most well-known, of course, are Cookies, which have been around since the early days of the Web; however, they are extremely limited. Cookies are key-value pairs of strings that are stored locally in a text file and are sent to the server with every HTTP request that goes to the same domain name. Among other popular attempts are Google Gears (a plug-in for Internet Explorer and Firefox), userData (which is IE specific), or Local Shared Object (a Flash Player plug-in). However, all are browser or plug-in dependant. HTML5 is trying to solve this problem by implementing its own offline storage functionality.

In this solution, you'll learn how to check to see if your browser supports this new functionality, and how you can use it.

What's involved

There are several Storage APIs available in HTML5 (webSQL, File, and Local), but we will focus on Local Storage (also called "Web Storage" or "DOM Storage"). Local Storage lets you store data between browser sessions, share data between tabs, and prevent data loss. The data is stored as strings (key-value pairs, so you will need to serialize your complex values) in a Storage object and, unlike cookies, never transmitted to the remote web server (unless you send it manually).

To store data in the Local Storage, you use `localStorage.setItem`:

```
localStorage.setItem("name", "Cyril Hanquez")
```

Or, you can use the square bracket syntax:

```
localStorage["age"] = 38
```

Or, you can use dot notation if you prefer:

```
localStorage.country = "Belgium"
```

In the same way, you can retrieve data using getItem:

```
localStorage.getItem("name")
```

Alternatively, you can also use square bracket syntax:

```
localStorage["age"]
```

Or, you can use dot notation:

```
localStorage.country
```

Other operations you can perform are:

- Removing data using `localStorage.removeItem("age")`
- Clear all storage data using `localStorage.clear()`
- Get the number of key/value pairs stored in local storage with `localStorage.length`
- Get the name of a key at a particular index using `localStorage.key(0)`

> Note: The storage properties are automatically associated with the domain under which the script is running. This means that http://google.com can't access the storage of http://yahoo.com.

There is also a variant of the long-term storage localStorage called sessionStorage, which maintains the storage only in the current browser window or tab. (It's there mostly for security purposes.)

By default, each origin gets a storage space of 5 megabytes. If you want more, the browser normally should issue a request to the user for additional space. However, none of the browsers currently support this.

Now let's see how to check for Local Storage support.

How to build it

Create the following HTML5 page that will look for window.sessionStorage and window.localStorage:

```
<!DOCTYPE HTML>

<html>

<head>
        <meta http-equiv="Content-Type" content="text/html; charset=utf-8">
        <title>Checking for HTML5 Storage support</title>

        <script language="javascript">
        function RunTest(){
                var supp = "";
                for (var i in window) {
                        switch (i) {
                                case "sessionStorage":↵
        document.getElementById("session").innerHTML = "supported";
                                break;
                                case "localStorage":↵
        document.getElementById("local").innerHTML = "supported";
                                break;
                        }
                }
        }
        </script>

</head>

<body onload="RunTest();">

<h3>Checking for HTML5 Storage support</h3>

<div>Session Storage: <span class="value" id="session">not supported</span></div>
<div>Local Storage: <span class="value" id="local">not supported</span></div>

</body>
</html>
```

Running this example will tell you whether or not your browser supports Local and Session Storage as shown in Figure 11-2.

Checking for HTML5 Storage support

Session Storage: supported
Local Storage: supported

Figure 11-2. Checking for Local and Session Storage

You can also achieve the same result by using the Modernizr JavaScript library and checking the sessionstorage and localstorage properties:

```
<!DOCTYPE HTML>

<html>

<head>
        <meta http-equiv="Content-Type" content="text/html; charset=utf-8">
        <title>Checking for HTML5 Storage support (alternate)</title>

<script language="JavaScript" src="modernizr-1.7.min.js"></script>
        <script language="javascript">
        function RunTest(){

                if (Modernizr.sessionstorage) {
                        document.getElementById("session").innerHTML = "supported";
                };

                if (Modernizr.localstorage) {
                        document.getElementById("local").innerHTML = "supported";
                };

        }
        </script>

</head>

<body onload="RunTest();">

<h3>Checking for HTML5 Storage support (alternate)</h3>

<div>Session Storage: <span class="value" id="session">not supported</span></div>
<div>Local Storage: <span class="value" id="local">not supported</span></div>
```

```
</body>
</html>
```

You should get the exact same result as in the first example.

To understand the difference between local and session storage, let's build a simple example.

Start by creating a new HTML5 page to test the online property of the navigator object.

1. Create the following HTML5 Form page to encode a key/value pair

```
<!DOCTYPE HTML>
<html>
 <head>
  <title>HTML5 localStorage/sessionStorage</title>
 </head>
 <body>
 <h1>HTML5 localStorage/sessionStorage</h1>

  <form name="entryForm">

    <div>
     <p>
         <label>value: <textarea style="vertical-align:text-top" name="data" cols="20"
rows="5"></textarea></label>
     </p>

     <p>
      <label>Name: <input name="name"></label>
     </p>
  </form>

 </body>
</html>
```

2. Now add before the end of the form some buttons to do basic operations on local or session storage

```
<p>
       <input type="button" value="get local Item" onclick="getItem('local')">
       <input type="button" value="set local Item" onclick="setItem('local')">
       <input type="button" value="remove local Item" onclick="removeItem('local')">
     </p>
     <p>
       <input type="button" value="get session Item" onclick="getItem('session')">
       <input type="button" value="set session Item" onclick="setItem('session')">
       <input type="button" value="remove session Item" onclick="removeItem('session')">
</p>
```

3. Add a table after the buttons that will display the stored values/pairs

```
<div>
       <h2>Items</h2>
```

```
    <table id="items_tbl"></table>
    <p>
    <label><input type="button" value="clear localStorage"
onclick="clearStorage('local')"></label>
    </p>
     <p>
    <label><input type="button" value="clear sessionStorage"
onclick="clearStorage('session')"></label>
    </p>
   </div>
```

4. Add the needed JavaScript functions after the item table

```
<script>

    function setItem(typ) {
      var name = document.forms.entryForm.name.value;
      var data = document.forms.entryForm.data.value;
      if (typ == "local") {
            localStorage.setItem(name, data);
      } else {
            sessionStorage.setItem(name, data);
      }

      showAll();
    }

    function getItem(typ) {
      var name = document.forms.entryForm.name.value;
      if (typ == "local") {
            document.forms.entryForm.data.value = localStorage.getItem(name);
      } else {
            document.forms.entryForm.data.value = sessionStorage.getItem(name);
      }
      showAll();
    }

    function removeItem(typ) {
      var name = document.forms.entryForm.name.value;
      if (typ == "local") {
            document.forms.entryForm.data.value = localStorage.removeItem(name);
      } else {
            document.forms.entryForm.data.value = sessionStorage.removeItem(name);
      }
      showAll();
    }

    function clearStorage(typ) {
      if (typ == "local") {
            localStorage.clear();
      } else {
            sessionStorage.clear();
      }
      showAll();
```

```
        }

    function showAll() {
        var key = "";
        var pairs = "<tr><th>Type</th><th>Name</th><th>Value</th></tr>\n";
        for (var s in window) {
            switch (s) {
                case "sessionStorage":
                    var j=0;
                    for (j=0; j<=sessionStorage.length-1; j++) {
                    key = sessionStorage.key(j);
                    pairs +=
"<tr><td>session</td><td>"+key+"</td>\n<td>"+sessionStorage.getItem(key)+"</td></tr>\n";
                    }
                break;
                case "localStorage":
                    var i=0;
                    for (i=0; i<=localStorage.length-1; i++) {
                    key = localStorage.key(i);
                    pairs +=
"<tr><td>local</td><td>"+key+"</td>\n<td>"+localStorage.getItem(key)+"</td></tr>\n";
                    }

                break;
            }
        }
        if (pairs == "<tr><th>Type</th><th>Name</th><th>Value</th></tr>\n") {
            pairs +=
"<tr><td><i>empty</i></td>\n<td><i>empty</i></td>\n<td><i>empty</i></td></tr>\n";
            }
        document.getElementById('items_tbl').innerHTML = pairs;
    }

</script>
```

5. Show existing key/values pairs when the page load by calling the showAll function

```
<body onload="showAll()">
```

By testing this example you will see that values/pairs stored in the localeStorage persist when you open or close a new tab or window in the same browser, but those stored in the sessionStorage are not passed even to another tab.

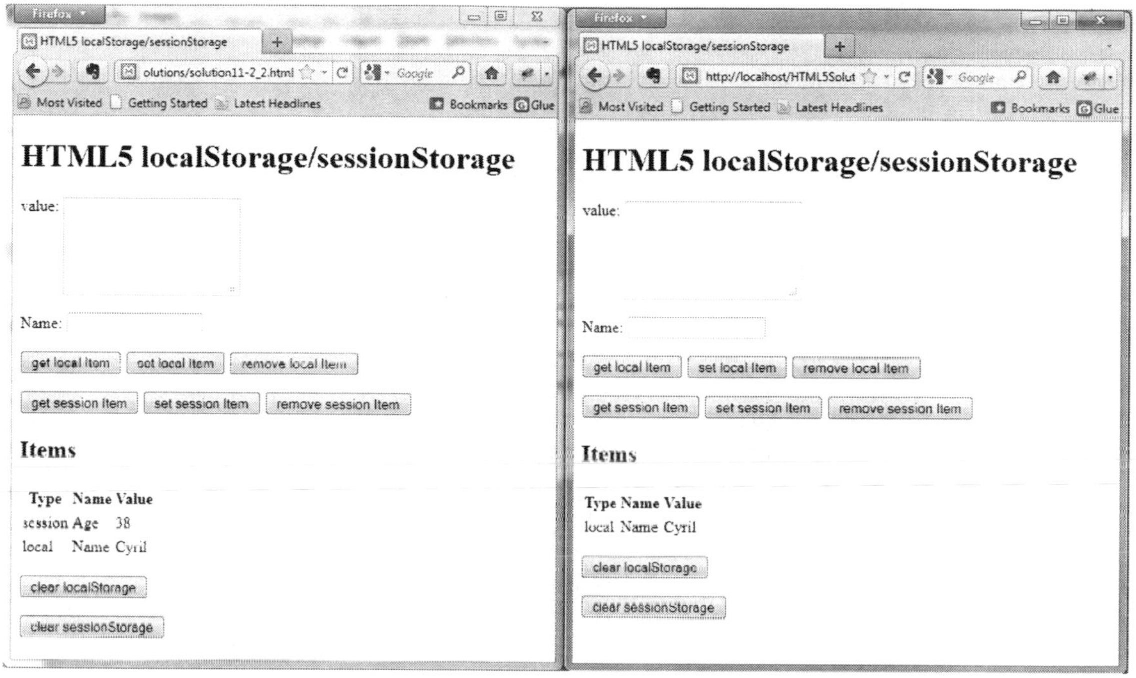

Figure 11-3. understanding the difference between local and session storage

> Note: unless localStorage, sessionStorage does not exist when a file is run locally
> except using the Chrome browser. So be sure to test your code using a webserver.

Solution 11-3: Declaring a manifest for your page

The manifest file is a simple text file located on your web server that contains a list of URLs pointing to the resources that you want to make available offline.

When you request an HTML file containing a reference to the manifest file for the first time, your browser will read it, download the specified resources (HTML, CSS, JavaScript, images, videos, and so forth), and store them in the local cache. Any subsequent requests for the same HTML file will load resources from the cache first (even if you are online), then check to see if there is a new version and update the Application Cache. The complete event flow will be detailed in the next solution. Please note that depending on your browser and the security level you might get a warning (per domain or not) asking permission to store data locally.

> Note: It's important to remember that even if the assets (images, for example) have
> been updated, the latest version only will be visible when the page is reloaded.

What's involved

First you need to point to the manifest file in your page using the manifest attribute on the `<html>` element.

```
<!DOCTYPE HTML>

<html manifest="./myAppCache.manifest">

<body>
...
</body>

</html>
```

The manifest file can be located anywhere on your web server, but it must be served with the MIME type text/cache-manifest. You will probably have to configure your web server. For Apache, you can add the following entry in the `mime.types` file in the conf folder:

```
text/cache-manifest      .manifest
```

> Note: It's a best practice to put a manifest attribute that points to the same cache manifest in every page of your application.

Now that everything is configured properly, you must write the manifest file using the proper syntax.

How to build it

Lines in the manifest end in CR, LF, or CRFL, but the text must be UTF-8 encoded.

1. The first line of a cache manifest begins with CACHE MANIFEST, and then the file is divided into three parts:

    - *Explicit section:* uses the header CACHE

    - *Fallback section:* uses the header FALLBACK

    - Online whitelist section: uses the header NETWORK

If there are no section headers defined in the cache manifest, all listed resources will fall into the explicit section by default. The hash symbol (#) is used to insert a comment. Here is a basic cache manifest:

```
CACHE MANIFEST

# this is a basic cache manifest
index.html
solution11-3.css
#version 1
```

In this example, the two files `index.html` and `solution11-3.css` are stored locally upon first request, and then any subsequent request, online or offline, will fetch them from the cache.

> Note: The HTML document pointing to the manifest file is implicitly included in the cache but, as there's usually more than one entry point, it's more convenient to list all of them in the cache manifest file.

2. The FALLBACK section entries define substitutions for resources that haven't been cached for whatever reason. Fallback files are automatically included in the cache.

Let's look at the following example:

```
CACHE MANIFEST

# a cache manifest with a fallback section
index.html
solution11-3.css

FALLBACK:
# while offline, visitor number is replaced by ------
counter.js        counter_offline.js
#version 2
```

When the user is online, index.html and solution11-3.css are fetched from the cache; the counter (counter.js) is reachable on the network.

When the user is offline, index.html and solution11-3.css are also fetched from the cache, but the counter (counter.js) is not accessible and so it is replaced by an offline version (counter_offline.js).

3. All requests to files or paths included in the NETWORK section must not be cached and are only accessible using the network, even if a matching cached resource is found.

```
CACHE MANIFEST

# a cache manifest with all 3 sections

NETWORK:
HTML5_logo.jpg

FALLBACK:
# while offline, visitor number is replaced by ------
counter.js        counter_offline.js

CACHE:
index.html
counter.js
solution11-3.css
#version 3
```

In this third example, we are explicitly telling the browser to not cache a picture, so when offline it will display a broken image placeholder. You also noticed that we reversed the order of the sections so that you can see that there's absolutely no impact on the global mechanism.

> Note: The caching restrictions imposed on pages served over SSL are overridden by cache manifests so that pages served over https can be made to work offline.

Solution 11-4: Using the ApplicationCache object

The window.applicationCache object is the one that gives information on the state of the cache and triggers events related to it.

What's involved

The applicationCache has a property status that indicates the state of the cache among six possible options, as shown in Table 11-3.

Table 11-3. The Six Cache States

Numeric value	Status
0	UNCACHED
1	IDLE
2	CHECKING
3	DOWNLOADING
4	UPDATEREADY
5	OBSOLETE

Let's define those cache states:

0. *UNCACHED state:* this is the default state when no cache manifest exists.

1. *IDLE state:* this is the most typical state, and it means that an application or web page has a cache manifest and that all specified resources are up to date and stored in the cache.

2. *CHECKING state:* the cache is put in this state when the browser is reading the manifest file.

3. *DOWNLOADING state:* the cache enters this state when new or updated resources specified in the manifest are downloaded from the server and saved in the cache.

4. *UPDATEREADY state:* the cache is in this state when the manifest file has been updated, and new or updated resources are now available in the cache.

5. *OBSOLETE state:* if at one point there was a valid cache but now the manifest file is missing, then the cache enters this state. Resources will be downloaded from the network even if they are available in the cache.

Most of these states have associated events. We will discuss this in the next solution.

How to build it

For this solution we will build a simple page that will display the status of the applicationCache.

1. Create the following HTML5 page

```
<!DOCTYPE HTML>
<html>
 <head>
  <title> HTML5 ApplicationCache Object</title>
 </head>
 <body>

 </body>
</html>
```

2. Add the following JavaScript code in the header section to check the value of the applicationCache

```
<script>
function init() {
var myAppCache = window.applicationCache;

switch (myAppCache.status) {
  case myAppCache.UNCACHED: // UNCACHED == 0
    document.write('UNCACHED');
    break;
  case myAppCache.IDLE: // IDLE == 1
    document.write('IDLE');
    break;
  case myAppCache.CHECKING: // CHECKING == 2
    document.write('CHECKING');
    break;
  case myAppCache.DOWNLOADING: // DOWNLOADING == 3
    document.write('DOWNLOADING');
    break;
  case myAppCache.UPDATEREADY:  // UPDATEREADY == 5
    document.write('UPDATEREADY');
    break;
  case myAppCache.OBSOLETE: // OBSOLETE == 5
    document.write('OBSOLETE');
    break;
  default:
    document.write('UKNOWN CACHE STATUS');
    break;
};
 }
 </script>
```

Call the init() function in the body of the page.

```
<body onload="init()">
```

If you run this page, it will display UNCACHED because no manifest have been specified.

3. create an empty file called myCache.manifest and just type CACHE MANIFEST to create a simple manifest. By default the document pointing to the manifest file is implicitly included so let's add a reference to it in our file

```
<html manifest="myCache.manifest">
```

Now if you run the page again you will see that the status will now display IDLE: as you specified a manifest file that exists, it automatically cache the calling page and update the applicationcache status.

Solution 11-5: The ApplicationCache events

In Solution 11-3, we briefly described how the manifest file is served. Nothing is magic, however, so let's look at the different scenarios in detail.

What's involved

In the previous solution, we mentioned that most of the states have an associated event. Table 11-4 lists common events and their associated cache states.

Table 11-4. Common Events Associated with Cache States

Event	Cache State
onchecking	CHECKING
ondownloading	DOWNLOADING
onupdateready	UPDATEREADY
onobsolete	OBSOLETE
oncached	IDLE
onprogress	-
onerror	-
onnoupdate	-

We will now describe the event flow in detail.

1. As soon as a manifest attribute is found, the browser executes the onchecking event on the applicationCache object. This event is always executed, even if the cache manifest has already been read.

2. The first time that the manifest is read, the following occurs:

- An ondownloading event is executed, and all resources specified in the manifest file start to download.

- While downloading, the browser periodically executes an onprogress event containing information on how many files have been downloaded and how many are still in the queue.

- If everything is downloaded successfully, then the browser executes a final oncached event, and the offline application is fully cached. Your application is now in the IDLE state.

3. If the manifest has already been read from another page, for example, then all the required resources must be in the cache, but you still need to check if the manifest changed since the last time.

- If the cache manifest is the same, then the browser will execute an onnoupdate event, and that's it. Your application will be in the IDLE state.

- If the cache manifest has changed, the browser executes an ondownloading event and all the resources will be downloaded again.

- While downloading, the browser executes an onprogress event periodically containing information on how many files have been downloaded and how many are still in the queue.

- After everything is downloaded successfully, this time the browser executes an onupdateready event. This means that the cache has been updated, but the new version is not yet in use! You need to tell the user to reload the page to display the latest version.

4. If something goes wrong in the flow, then the browser executes an onerror event and stops.

5. You can also programmatically force the browser to check the manifest again using applicationCache.update(). Then you can force the switch to the new version of the cache using applicationCache.swapCache(), but here again the page needs to be reloaded manually.

How to build it

Now let's build an example that will display the event flow on screen.

1. Create the following HTML5 page

```
<!DOCTYPE HTML>
<html>
 <head>
  <title> HTML5 ApplicationCache Event</title>
 </head>
 <body>
```

```
    </body>
</html>
```

2. Add the following JavaScript code to listen to the different applicationCache events

```
<script>
var appCache = window.applicationCache;

appCache.addEventListener('checking',
                        function(e) {
                        document.write("Checking for application update<BR>");
                        }, false);
appCache.addEventListener('cached',
                        function(e) {
                        document.write("Application cached<BR>");
                        }, false);
appCache.addEventListener('noupdate',
                        function(e) {
                        document.write("No application update found<BR>");
                        }, false);
appCache.addEventListener('obsolete',
                        function(e) {
                        document.write("Application obsolete<BR>");
                        }, false);
appCache.addEventListener('error',
                        function(e) {
                        document.write("Application cache error<BR>");
                        }, false);
appCache.addEventListener('downloading',
                        function(e) {
                        document.write("Downloading application update<BR>");
                        }, false);
appCache.addEventListener('progress',
                        function(e) {
                        document.write("Application Cache progress<BR>");
                        }, false);
appCache.addEventListener('updateready',
                        function(e) {
                        document.write("Application update ready<BR>");
                        }, false);
</script>
```

3. create an empty file called myCache.manifest and just type CACHE MANIFEST to create a simple manifest And add a reference to it in our file

```
<html manifest="myCache.manifest">
```

Now run the page and play with it by, for example, changing the name of the manifest file to throw errors, etc...

To achieve the result in the screenshot, you can do the following:

- launch the page a first time.

- on your webserver, rename the file myCache.manifest into myCache2.manifest: when you will refresh the page, it should display Application cache error as the reference to the manifest didn't change in the html page.

- now rename the manifest file back to his original name: refreshing the page should display the screenshot (Figure 11-4).

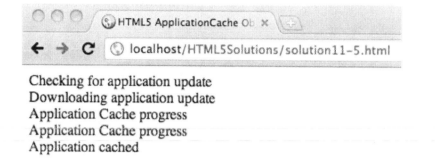

Checking for application update
Downloading application update
Application Cache progress
Application Cache progress
Application cached

Figure 11-4. The ApplicationCache Events

Expert tips

You can force a page to refresh by monitoring the updateready event by doing the following:

```
// Check if the cache manifest has been updated.

if (window.applicationCache.status == window.applicationCache.UPDATEREADY) {
        // Swap the applicationCache
        window.applicationCache.swapCache();
        // force a reload the page
        window.location.reload();
} else {
        // Manifest didn't changed.
}
```

Solution 11-6: Deleting the local cache

You can really get a headache while playing with the cache manifest. You will also have to deal with your browser and web server caching mechanism and, at some point, you will just want to start over again and clear the cache.

What's involved

At the moment, you can't do it using the applicationCache object. You will need to clear the cache directly in your browser. However, clearing the normal cache won't be enough—you will have to find the options normally hidden in your browser's menu and options.

How to clear the cache

To clear the cache, let's first use the second example of Solution 11-2 and store some information in the local cache (see Figure 11-5).

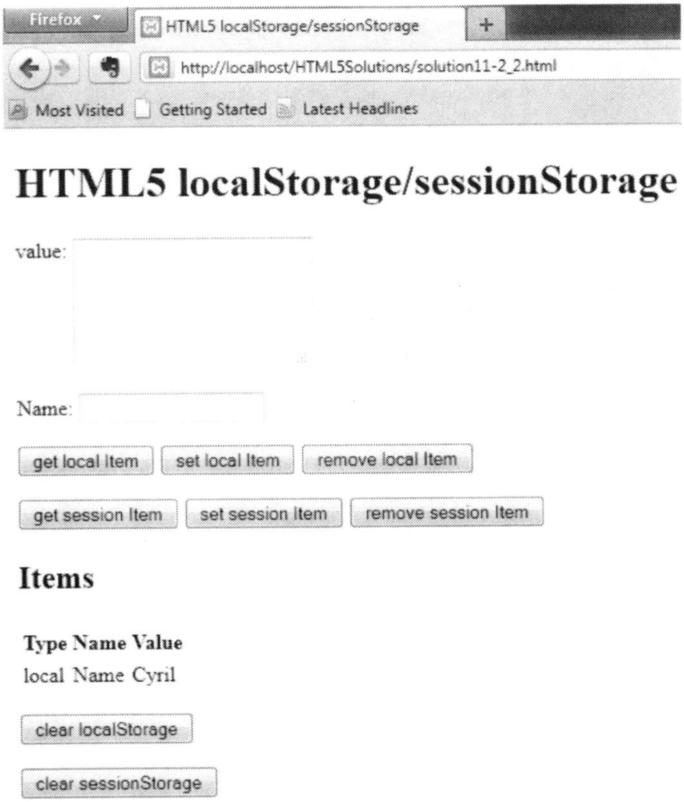

Figure 11-5. Storing an item in the Local Storage

Now let's try to find and clear the application cache for the most common browsers.

In Firefox (see Figure 11-6):

- On Windows:

    Tools ➤ Options ➤ Advanced ➤ Network ➤ Offline Storage

- On OSX:

    Firefox ➤ Preferences ➤ Advanced ➤ Network ➤ Offline Storage

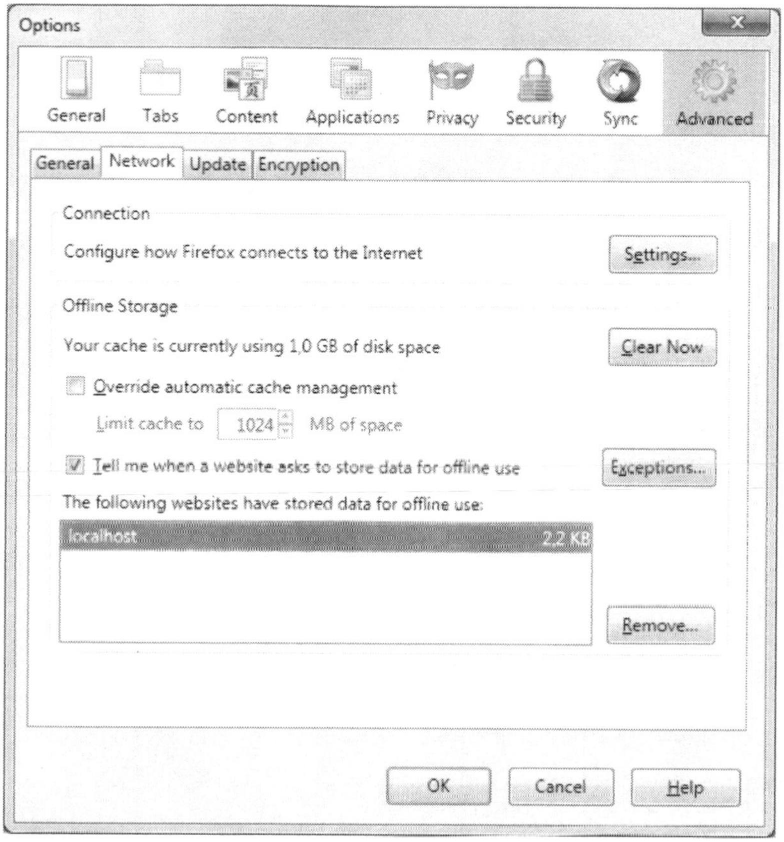

Figure 11-6. The Firefox 3 Offline Storage menu

In Chrome (see Figure 11-7):

The best way to find out about the different kinds of caches in Chrome is to use the built-in developer tools. To enable them, click in the menu on Tools ➤ Developer tools. Then select Resources in the toolbar, and you will get access to a detailed view of all kinds of storage and caches, from Cookies to Application Cache.

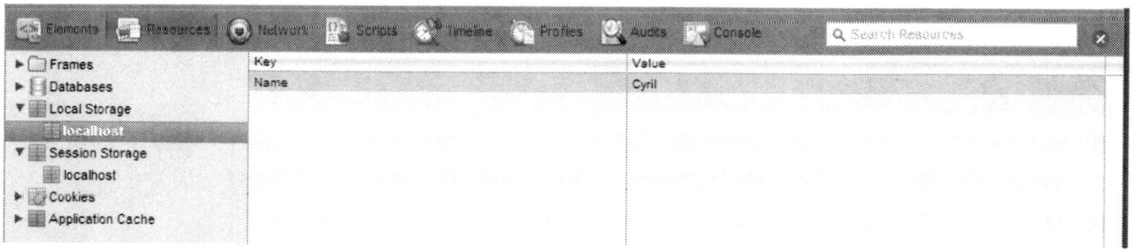

Figure 11-7. The Google Chrome 10 Resources developer tool

In Opera (see Figure 11-8):

- On Windows:

    Menu ➤ Settings ➤ Preferences ➤ Advanced ➤ Storage

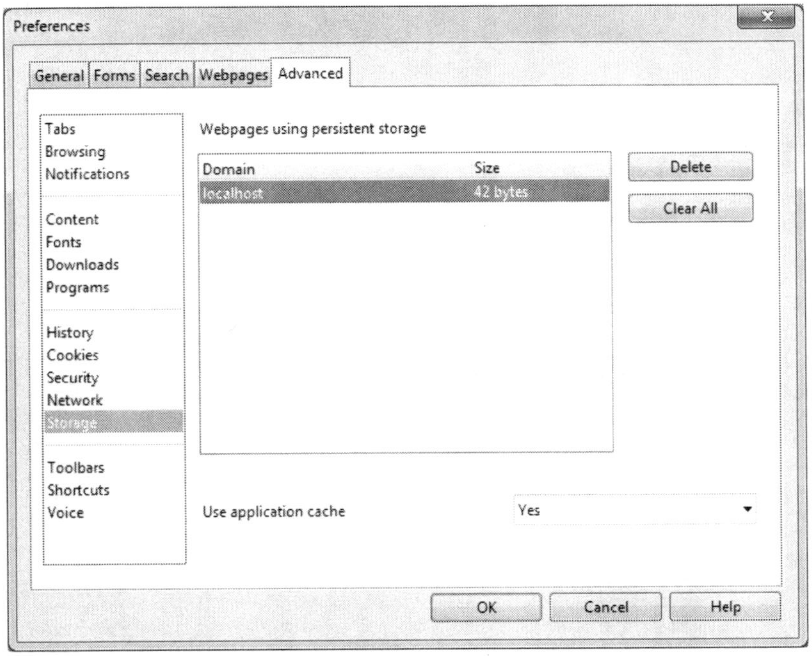

Figure 11-8. The Opera 11.10 Persistent Storage menu

In Safari (see Figure 11-9):

As with Google Chrome, you have to enable the developer tools. To do so, in the Settings menu, select Preferences ➤ Advanced and click Show Develop in the menu bar. Then, in the menu, click on Develop ➤ Show Web Inspector and click on Storage.

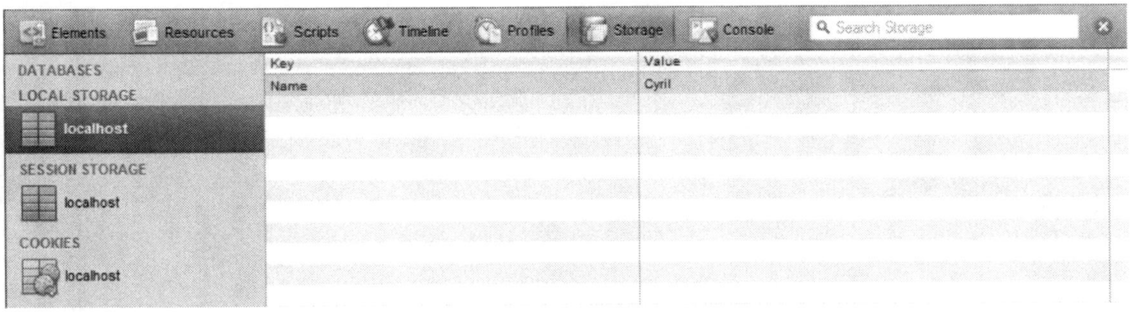

Figure 11-9. The Safari 5 Storage developer tool

There is currently no easy way to inspect the caches of mobile browsers, but most of them have only one option to clear the cache that clears all type of cache.

Summary

This HTML5 Local Storage feature opens up new opportunities for developers to create rich applications that run on multiple platforms and devices—users will even be able work offline and sync up when connected without relying on any proprietary technology. In view of the growing mobile market and more support for this capability in browsers, HTML5 Local Storage will be one of the most useful new specifications.

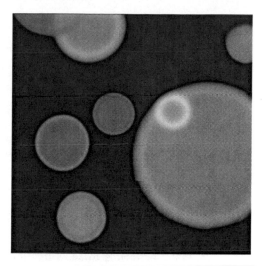

Chapter 12

HTML5 Accessibility

Accessibility for web applications is a very hot issue. Not only is the number of disabled persons who use the Web increasing every day, but the context in which people in difficult situations are navigating the Web is also increasing. Filling in web forms using the keyboard instead of a mouse, dragging objects on screen using a touch-based device, or using a multimedia element from a slow UMTS connection (http://en.wikipedia.org/wiki/UMTS) on a cell phone are constant barriers that the disabled must face. The reason for making an application accessible and the techniques for doing so do not encompass all disabilities that affect access to the Web, which include visual, auditory, physical, speech, cognitive, and neurological disabilities. Rather, it involves improving access for anyone who experiences certain difficulties accessing the Web.

The four principles of accessibility

The guidelines and Success Criteria are organized around the following four principles, which lay the foundation necessary for anyone to access and use Web content (http://www.w3.org/TR/UNDERSTANDING-WCAG20/intro.html#introduction-fourprincs-head). Anyone who wants to use the Web must have content that is:

1. **Perceivable:** Information and user interface components must be presentable to users in ways they can perceive.

    This means that users must be able to perceive the information being presented (it can't be invisible to all of their senses).

2. **Operable:** User interface components and navigation must be operable.

    This means that users must be able to operate the interface (the interface cannot require interaction that a user cannot perform).

3. **Understandable:** Information and the operation of user interface must be understandable.

    This means that users must be able to understand the information as well as the operation of the user interface (the content or operation cannot be beyond their understanding).

4. **Robust:** Content must be robust enough that it can be interpreted reliably by a wide variety of user agents, including assistive technologies.

    This means that users must be able to access the content as technologies advance (as technologies and user agents evolve, the content should remain accessible).

There are many acronyms to know that involve this issue: W3C, WCAG, WAI, ATAG (Authoring Tool Accessibility Guidelines), and UAAG (User Agent Accessibility Guidelines). Let's try and clarify them a bit as sometimes things can appear to be more complicated than they actually are.

The World Wide Web Consortium (W3C), with the Web Accessibility Initiative (WAI), released the second version of the Web Content Accessibility Guidelines (WCAG) on December 11, 2008.

The purpose of these guidelines is to explain how to make web content accessible to people with disabilities by defining accessibility levels. In practice, the Consortium wants to allow all web users to obtain the same information and to use the same functions.

The purpose of the WCAG

Web Content Accessibility Guidelines (WCAG) are part of a series of Web accessibility guidelines for helping developers on making content accessible, primarily for disabled users, but also for all user agents, including highly limited devices, such as mobile devices.

These set of guidelines are maintained by the W3C (Figure 12-1):

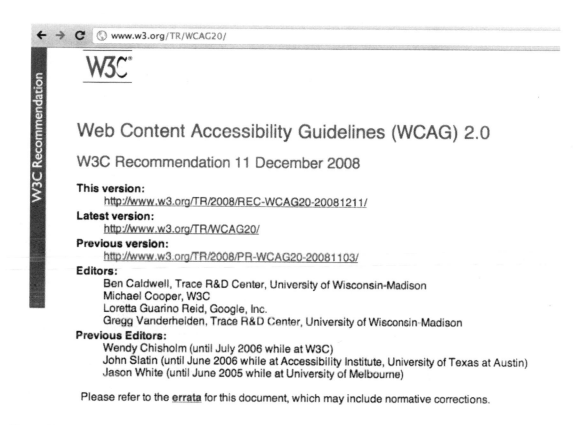

Figure 12-1. The WCAG specification page on the W3C site

The three levels of the guidelines are as follows.

Level 1: Overview of design principles, guidelines, and success criteria

Level 1 provides an introduction to the WCAG 2 (the second generation of the accessibility guidelines), the four principles of accessibility, the 13 guidelines that aren't linked to technologies, and the regulations and definitions of examples for every guideline, as well as a final appendix.

Level 2: Technology-specific checklists

Level 2 is designed to support the general guidelines. It includes a series of documents and checklists that help define the information about the technologies to use to comply with the WCAG 2 specifications.

Level 3: Technology-specific application information

Level 3 includes examples of code, screen shots, and other technical information. The examples include:

General Techniques

- Techniques for using HTML and XHTML

- Techniques for cascading style sheets (CSS)

- Techniques for server-side scripting

- Techniques for client-side scripting

- Techniques for Scalable Vector Graphics (SVG)

- Techniques for Synchronized Multimedia Integration Language (SMIL)

- Techniques for Extensible Markup Language (XML)

It is therefore through the study and application of best practices described in the WCAG that you can make a web application accessible.

There is one more issue to add to the conversation: the software used to update web content. Most content on the Web is created by using development tools (such as a Content Management System, or CMS). This software often determines how and to what extent content can be accessible, so it plays a fundamental role in the creation of content that complies with the WCAG. It is therefore an essential requirement for developers of these tools to follow the WCAG specifications to make their software more versatile and appropriate for the creation of accessible content.

The Authoring Tool Accessibility Guidelines, or ATAG, were born with these requirements in mind.

On the other hand, the User Agent Accessibility Guidelines, or UAAG, guide the development of user agents, which break the barriers to accessibility for differently-able individuals (visual, auditory, psychological, cognitive, and neurological disabilities). User agents include browsers, media players, and all software that executes the rendering and parsing of web content.

Solution 12-1: Creating skip links with the nav element

From Wikipedia (http://en.wikipedia.org/wiki/Screen_reader): A screen reader is a software application that attempts to identify and interpret what is being displayed on the screen (or, more accurately, sent to standard output, whether a video monitor is present or not). This interpretation is then re-presented to the user with text-to-speech, sound icons, or a Braille output device. Screen readers are a form of assistive technology (AT) potentially useful to people who are blind, visually impaired, illiterate, or learning disabled, often in combination with other AT such as screen magnifiers.

People with disabilities, such as those who surf the Web using a screen reader, have different sets of user needs. Some may want to skip quickly to specific portions of a web page, while others may wait for the screen reader to read the page content in sequence.

The former user type can take advantage of shortcuts ("skip links") the screen reader provides to determine quickly what content they may skip; the screen reader can also provide certain elements upon request, such as navigation elements, contents, headers, footers, and so on. The developer obviously has to design the page so that it can provide these tips to the screen reader.

Let's see how to create these functions with HTML5.

What's involved

Most web pages can be reduced to the following logic structure: headers, footers, navigational menu, body, columns, and so on.

With HTML4, this structure often used to be created by using the DIV tag, associated with the id attribute.

```
<body>
<div id="header"></div>
<div id="body">
  <div id="menu"></div>
  <div id="page content"></div>
  <div id="right_sidebar"></div>
</div>
<div id="footer"></div>
</body>
```

In this example, we created the following page structure: header, body, menu, page content, right sidebar, and footer. The content is inserted into this structure and then formatted with CSS statements.

The mass use of DIV blocks was necessary due to the lack of semantics in HTML4 to describe the logic partition of the page.

To allow fast navigation with skip links, there were a couple of techniques. Skip links are used to enable someone using assistive technologies from avoid having to listen to an entire page, rather than just the content in which they are interested. This approach is also discussed in the WCAG at Checkpoint 13.6: "Group related links, identify the group (for user agents) and, until user agents do so, provide a way to bypass the group."

One approach uses visible skip links, while others use hidden skip links. Regardless of the approach, the skip links concept was based on the name attribute of the <a> tag. Basically, you created an anchor link in the page that, when selected, brought the user to a specific portion of the page.

Here is a practical example of a skip link that allows the screen reader to skip the navigation menu to the main content:

```
<div id="body">
  <div id="menu">
<ul>
<p><a href="#main_content">skip to main content</a></p>
<li>Menu links</li>
<li>Menu links</li>
<li>Menu links</li>
  ...
</ul>
</div>
  <div id="page content">
```

```
<a name="main_content" id="contentjump"></a>
  <p>Content</p>
</div>
</div>
  <div id="right_sidebar"></div>
</div>
```

Another example of skip links navigation, implemented by many portals that were rich in content, created an actual menu to navigate quickly to portions of a page:

```
<div class="skiplinks">
<strong>Welcome to XYZ Portal</strong>
Skip directly to: <a href="#main">Main Content</a>,
<a href="#nav">Navigation menu</a>,
<a href="#news">News section</a>.
<a href="#video">Video section</a>.
</div>
```

With HTML5, this approach changed radically. HTML5 introduces a whole set of new elements that make it easier to structure web pages.

You have already seen the structural and semantic elements of HTML5 in Chapter 3. You will now use these elements to create quick navigation functions in a web page without needing to create specific skip links.

Not all screen readers currently recognize the new semantic elements of HTML5, for example the nav markup. However, companies that produce this software are working closely with the W3C to provide this support.

How to build it

By using the new <nav> tag, browsers now have a standard HTML element to specify navigational content. As such, the old approach of creating skip links to let the user skip quickly to a section of a page becomes obsolete.

With the new <nav> element, it's now possible to specify navigational content within the page for screen readers, as a note in the HTML5 specification explains:

User agents (such as screen readers) that are targeted at people who can benefit from navigational information being omitted in the initial rendering, or those who can benefit from navigational information being immediately available, can use this element as a way to determine what content on the page to skip initially and/or provide on request.

When the screen reader software recognizes the <nav> element, it will be able to provide the user with a way to skip over the navigation section.

It's possible to use more than one <nav> element in the same page. In the next example, there are two <nav> elements. The first one lets the user connect to external web pages, while the second one is designed to navigate within the page:

```
<!DOCTYPE html>

<html>

    <head>

    <title>
     Solution 12-1: Creating skip links with the nav element
    </title>

    </head>
<body>

        <header>

            <h1>Solution 12-1: Creating skip links with the nav element </h1>

        </header>

<nav>
 <ul>
  <li><a href="http://casario.blogs.com">My Blog</a></li>
  <li><a href="http://it.linkedin.com/in/marcocasario">My LinkedIn Profile</a></li>
  <li><a href="http://twitter.com/#!/marcocasario">My Twitter</a></li>
 </ul>
</nav>

 <header>
  <h1>Stop using custom skip links!</h1>
  <p>And start using the semantic HTML5 tags.</p>
 </header>

 <nav>
  <ul>
   <li><a href="#navtag">The NAV tag</a></li>
  </ul>
 </nav>


 <section id="navtag">
  <h1>The Nav tag</h1>
  <h3>From the W3C NAV specs</h3>
  <p>

  A section with navigation links.
  </p>
 </section>

    </body>
</html>
```

Not all groups of links on a page need to be in a <nav> element. Only sections that consist of major navigation blocks are appropriate for the <nav> element. In particular, it is common for footers to have a short list of links to various pages of a site, such as the terms of service, the home page, and a copyright page. The footer element alone is sufficient for such cases, without a <nav> element.

Expert tips

Speaking of menus and skip links, there is a new element to consider in the HTML5 specifications: <menu>.

The <menu> element can be used for navigation instead of the <nav> element. Here's the deal: <menu> is used for a list of commands, and it is an interactive element that has several possibilities for being used exclusively in web applications:

```
<menu type='toolbar'>
  <menu type='list' label='File' >
     <command label='New'/>
     <command label='Save'/>
     <command label='Close'/>
  </menu>
  <menu type='list' label='Edit'>
      <command label='Cut'/>
      <command label='Copy'/>
<command label='Paste'/>
  <menu>
</menu>
```

You can think of the menu element like a classic desktop application menu system.

Solution 12-2: Creating accessible tabular data

Tables are a tool used to represent data in tabular format. All too often in the past, however, they were used to control page layout. This use created a lot of problems in making web pages accessible because assistive technologies could obtain very confusing results. In particular, users of accessibility tools such as screen readers were likely to find it very difficult to navigate pages with tables used for layout.

On the other hand, HTML tables are necessary to display data with more than one dimension (just as the W3C specifications provide).

To make a table highly accessible, we have to ensure that it has the necessary formatting to be transformed elegantly, and that it can also be read by devices such as screen readers.

This is where some specific properties can help. If used intelligently, these properties make data in a table accessible to anyone.

What's involved

Designing an accessible data table requires specific attention to the use of a series of attributes, which allows user agents to optimally understand and interpret the content and structure of the table itself.

Each table must provide information regarding the data that it contains. This information will be critical for users of assistive technologies to navigate such tables because of how they will be read and interpreted.

This is why HTML5 has a `<caption>` tag, which associates a label with the table; and the summary attribute, which is not displayed on the standard web browser but provides text that is legible to a user agent and that describes the content, structure, and purpose of the table itself:

```
<table summary="Last season records">
<caption>
  <strong>List of team and their records</strong>
  <p>This is a collection of the latest results in 2010</p>
</caption>
```

Every table, by definition, can represent data from one or more dimensions. It is therefore necessary to associate the reading of each line with the corresponding column. This is the only way to guarantee the correct reading of information to the users who, for example, use screen reader tools to navigate.

In fact, the scope attributes and the id and headers couple allows for the identification of headers and the relationship between them and the cells that permits an easier consultation of the data:

```
<tr>
    <th id="year">Year</th>
    <th id="team">Team</th>
    <th id="record" abbr="Record">Current Year Record</th>
  </tr>
  <tbody>
  <tr>
   <td headers="year">1915</td>
   <td headers="team">Philadelphia Phillies</td>
   <td headers="record">101-50</td>
  </tr>
  </tbody>
```

This association provides the exact column for every value in a cell, which is very useful for screen readers as they will be able read the header of the column before reading the data contained in it at any time.

Now let's build a complete example.

How to build it

Keep in mind how a screen reader works. It does not read the screen as you might imagine — it reads the underlying source code for the HTML page instead. That's why it is important to make tabular data accessible using attributes and properties that provide information about the data that the table contains.

You can see how to do this from the following solution:

```
<!DOCTYPE html>
<html>
    <head>
    <title>
     Solution 12-2: Creating accessible tabular data
    </title>
```

```
    </head>
<body>

<table summary="Last season records">
<caption>
  <strong>List of teams and their records</strong>
  <p>This is a collection of the latest results in 2010</p>
 </caption>
 <thead>
 <tr>
    <th id="year">Year</th>
    <th id="team">Team</th>
    <th id="record" abbr="Record">Current Year Record</th>
 </tr>

  <tbody>
  <tr>
   <td headers="year">1915</td>
     <td headers="team">Philadelphia Phillies</td>
     <td headers="record">101-50</td>

  </tr>
  <tr>
    <td headers="year">1916</td>

     <td headers="team">Brooklyn Robins</td>

     <td headers="record">91-63</td>

  </tr>
  <tr>
       <td headers="year">1915</td>

     <td headers="team">Philadelphia Phillies</td>

     <td headers="record">101-50</td>
  </tr>
</tbody>
</table>

</body>
</html>
```

Now add a few styles to this table, only to make it more pleasant from a visual standpoint. Create a CSS file where you can create style selectors for the table and cells:

```
/* CSS Document */

table {
border-top: 1px solid #999;
border-left: 1px solid #999;

border-collapse:collapse;
}
```

```
th, td {
padding: 5px;
border-right: 1px solid #999;
border-bottom: 1px solid #999;
}

caption {
font-family:Geneva, Arial, Helvetica, sans-serif;
color:#993333;
padding-bottom: 5px;
}

th {
background-color:#cccccc;
font-family:"Courier New", Courier, mono;
}
```

Save this file as table.css. Now to apply the CSS to the page, first import it with the style tag within the head tag:

```
<!DOCTYPE html>
<html>
    <head>
    <title>
     Solution 12-2: Creating accessible tabular data
    </title>

<link href="table.css" rel="stylesheet" />
    </head>
```

The table is now formatted as shown in Figure 12-2.

List of team and their records

This is a collection of the latest results in 2010

Year	Team	Current Year Record
1915	Philadelphia Phillies	101-50
1916	Brooklyn Robins	91-63
1915	Philadelphia Phillies	101-50

Figure 12-2. The accessible tabular data inherits the styles.

Expert tips

HTML5 introduces a new control to represent data: the `<datagrid>`.

The `<datagrid>` element works as a container for the table as well as for trees and lists. It allows you to select rows, columns, and cells, and to carry out operations such as collapsing rows/columns, sorting the grid, and interacting with the data directly in the browser on the client:

```
<datagrid>
<table summary="Last season records">
  <tr>
   <td headers="year">1915</td>
     <td headers="team">Philadelphia Phillies</td>
     <td headers="record">101-50</td>

  </tr>
  <tr>
    <td headers="year">1916</td>

    <td headers="team">Brooklyn Robins</td>

    <td headers="record">91-63</td>

  </tr>
  <tr>
      <td headers="year">1915</td>

    <td headers="team">Philadelphia Phillies</td>

    <td headers="record">101-50</td>
  </tr>
</table>

</datagrid>
```

The DataGridDataProvider interface represents the interface that objects must implement to be used as custom data views for <datagrid> elements. You can use the DataGridDataProvider to load data from databases, XmlHttpRequest, or anything else JavaScript code can talk to.

Solution 12-3: Creating accessible forms

We have already discussed the importance of forms in great depth in Chapter 4, and you have seen how they can be tools that allow the user to interact with the website. A good form design is not only important in terms of accessibility, but also for usability itself. In fact, design and construction errors in forms can compromise the good results of an application by making it less comprehensible or even leading the user to abandon the page.

Making a good form is therefore an extremely difficult task the web designer must cope with.

HTML5 introduces 13 new values for the type attribute of the HTML <input> element: search, tel, url, email, datetime, date, month, week, time, datetime-local, number, range, and color. These already allow screen readers to recognize and transmit more correct data to users.

With other small adjustments, such as the possibility of navigating the form using the keyboard, you can substantially improve the user experience.

What's involved

Once an accessible form is created most of the work will be carried out by the assistive technologies themselves.

The first adjustment is to lead with a clear and explanatory title that immediately allows the user to understand what kind of form he or she is completing. Beyond the title, it is almost always useful to provide a brief explanation of the reasons for the requested information or simply to specify whether or not some fields are compulsory. This is why we can use the `<legend>` tag to represent a caption for the rest of the contents:

```
<form id="thisform">
    <legend>This is a sign in form. Insert your email and password to access:</legend>
</form>
```

Furthermore, especially when the form is very long and includes several inputs, a coherent group of fields to be filled in is another important choice. Mixing data up is a great way to confuse users. There is, in fact, the `<fieldset>` tag, which represents a set of form controls that can be optionally grouped under a common name:

```
<form id="thisform">
 <fieldset name="signin">
```

Another useful consideration is the possibility of navigating the form with keyboard shortcuts (with the accesskey attribute) and unambiguously associating the input types to labels:

```
    <p><label for="name" accesskey="N" >Name:</label><br />
    <input type="text" id="name" name="name" tabindex="2" /></p>
```

How to build it

The following example shows an accessible form:

```
<!DOCTYPE html>

<html>

    <head>

    <title>
     Solution 12-3: Creating accessible form
    </title>

    </head>
<body>

<form id="thisform">
 <fieldset name="signin">

    <legend>This is a sign in form. Insert your email and password to access:</legend>
```

```
<p><label for="email" >Email:</label><br />

<input type="email" id="email" name="email" tabindex="1" autofocus /></p>

 <p><label for="password" accesskey="P" >Password:</label><br />

<input type="text" id="password" name="password" tabindex="2" /></p>

<p><label for="name" accesskey="D" >Insert your birthday:</label><br />

<input type="date" id="date" name="date" tabindex="3" /></p>

<p><input type="checkbox" id="remember" name="remember"   tabindex="4" />

<label for="remember">Remember this info?</label></p>

<p><input type="submit" value="submit" tabindex="5" /></p>
</fieldset>

</form>

</body>
</html>
```

To make the form more pleasant, add CSS statements. To do so, create an external CSS file, which we save as form.css, and insert the following code:

```
#thisform label {
font-family:Verdana, Arial, Helvetica, sans-serif;
font-size:1.2em;
font-weight: bold;
color:#666666;
}


#password, #email {

width: 200px;

}
#thisform legend {
            font-weight: bold;
            font-size: 90%;

            color: #666;
            background: #eee;

            border: 1px solid #ccc;

            border-bottom-color: #999;

            border-right-color: #999;
```

```
            padding: 4px 10px;


            }


#thisform fieldset {

            border: 1px dotted #ff0000;
            padding: 5px 20px 10px 10px;


            }
```

Save the file again. Now open the HTML file you created in this solution. To apply the styles file to the form, you import it with a <link> tag declared within the head:

```
<head>
    <title>
     Solution 12-3: Creating accessible form
    </title>
<link href="form.css" rel="stylesheet" />
    </head>
```

Save the file, and execute the HTML file in a browser to see the final result as shown in Figure 12-3:

Figure 12-3. The formatted and accessible form

Solution 12-4: Captioning and annotations using video elements

The video element presents issues in the field of accessibility. There are users with disabilities who are not, for example, able to hear audio. To be considered accessible to all users, a video must be accompanied by equivalent text alternatives. Even the WCAG describe the importance of text alternatives for videos.

Subtitles or text transcriptions are undoubtedly useful for people with auditory disabilities, but also for users who don't have fast connections. Therefore, the developer can choose one of the following operations:

- Insert a brief summary of the content of the video directly in the HTML code of the page where the video is published.

- Insert a complete text transcript of the spoken audio in HTML, with a link to download the text file with the complete transcript of the spoken audio.

- Insert subtitles in the video.

The final choice is up to the developer, and it will also obviously be tied to the level of importance of the video, the duration of the video itself, and to any technical difficulties in creating subtitles.

To create subtitles, it is necessary to use subtitling software that allows the developer to export the subtitle file in the required format (QuickTime, Windows Media Player, Real Player, or Flash) and publish it on the Web. The developer may also write the programming code that enables the text to be synchronized with video sequences automatically. With HTML5 and the new video element, it is possible to create this kind of function by synchronizing the text with the video.

What's involved

There are various approaches to adding subtitles to a video. You can write JavaScript code to synchronize an external text file programmatically to the video, or you can use one of the available software programs to do most of the work for you.

The first important distinction to make relates to closed captions vs. open captions:

- Open captions are part of the video sequence and cannot be switched off.

- Closed captions underlie the video sequence, as they are in a different file and can be turned on and off by the user.

Neither method is necessarily preferable, but closed captions allow the user more customization options by providing the choice of language, turning the captions on and off, and an indexing system for searching the subtitle text.

Once the type of subtitles to be embedded in the video is decided, you have to choose the software. These are the most common software programs for adding captions, as suggested by National Center for Accessible Media (NCAM) guidelines (http://ncam.wgbh.org/invent_build/web_multimedia/tools-guidelines):

- MAGpie: Free software for adding captions and video descriptions to QuickTime, Windows Media, Real player, and Flash multimedia.

- CCforFlash: A free Flash component that can be used to display captions of Flash video and audio content.

- ccPlayer and ccMP3Player: Free players that incorporate CCforFlash components; useful for non-Flash authors who want to add captions to Flash video or audio.

- CaptionKeeper: Software that converts television closed-caption data into web streaming formats.

- NCAM QA Favelet: A tool to help developers identify accessibility problems on web pages.

- STEP: The Simple Tool for Error Prioritization (STEP) for Section 508 compliance.

In this solution, we use MAGpie Media Access Generator, which is a free authoring tool to create caption- and audio-description information in multimedia contexts. It allows you to work with the following formats: QuickTime, Windows Media, Real, Flash, MP4, and 3GP source files.

> Note: Mac users: MAGpie is a Java-based application that requires QuickTime Java in order to run properly. Unfortunately, Apple has deprecated the QuickTime Java interface and no longer provides support for it. Therefore, MAGpie will no longer run on the Mac.

You can download MAGpie at the following address: http://ncam.wgbh.org/invent_build/web_multimedia/tools-guidelines/download-magpie

How to build it

By using MAGpie for the subtitles, you are able to import the subtitles from a text file or insert the spoken text manually. You can synchronize the text with the video sequence and then export the subtitle file in the required format.

The procedure to carry this out is quite simple. Once you've installed MAGpie, open it.

Then open a new project from the File ➤ New menu, and select the video to be subtitled in the initial window. Now you are asked to choose the video format with which you want to work. You can choose the QuickTime format by selecting "Apple QuickTime Player," whereas for RealPlayer and Windows Media Player format videos, select "Oratrix GRiNS Player".

Now you have to specify the style in which you want the subtitles to display, and then insert the width and height of the video file.

If the text of the subtitles is inserted manually, select captions from the Track ➤ Track Properties menu in the Magpie window and insert the subtitles in this field.

If the text comes in from an external file, import the text using the "Track ➤ Import Track" menu.

To synchronize the text with the video, use the buttons on the toolbar and start the video by inserting the beginning and end of the subtitles.

With these few steps, you have synchronized the subtitles with the video. Now it is necessary to export the subtitles into a format that can be played by the video object of HTML5 — MP4, for example.

From the MAGpie File ➤ Properties menu, you can check that you have selected "Apple QuickTime Player" and export the data by choosing "QuickTime SMIL 1.0" from the "Export" menu. When you click on the OK button, MAGpie generates 2 files: a TXT file and a file with an SMIL extension.

SMIL stands for Synchronized Multimedia Integration Language, and it enables simple authoring of interactive audiovisual presentations. SMIL is typically used for "rich media" (multimedia) presentations that integrate streaming audio and video with images, text, or any other media type. SMIL is an easy-to-learn HTML-like language, and many SMIL presentations are written using a simple text editor.

To test the function of the subtitles, open the SMIL file you exported with the QuickTime player and start the video.

The text file MAGpie created contains the style data of the subtitles, the synchronization data, and the subtitle text. The final result is shown in Figure 12-4.

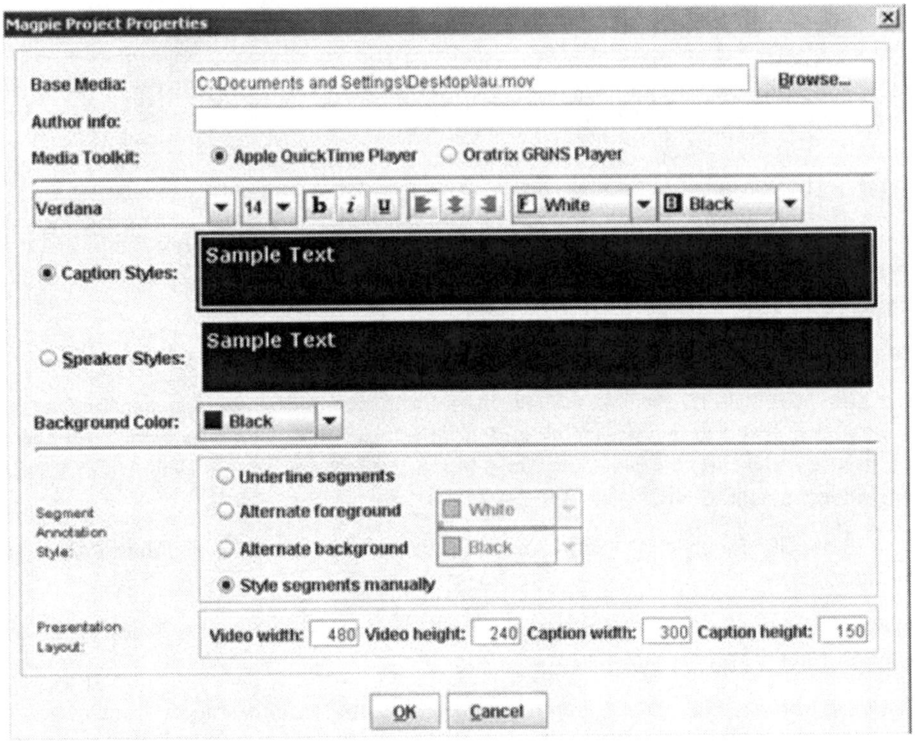

Figure 12-4. The MAGpie properties menu

Expert tips

Speaking of subtitles, there is an interesting article published by Bruce Lawson on the Dev.Opera website: `http://dev.opera.com/articles/view/accessible-html5-video-with-javascripted-captions/`. The article illustrates an approach to add subtitles to a video object dynamically.

It uses a new HTML5 feature that allows any element to have custom data attributes and to pass data to scripts:

```
<span data-begin=1 data-end=6>
```

This is the subtitle that starts at sec 1 until second 6</span>.

The solution requires some JavaScript knowledge, but it is worth studying because it could be handy in many contexts.

Solution 12-5: Using the ARIA project

When developing a website or a web application and trying to make it accessible, you soon realize that HTML was not created to write these kinds of applications. HTML was developed to provide a means for navigating documents (hence the hypertext language) through elements that have their specific identification and function and with client-server interactions which, in most cases, are in a sequential order. HTML was created with the concept of a one-click, one-page web application, meaning that every click to navigate within the website corresponds to a request to the server, which is then processed and the response is returned to the client. However, things have changed somewhat recently for web applications.

First with Flash Player and then with JavaScript and AJAX, the one-click, one-page model was changed with the one-page application approach. This means that the user can navigate the application without requiring all the content of the entire page to update—all the data in a table, for example. In fact, the application updates the content of the page silently in the background in response to user events, maintaining user interface elements that are fixed in the page. Navigation is carried out between "states" defined in the web application, and not between pages.

Most of the work, in fact, is entrusted to the client instead of the server, as opposed to the reverse situation in the past.

Besides being more user friendly, this approach also minimizes server requests, which are optimized to those for data that is strictly necessary for the application. The web application behaves like a desktop application that is loaded in a container, which is the user agent.

Unfortunately, not all that glitters is gold.

In fact, this new event-based system is often a problem for assistive technologies, which expect the old request-response model.

The states of a page — that is, the custom user interface components and their properties that the AJAX frameworks provide to users — are not available to assistive technologies. Furthermore, because there is no longer a request-response model in which a new page is loaded for each click, the back button of the browser is often compromised.

To deal with this type of problem, the W3C is working on a project called WAI-ARIA (http://www.w3.org/WAI/intro/aria.php). Basically, ARIA provides for the implementation of a parsing system in browsers that is able to recognize certain properties associated with the HTML elements

323

of a web page, which "explain" the roles and functions associated with them to the assistive technologies. This makes the content of the page clear to those who are not able to see what happens when a certain event is triggered.

The project is still a working draft, not yet in the final recommendation stage. Nevertheless, we can already use its functions, so there are no negative effects from the use of ARIA in web applications. The leading browsers and screen readers have already started supporting this project.

Opera 9.5, Firefox 1.5, and Internet Explorer 8, for example, have already started implementing ARIA specifications; whereas WebKit browsers, such as Safari and Chrome, are working on supporting the ARIA specs in upcoming versions.

As far as assistive technologies are concerned, Jaws 7.1, Zoomtext 9, Windows Eyes 5.5, and others also support ARIA.

What's involved

The ARIA project can help assistive technologies in the following scenarios:

- Silent background interaction with the server

- Keyboard navigation for custom components (widgets)

- Navigation between states within an application or a widget

- Definition of roles in the page structure

The ARIA project extends and adds a series of properties that the developer declares in the tags, which are interpreted by the browsers and assistive technologies.

Silent background interaction with the server

The contexts in which the application loads data in the background and updates the user interface elements are the most difficult for the screen reader to interpret. ARIA provides a set of new properties that declare special regions in the page, and will warn the user agent when things change.

The properties are:

aria-live: This property specifies that an element will be updated, and it describes the types of updates the user agents, assistive technologies, and users can expect from the live region. It accepts the off (the region is not live), polite (notifies users of updates, but generally does not interrupt the current task), and assertive (the update is communicated to the user urgently) values:

```
<div id="liveRegion"
        role="contentInfo"
        aria-live="assertive" > This is a live region.
</div>
```

aria-atomic: Indicates whether assistive technologies will present all or part of the changed region to the user. It accepts true or false as values:

```
<div id="liveRegion"
        role="contentInfo"
        aria-live="assertive"
         aria-atomic="true" > This is a live region.
</div>
```

aria-relevant: Indicates what changes are relevant within a region. It accepts the values listed in Table 12-1.

Table 12.1. aria-relevant values

Value	Description
additions:	Element nodes are added to the DOM within the live region.
removals:	Text or element nodes within the live region are removed from the DOM.
text:	Text is added to any DOM descendant nodes of the live region.
all:	Equivalent to the combination of all values; "additions removals text".
additions text (default):	Equivalent to the combination of values, "additions text"

aria-busy: Indicates whether an element is being updated. It accepts the value true or false

More than we think, users use their keyboards to move within an application. It is therefore essential to support this and not link the application to events that depend on specific devices, such as the mouse (for example, the rollover event).

On this front, ARIA extends its support to the tabindex property, which allows you to assign a navigation order to objects on a page using the Tab key. There was support for this property previously in HTML, but only for the a, area, button, object, input, select, and textarea properties. On this front, ARIA extends the support to the tabindex property, which allows you to assign an order of navigation to any visible element in a page:

```
<div>

  <h3 id="radio_btn">Choose your favorite movie:</h3>

  <ul class="radiogroup"
      id="rg1"
      role="radiogroup"
      aria-labelledby="radio_btn">

    <li id="r1"
      tabindex="1"
      role="radio">
      Matrix
    </li>
    <li id="r2"
        tabindex="2"
        role="radio">
```

```
    Inception
  </li>
  <li id="r3"
      tabindex="3"
      role="radio">
   Avatar
  </li>
  <li id="r4"
      tabindex="5"
      role="radio">
   Blade Runner
  </li>
  <li id="r5"
      tabindex="4"
      role="radio" >
   The silent of the lambs
  </li>
  </ul>
  </div>
```

In this example, we've associated a `tabindex` to LI elements of a UL, which simulates a radio button group component.

The `tabindex` property of ARIA also accepts negative values that allow you to exclude the object but still receive the focus programmatically from navigation using the keyboard.

Navigation between states in an application or a widget

The state of a page or component conveys specific information about that object. For example, one page can have a Logged state that loads certain user interface elements according to the user who is logged in. Also, a radio button component can have a selected state that is launched when the user selects the object.

ARIA provides a set of states and properties that can be used in various contexts to provide specific information to the user agents and screen readers during the life cycle of the application. There are, for example, properties provided by ARIA that are specific to common user interface elements that receive user input and process user actions:

- aria-autocomplete
- aria-checked (state)
- aria-disabled (state)
- aria-expanded (state)
- aria-haspopup
- aria-hidden (state)
- aria-invalid (state)

- aria-label
- aria-level
- aria-multiline
- aria-multiselectable
- aria-orientation
- aria-pressed (state)
- aria-readonly

- aria-required
- aria-selected (state)
- aria-sort
- aria-valuemax
- aria-valuemin
- aria-valuenow
- aria-valuetext

Using the previous example, you can use the aria-checked property to point out which object in the list has been selected by default. (By adding a bit of JavaScript code, you can display an image for the selected state of that object.)

```
<div>
  <h3 id="radio_btn">Choose your favorite movie:</h3>

  <ul class="radiogroup"
      id="rg1"
      role="radiogroup"
      aria-labelledby="radio_btn">

    <li id="r1"
      tabindex="1"
      role="radio"
      aria-checked="false">
      Matrix
    </li>
    <li id="r2"
        tabindex="2"
        role="radio"
        aria-checked="false">
      Inception
    </li>
    <li id="r3"
        tabindex="3"
        role="radio"
        aria-checked="false">
      Avatar
    </li>
    <li id="r4"
        tabindex="5"
        role="radio"
        aria-checked="true">
      Blade Runner
    </li>
    <li id="r5"
        tabindex="4"
        role="radio"
        aria-checked="false">
      The silence of the lambs
    </li>
  </ul>
  </div>
The following element therefore has a selected state:
<li id="r4"
        tabindex="5"
        role="radio"
        aria-checked="true">
      Blade Runner
    </li>
```

Defining roles in the page structure

HTML5 has added new tags to define the semantic structure of a page (see Chapter 1 and Chapter 3). ARIA also defines a subset of properties for pages and widgets to help define their structure. These properties are called "roles." Among these are landmark roles, which are regions of the page intended as navigational landmarks; and widget roles, which either represent standalone user interface widgets or are part of larger, composite widgets.

Landmark roles include:

- application
- banner
- complementary
- contentinfo

- form
- main
- navigation
- search

Widget roles include:

- alert
- alertdialog
- button
- checkbox
- dialog
- gridcell
- link
- log
- marquee
- menuitem
- menuitemcheckbox
- menuitemradio

- option
- progressbar
- radio
- scrollbar
- slider
- spinbutton
- status
- tab
- tabpanel
- textbox
- timer
- tooltip

- treeitem
- combobox
- grid
- listbox
- menu
- menubar
- radiogroup
- tablist
- tree
- treegrid

How to build it

Here is a complete example that implements some functions of the ARIA project:

```
<!DOCTYPE html>

<html>

    <head>
```

```
    <title>
     Solution 12-5: Using the ARIA project
    </title>


   </head>
<body>

<div role="banner">

<a href="http://www.comtaste.com"><img src="http://www.comtaste.com/images/logo_comtaste.png"
title="Comtaste Logo" alt="Comtaste" /></a>

</div>

<div role="application">

  <h3 id="radio_btn">Choose your favorite movie:</h3>

  <ul class="radiogroup"
      id="rg1"
      role="radiogroup"
      aria-labelledby="radio_btn">

    <li id="r1"
      tabindex="1"
      role="radio"
      aria-checked="false">
      Matrix
    </li>
    <li id="r2"
       tabindex="2"
       role="radio"
       aria-checked="false">
      Inception
    </li>
    <li id="r3"
       tabindex="3"
       role="radio"
       aria-checked="false">
     Avatar
    </li>
    <li id="r4"
       tabindex="5"
       role="radio"
       aria-checked="true">
     Blade Runner
    </li>
    <li id="r5"
       tabindex="4"
       role="radio"
       aria-checked="false">
     The silence of the lambs
    </li>
```

```
    </ul>
    </div>
      </body>

  </html>
```

Expert tips

The ARIA project won't only be supported by user agents. In fact, Adobe has also begun to work on supporting this project in Flash Player. In this article from the accessibility section of the Adobe blog (http://blogs.adobe.com/accessibility/2010/03/flash_player_and_flex_support.html), we read:

The upgrades expand on Flash Player's existing support for accessibility via the Microsoft Active Accessibility interface (MSAA) and will enable accessibility across all three major operating systems (Windows, Mac, and Linux). The Flash Player will employ IAccessible2 from the Linux Foundation and the WAI-ARIA specification from the W3C to address user and developer needs and to ease interoperability with assistive technology vendors. Additionally, enhancements are planned to the free and open-source Flex software developer's kit (SDK), including improvements to complex components such as Flex datagrids and adding support for WAI-ARIA to simplify development of custom user interface components. These improvements are expected to start with the next major release of Adobe Flash Player (following Flash Player 10.1), and the first successive release of the Flex SDK.

Summary

Accessibility is a very important "social" issue for web development. When a web application or a website is well-designed and well-developed, all users have equal access to information and functionalities.

HTML5 provides new elements, properties, and attributes to be used by developers in order to make content more accessible. In this chapter, you've learned how to avoid the use of the skip-links approach, how to create more accessible tabular data and forms, and how to synchronize subtitles with the new HTML5 video element. Moreover, HTML5 supports the ongoing process of integrating WAI-ARIA, the Accessible Rich Internet Applications Suite discussed in Solution 12-5. Here is a useful resource to learn more about the new HTML5 accessibility support features: http://html5accessibility.com/.

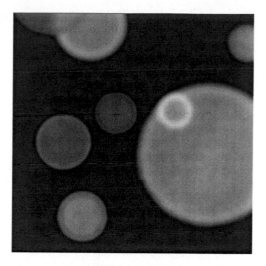

Index

A

\<a> tag, 45
abort(), 234
absolute font size, 167
Access-Control-Allow-Origin header, 220
accessibility
  accesskey attribute, 317
  assistive technology (AT), 308
  Authoring Tool Accessibility Guidelines
    (ATAG), 308
  building an accessible form, code listing,
    317–319
  building an accessible table, code
    listing, 313–315
  \<caption> tag, 313
  captioning and annotations for videos
    (Solution 12-4), 319
  CaptionKeeper, 321
  CCforFlash, 320
  ccMP3Player, 321
  ccPlayer, 321
  closed captions versus open
    captions, 320
  creating accessible forms (Solution
    12-3), 316
  creating accessible tabular data
    (Solution 12-2), 312
  creating skip links with the \<nav> tag
    (Solution 12-1), 308

\<datagrid> tag, 315
DataGridDataProvider, 316
\<fieldset> tag, 317
four principles of accessibility, 305
functions of the ARIA project, code
  example, 328–330
IAccessible2, 330
\<input> tag, 316
landmark roles, 328
Lawson, Bruce, 322
\<legend> tag, 317
MAGpie Media Access Generator, 320
\<menu> tag, 312
Microsoft Active Accessibility interface
  (MSAA), 330
National Center for Accessible Media
  (NCAM), 320
NCAM QA Favelet, 321
one-click, one-page model, 323
one-page application approach, 323
options for adding subtitles to a video,
  320
roles, definition of, 328
screen readers, 308
Simple Tool for Error Prioritization
  (STEP), 321
specifying navigational content within a
  page for screen readers, 310
subtitling software, using, 320
summary attribute, 313

accessibility (*continued*)

    Synchronized Multimedia Integration Language (SMIL), 322

    User Agent Accessibility Guidelines (UAAG), 308

    user agents, 306, 308, 310, 313

    using more than one <nav> tag in the same page, code listing, 310

    using the ARIA project (Solution 12-5), 323

    WAI-ARIA, 330

    Web Accessibility Initiative (WAI), 306

    Web Content Accessibility Guidelines (WCAG), 306

    widget roles, 328

    World Wide Web Consortium (W3C), 306

accesskey attribute, 317

addEventListener(), 110, 120, 129, 216, 221, 238

<address> tag, 8

Adobe Flash Player, 24, 105

    Flash Video, definition of, 98

    FLV files, 98

    supported audio formats, 134

    SWF files, 98

Adobe Illustrator, AI2Canvas plug-in, 150

AJAX, 171

Allsopp, John, 153

alpha channel, 132

    adding to a color, 155

    rgba() property, 155

animate(), 210–211

annotations, 26, 28

append(), 236

applicationCache object

    applicationCache.swapCache(), 297

    applicationCache.update(), 297

    clearing the local cache (Solution 11-6), 299

    common events and their associated cache states, table of, 296

    displaying the status of the applicationCache, code listing, 295–296

    finding and clearing the cache for the most common browsers, 300

    forcing a page to refresh, 299

    inspecting the caches of mobile browsers, 303

    listening to the various applicationCache events, code listing, 297–299

    onchecking event, 296

    ondownloading event, 297

    table of property statuses, 294

    table of supporting browsers, 282

    updateready event, 299

arc(), 143, 151

<area> tag, 45

    code example, 28

    creating hyperlinks using image mapping (Solution 2-4), 25

    href attribute, 29

    hreflang attribute, 29

    media attribute, 28

    rel attribute, table of values, 26

    using with the <map> tag, 29

ARIA project

    Adobe's support for, 330

    aria-atomic property, 324

    aria-busy property, 325

    aria-checked property, code example, 327

    aria-live property, 324

    aria-relevant property, table of values, 325

    browser support for, 324

    defining roles in the page structure, 328

    functions of the ARIA project, code example, 328–330

    how it helps assistive technologies, 324

    IAccessible2, 330

    landmark roles, 328

    list of properties specific to common user interface elements, 326

    Microsoft Active Accessibility interface (MSAA), 330

    navigation between states in an application or a widget, 326

    roles, definition of, 328

    silent background interaction with the server, 324

    tabindex property, 325

    WAI-ARIA, 330

    widget roles, 328

<article> tag, 4, 9

asides

    adding two aside elements, code listing, 56

    <aside> tag, 5–6, 56

    associating additional text (a tangent) to an article or page (Solution 3-6), 56

    creating (Solution 1-5), 5

attributes

    class attributes, 4

element-specific attributes, 4
event handler content attributes, 4
global attributes, 4
id attributes, 4
audio
Adobe Flash Player, supported audio
formats, 134
\<audio\> tag, declaring, 134
\<audio\> tag, list of attributes, 135
browsers supporting the HTML5 video
and audio elements, 98
FLV files, 98
source attribute, 134–135
specifying the MIME type, 135
SWF files, 98
using the audio element (Solution
5-9), 134
using the audio element, code
example, 135
using third-party plug-ins to deliver
audio content on the Web, 134
Authoring Tool Accessibility Guidelines
(ATAG), 308
autobuffer attribute, 117
autoplay attribute, 117

B

beginPath(), 143, 151
Berners-Lee, Tim, 31
bezierCurveTo(), 143–144
browsers
adding fallback content for non-canvas-
compliant browsers, 176, 184
ARIA project support among browsers
and screen readers, 324
browser support for HTML5 form
elements, table of, 63
caniuse.com, 16
checking for WebSocket browser
support (Solution 9-1), 241
findmebyip.com, 15
Geolocation API support in desktop and
mobile devices, table of, 263
Internet Explorer and HTML5, 15
modernizr.com, 16, 189
sandbox security, definition of, 216
seamless attribute and lack of browser
support, 22
support for HTML5 video, 24
testing for browser compability (Solution
1-11), 15
\<button\> tag, 109

C

CACHE section, 292
caniuse.com, 16
canPlayType property, testing, 103
canvas element and 2D API
absolute versus relative font sizes, 167
accessing a canvas through its id
attribute, 176
accessing a canvas through the DOM
using JavaScript, 138, 140
adding a border to a canvas using
CSS, 139
adding a canvas programmatically, code
example, 176
adding an alpha value to a color, 155
adding fallback content for non-canvas-
compliant browsers, 140, 176, 184
AI2Canvas plug-in, 150
Allsopp, John, 153
animate(), 210–211
animating a ball to detect wall collisions,
procedure for, 209–213
applying blurred shadows to rectangles,
procedure for, 202–206
applying color filters through pixel
manipulation, procedure for,
196–201
applying custom styles to shapes, lines,
and strokes, 146
arc(), 143, 151
beginPath(), 143, 151
bezierCurveTo(), 143–144
browser and mobile device compatibility,
table of, 137
Canvas Console, 153
canvas coordinates system,
understanding, 142
\<canvas\> tag, 138–139, 176
canvas text plug-in, 166
canvasPixelArray, 195–196
clearing a canvas by resetting its height
and width, 177, 213
clearInterval(), 207
clearRect(), 151, 183, 210
clearTimeout(), 208–209
closePath(), 143, 151
combining CSS and the drawing
API, 158
connecting multiple subpaths to draw
complex shapes, 143
createImageData(), 195
createLinearGradient(), 158

canvas element and 2D API (*continued*)

createRadialGradient(), 159

creating a canvas, 138–139

creating a canvas in an HTML5 page (Solution 7-1), 178–181

creating a linear gradient, 158

creating a loop that repeats at a defined interval, procedure for, 207

creating a radial gradient, 159

creating animations inside the canvas (Solution 7-6), 207

creating blurred shadow effects (Solution 7-5), 201

creating image data, 195

creating two canvases as overlapping layers, procedure for, 181–183

creating two functions that check for canvas and canvas text support, 185–189

detecting canvas and canvas text support (Solution 7-2), 184

download.php, 172, 174

draw(), 179, 192

drawBall(), 211

drawGradientShapes(), 160

drawGraph(), 182

drawing a Bezier curve, 144

drawing a circle and two rectangles programmatically, code listing, 151–153

drawing a line path, 143

drawing a path, procedure for, 143

drawing a quadratic curve, 144

drawing an arc, 145

drawing as processor-intensive, 158

drawing circles (Solution 6-3), 151

drawing rectangles (Solution 6-3), 150

drawing text (Solution 6-6), 163

drawing the friendsofED logo, procedure for, 147–149

drawing using the canvas element's drawing API (Solution 6-1), 138

drawLogo(), 149

drawShape(), 170

drawShapes(), 152–153, 157

drawText(), 165

em value, 167

exporting a vector file in SVG format, 150

fill(), 143, 151, 154, 156, 161

filling shapes with solid colors (Solution 6-4), 154

filling the stroke of a shape with a gradient, 160

fillRect(), 151, 153–154

fillStroke property, 155

fillStyle property, 154

fillText(), 164, 185

getContext(), 138, 177, 184–185

getElementById(), 138

getImageData(), 196, 198

having only one context per canvas, 181

identity matrix, 191

ImageData object, 195

immediate mode renderer, 177

init(), 171, 178–179, 205, 210

Internet Explorer and, 137

JavaScript and, 138, 176

line properties and styles, 146

lineCap property, 146

lineTo(), 143

lineWidth property, 146

manipulating pixels inside the canvas (Solution 7-4), 195

manipulating the coordinate system for transform operations (Solution 7-3), 190

matrix-transforming values, table of, 191

modernizr.com, 189

moveTo(), 143–144

online reference of 2D context API methods, 177

onreadystatechange property, 172

origin point, 142

painting image data on the context, 196

performance issues related to drawing shadows, 206

performance issues related to pixel manipulations, 201

preserving the original coordinate system by saving the canvas state, 191

putImageData(), 196

quadraticCurveTo(), 143–144

readyState property, 172

rect(), 150

rendering 2D shapes and bitmap images on the fly, 137

rendering a simple graph, 182

restore(), 177, 179–180, 191–192

retrieving a pixel array, 196

retrieving the context object, 138, 140

rgb() property, 155

rgba() property, 155

rotate(), 191–192
rotating an image from its center, 194
rotating canvas objects, 191
save(), 177, 179–180, 191
saveCanvas(), 171
saveImage.php, 172–173
saveImage(), 171
saving a shape as a PNG file (Solution 6-8), 169
scale(), 190
scaling canvas objects, 190
setInterval(), 207
setTimeout(), 208–209
setting relative font sizes (Solution 6-7), 167
setting the font property and its attributes, 163
setting the text baseline attributes, 164
setTransform(), 191
shadowBlur property, 202
shadowColor property, 202
shadowOffsetX property, 202
shadowOffsetY property, 202
Solution 6-1, complete code listing, 139–141
Solution 6-4, complete code listing, 155–157
Solution 6-5, complete code listing, 160–163
Solution 6-6, complete code listing, 165–166
Solution 6-7, complete code listing, 167–169
Solution 6-8, complete code listing, 173–174
storing and resetting the state of the canvas, 177
stroke(), 143, 148, 151, 155–156, 161
strokeFill(), 160, 164
strokeRect(), 151
strokeStyle property, 155
strokeText(), 164
Studt, Jim, 166
textAlign property, 163
toDataURL(), 170, 201
transform(), 191
translate(), 190
translating canvas objects, 190
using gradients to fill shapes (Solution 6-5), 158
using paths and coordinates (Solution 6-2), 141

using the transformation matrix, 191
using transformations with the coordinate system, procedure for, 191–194
Web Hypertext Application Technology Working Group (WHATWG), 175
WebGL and future support for 3D drawing, 177
canvas text plug-in, 166
canvasPixelArray, 195–196
CaptionKeeper, 321
<caption> tag, 313
captions, closed versus open, 320
CCforFlash, 320
ccMP3Player, 321
ccPlayer, 321
change event, 120
character encoding
creating a character encoding declaration (Solution 1-2), 3
ISO-8859-1, 3
UTF-8, 3
UTF-16, 3
chatIframe.html, complete code listing, 225
class attributes, 4
clearInterval(), 207
clearRect(), 151, 183, 210
clearTimeout(), 208–209
clearWatch(), 266, 276
close(), 244, 256
closePath(), 143, 151
codecs supporting HTML5 video, 24
Communication APIs
Cross-Origin Resource Sharing (CORS), 215
postMessage API, 216
XMLHttpRequest, 215
XMLHttpRequest Level 2, 232
contentWindow property, 223
context object, retrieving, 138, 140
controls attribute, 106
cookie, definition of, 284
Course element
code listing, 41
custom vocabulary, creating, 41
HTML page example, 43
properties, table of, 43
createImageData(), 195
Cross-Origin Resource Sharing (CORS)
definition of, 215, 220
sending messages between windows and iframes (Solution 8-2), 221

cross-origin communication, 216
currentTime property, 108, 118

D

<datagrid> tag, 315
DataGridDataProvider, 316
<datalist> tag
    code example, 81
    explanation of, 81
date control, example of, 93
<div> tag, 3–4
DOCTYPE
    example of, in a traditional HTML or
        XHTML document, 2
    procedure for creating (Solution 1-1), 1
documents
    <address> tag, 8
    <article> tag, 4, 9
    <aside> tag, 5–6, 56
    asides, creating (Solution 1-5), 5
    associating additional text (a tangent) to
        an article or page (Solution 3-6), 56
    connecting images to their captions
        (Solution 3-5), 52
    creating a semantic representation of a
        section's headings, 49
    creating nested section content
        elements, 49
    <div> tag, 3–4
    dividing a document into meaningful
        sections (Solution 1-3), 3
    <figcaption> tag, 14, 52
    <figure> tag, 13, 52
    figures, inserting (Solution 1-10), 13
    <footer> tag, 8–9, 12
    footers, creating (Solution 1-8), 9
    grouping headings together (Solution
        1-7), 8
    header and hgroup elements (Solution
        3-4), 48
    <header> tag, 7, 49–50
    headers, creating (Solution 1-6), 7
    <hgroup> tag, 7–8, 48–50
    <hr> tag, 7
    making parts of a document
        distributable (Solution 1-4), 4
    <nav> tag, 11
    navigational links, creating (Solution
        1-9), 11
    nesting multiple images in a single
        caption, 53

<section> tab, 3–4
    Solution_3_4.css, 51
download.php, 172, 174
draw(), 179, 192
drawBall(), 211
drawGradientShapes(), 160
drawGraph(), 182
drawLogo(), 149
drawShape(), 170
drawShapes(), 152–153, 157
drawText(), 165
Dreamweaver CS5, using as a code
        editor, 2
duration property, 118, 124

E

elements
    defining machine-readable custom
        elements in a web page, 31
    defining the scope of an element, 32
    element-specific attributes, 4
    items, definition of, 31
    properties, definition of, 31
em value, 167
e-mail input type
    table of valid attributes, 66
    using (Solution 4-1), 65
<embed> tag, 98
    Adobe Flash Player, 24
    browser support for HTML5 video, 24
    code example, 25
    codecs supporting HTML5 video, 24
    differentiating <embed> from the <img>
        tag, 24
    embedding media into a host web page
        (Solution 2-3), 23
    H.264, 24
    identifying video types, 25
    src attribute, 25
    Theora, 24
    type attribute, 25
enableHighAccuracy property, 269, 274
end(), 125
establishSocket(), 245, 256
event handler content attributes, 4
EventSource(), 226
    Opera browser and, 230
    viewing the EventSource() constructor in
        action, code listing, 228–230
external resources, 26, 28

F

failGeo(), 267, 274
fallback content, adding for non-canvas-
        compliant browsers, 140, 176, 184
FALLBACK section, 293
<fieldset> tag, 67, 317
figures
    business card example, code listing, 54
    connecting images to their captions
        (Solution 3-5), 52
    <figcaption> tag, 14, 52
    <figure> tag, 13, 52
    inserting (Solution 1-10), 13
    nesting multiple images in a single
        caption, 53
fill(), 143, 151, 154, 156, 161
fillRect(), 151, 153–154
fillStroke property, 155
fillStyle property, 154
fillText(), 164, 185
findmebyip.com, 15
Flash Video, definition of, 98
Flowplayer JavaScript library, 105
FLV files, 98
footers
    creating (Solution 1-8), 9
    <footer> tag, 8–9, 12
forceFullScreen(), 129
formData object, 234, 236
forms
    adding a slider control using the range
        input type (Solution 4-4), 75
    adding a URL input type control to an
        HTML page, code listing, 70
    associating a <datalist> tag to an
        <input> control, 81
    browser support for HTML5 form
        elements, table of, 63
    creating a spinner control, code listing, 73
    creating a suggest-like autocomplete
        with the datalist control (Solution
        4-6), 81
    creating accessible forms (Solution
        12-3), 316
    creating custom input types using
        regular expressions (Solution
        4-8), 88
    creating date and time controls (Solution
        4-10), 92
    <datalist> tag, 81
    date and time input types, code
        example, 94

date control, example of, 93
delegating some data-verification
        functions to the browser, 84
e-mail input type (Solution 4-1), 65
e-mail input type, table of valid
        attributes, 66
<fieldset> tag, 67
form attribute, 65
form controls in HTML 4, 63
input types for handling date/time
        pickers, 93
inserting placeholder text in an input
        field (Solution 4-9), 91
Kayak.com, 92
<label> tag, 67
<legend> tag, 67
list attribute, 81
multiple attribute, 79–80
new form attributes in HTML5, 65
new form elements introduced in
        HTML5, 64
novalidate attribute, 87
number input type, JavaScript
        methods, 75
number input type, table of valid
        attributes, 73
onblur event, 88
onforminput event, 83
Opera, 65, 67, 69
<option> tag, 81
<output>tag, 78, 83
overriding the default validation system
        of the browser, 87
pattern attribute, 88–89
placeholder attribute, 91
range input type, code example, 77
range input type, table of valid
        attributes, 76
required attribute, 84
<select> tag, 83
sending multiple files (Solution
        4-5), 79
slider control, definition of, 75
spinner control, definition of, 72
time control, example of, 94
title attribute, 89, 92
URL input type (Solution 4-2), 69
using a regular expression to validate
        an American Zip code, code
        example, 89
using a spinner control to insert
        numbers (Solution 4-3), 71

forms (*continued*)
　using CSS pseudo-classes to provide a
　　user with feedback clues for
　　mandatory fields, 85
　using JavaScript to create more
　　complex and robust form-validation
　　routines, 87
　validating an e-mail address on the
　　client side, 65, 68
　validating form controls (Solution 4-7), 84
　Web Forms 2 library, downloading and
　　importing, 90
　week and month input types, 94
four principles of accessibility, 305

G

geo.js
　adding support for older mobile
　　devices, 278
　calling init(), 279
　downloading, 278
　geo_position_js_simulator, 280
　successGeo(), 279
　testing code that tracks a moving
　　user, 279
　using the open source geo.js library
　　(Solution 10-6), 278
Geolocation API
　accessing the user's geolocation
　　position (Solution 10-2), 266
　alerts triggered after obtaining the user's
　　location, 271
　calculating the distance between two
　　latitude and longitude pairs, code
　　listing, 277
　catching and handling position errors
　　(Solution 10-4), 273
　clearWatch(), 266, 276
　detecting if the user's browser supports
　　the Geolocation API, code
　　example, 265
　enableHighAccuracy property, 269, 274
　failGeo(), 267, 274
　getCurrentPosition(), 266–267, 269,
　　272, 274–275
　haversine formula, 277
　how the browser determines a user's
　　approximate location, 264
　IP-based geolocation, 264
　location-aware applications, 263
　MAC address, 264
　maximumAge property, 269

　monitoring the user's position over time
　　(Solution 10-5), 275
　Position object (Solution 10-3), 270
　PositionError object, 268, 273–274
　prompting users to share their location
　　or deny access, 267
　reasons for position errors, 273
　SSID, 264
　successGeo(), 267, 279
　support in desktop and mobile devices,
　　table of, 263
　testing geolocation features reliably
　　across browsers, 267
　timeout property, 269
　tracking the location of a moving user,
　　code example, 275
　using high accuracy location detection
　　on mobile devices, 269
　using the Google Maps API, 272
　using the navigator object (Solution
　　10-1), 264
　using the open source geo.js library
　　(Solution 10-6), 278
　visualizing what a latitude and longitude
　　correspond to, 272
　watchPosition(), 266, 275–276
　when obtaining the user's location
　　succeeds or fails, 266
　Wi-Fi signal geolocation, 264
getContext(), 138, 177, 184–185
getCurrentPosition(), 266–267, 272,
　　274–275
　list of options, 269
getElementById(), 110, 119, 138
getElementsByTagName(), 110
getImageData(), 196, 198
getResponseHeaders(), 234
global attributes, 4
Google
　custom vocabularies defined by Google,
　　list of, 34, 41
　Google Gears, 285
　Google Maps API, 272
　Rich Snippets Testing Tool, 44

H

H.264 codec, 24, 99
haversine formula, 277
headers
　creating (Solution 1-6), 7
　header and hgroup elements (Solution
　　3-4), 48

<header> tag, 7, 49–50
headings
    grouping together (Solution 1-7), 8
    header and hgroup elements (Solution
        3-4), 48
    <hgroup> tag, 7–8, 49–50
<hr> tag, 7
    code example, 20
    confusion over its purpose, 19
    separating topics within a section, 20
    using in HTML5 (Solution 2-1), 19
    using with CSS, 21
href attribute, 29
hreflang attribute, 29
HTML5media project, 105
hyperlinks, 26, 28

I

IAccessible2, 330
id attribute, 4, 176
identity matrix, 191
<iFrame> tag
    code example, 22
    creating a browser within a browser
        (Solution 2-2), 21
    sandbox attributes to improve security, 23
    seamless attribute, 22
ImageData object, 195
<img> tag, usemap attribute, 29
immediate mode renderer, 177
init(), 171, 178–179, 205, 210, 222, 245
initSeekBar(), 120, 124
innerHTML, 114, 218
<input> tag, 316
Internet Explorer, compatibility with HTML5,
    15, 137
ISO-8859-1, 3
itemprop attribute, 32
    declaring properties, 36
    definition of, 34
items
    creating, 32
    definition of, 31
itemscope attribute, 32
    creating a new element, 35
    definition of, 34
itemtype attribute
    assigning to a Uniform Resource
        Locator (URL), 33
    definition of, 34
    specifying a custom vocabulary, 35

J

JavaScript
    canvas element and, 138, 176
    creating more complex and robust
        form-validation routines, 87
    getContext(), 138
    getElementById(), 138
    modernizr.com, 189
    typeof operator, table of possible
        returned values, 218, 242

K

Kayak.com, 92
keycode property, 260

L

<label> tag, 67
landmark roles, 328
Lawson, Bruce, 322
<legend> tag, 67, 317
linear gradient
    createLinearGradient(), 158
    creating, 158
lineCap property, 146
lineTo(), 143
lineWidth property, 146
link types and relations
    <a> tag, 45
    annotations, 26, 28
    <area> tag, 45
    hyperlinks, 26, 28, 45
    <link> tag, 45
    link types, table of, 46
    links to external resources, 26, 28, 45
    rel attribute, 46
    three categories of links, 25
    tips on using, 47
    understanding (Solution 3-3), 45
list attribute, 81
loadedmetadata event, 129
Local Shared Object, 285
Local Storage
    checking for Local Storage support,
        code listing, 286
    checking the sessionstorage and
        localstorage properties using the
        Modernizr JavaScript library, 287
    Chrome browser and, 291
    features of, 285
    localStorage.setItem, syntax for, 285

Local Storage (*continued*)
sessionStorage, 286
showAll(), 290
table of supporting browsers, 282
understanding the difference between local and session storage, code listing, 288–290
location-aware applications, 263
lossy data compression, 97

M

MAC address, 264
Macromedia, 98
MAGpie Media Access Generator, creating subtitles with, 321
makeVisible(), 129
manifest file
CACHE section, 292
creating a manifest file, procedure for, 292
declaring a manifest file (Solution 11-3), 291
FALLBACK section, 293
manifest attribute, 292
NETWORK section, 293
<map> tag, using with the <area> tag, 29
matrix-transforming values, table of, 191
max property, 119
maximumAge property, 269
media attribute, 28, 127
<menu> tag, using instead of the <nav> tag, 312
message parameter, 216
MessageChannel(), 232
messageHandler event handler, 221
MessagePort objects, 231
microdata
<a> tag, 45
<area> tag, 45
<aside> tag, 56
associating additional text (a tangent) to an article or page (Solution 3-6), 56
connecting images to their captions (Solution 3-5), 52
creating a custom vocabulary for defining an element's valid properties, 32
creating a Recipe element (Solution 3-1), 34
custom vocabularies defined by Google, list of, 34, 41

custom vocabulary, creating (Solution 3-2), 40
defining a name-value pair group, 40
defining machine-readable custom elements in a web page, 31
definition of, 31
executing the markup of HTML content in a structured manner, 33
header and hgroup elements (Solution 3-4), 48
<header> tag, 49–50
<hgroup> tag, 49–50
hyperlinks, 45
itemprop attribute, 32, 34, 36
items, definition of, 31
itemscope attribute, 32, 34–35
itemtype attribute, 33–34
<link> tag, 45
link types and relations, understanding (Solution 3-3), 45
link types, table of, 46
links to external resources, 45
making a web page more search-friendly for search engines, 33
meta tags, 40
properties, definition of, 31
Recipe element, complete code listing, 38
rel attribute, 46
Rich Snippets Testing Tool, 44
Search Engine Optimization (SEO), 47
semantic web and Tim Berners-Lee, 31
Solution_3_4.css, 51
specifying a custom vocabulary using the itemtype attribute, 35
using with meta tags, 40
Microsoft Active Accessibility interface (MSAA), 330
Modernizr JavaScript library
code example, 103–104
modernizr.com, 16
using, 189
moveTo(), 143–144
multiple attribute
browser support for, 79
code example, 80

N

National Center for Accessible Media (NCAM), 320

<nav> tag
    creating skip links with (Solution 12-1),
        308
    navigational links, creating (Solution
        1-9), 11
    specifying navigational content within a
        page for screen readers, 310
    using more than one <nav> tag in the
        same page, code listing, 310
navigator object, using (Solution 10-1), 264
navigator.onLine property, 283
NCAM QA Favelet, 321
NETWORK section, 293
novalidate attribute, 87
number input type, table of valid
        attributes, 73

O

<object> tag, 98
Occasionally-Connected Applications,
        description of, 282
offline storage
    applicationCache object, table of
        property statuses, 294
    applicationCache, table of supporting
        browsers, 282
    applicationCache.swapCache(), 297
    applicationCache.update(), 297
    checking for HTML5 storage support
        (Solution 11-2), 284
    checking for Local Storage support,
        code listing, 286
    checking the sessionstorage and
        localstorage properties using the
        Modernizr JavaScript library, 287
    Chrome browser and, 291
    clearing the local cache (Solution
        11-6), 299
    common events and their associated
        cache states, table of, 296
    cookie, definition of, 284
    creating a manifest file, procedure
        for, 292
    declaring a manifest file (Solution
        11-3), 291
    displaying the status of the
        applicationCache, code listing,
        295–296
    finding and clearing the cache for the
        most common browsers, 300
    forcing a page to refresh, 299

Google Gears, 285
HTML5 caching mechanism, using
        when online, 282
HTML5 Storage APIs, 285
inspecting the caches of mobile
        browsers, 303
listening to the various applicationCache
        events, code listing, 297–299
Local Shared Object, 285
Local Storage, 282, 285
localStorage.setItem, syntax for, 285
manifest attribute, 292
navigator.onLine property, 283
onchecking event, 296
ondownloading event, 297
registering listeners for online and offline
        events, 283
sessionStorage, 286
showAll(), 290
testing the online property of the
        navigator object, code listing,
        283–284
understanding Occasionally-Connected
        Applications (Solution 11-1), 282
understanding the difference between
        local and session storage, code
        listing, 288–290
updateready event, 299
userData, 285
Ogg Theora codec, 98
onblur event, 88
onchecking event, 296
ondownloading event, 297
one-click, one-page model, 323
one-page application approach, 323
onforminput event, 83
onkey(), 260
onkeypress event, 260
onreadystatechange property, 172
open(), 233–234
Opera browser, 65, 69
    displaying an error message if an e-mail
        address is invalid, 67
    using the Event Source interface as an
        HTML element, 230
<option> tag, 81
origin point, 142
origin property, 217, 221
outerHTML, 218
<output> tag, 236
    displaying a calculated result, 78
    displaying a user-selected value, 83

P

pattern attribute, 88–89
pause(), 112
PHP, 171
phpwebsocket, downloading and
        installing, 254
placeholder attribute, code example, 91
play(), 108, 112
PNG format
        download.php, 172, 174
        drawShape(), 170
        init(), 171
        onreadystatechange property, 172
        readyState property, 172
        saveCanvas(), 171
        saveImage.php, 172–173
        saveImage(), 171
        saving a shape as a PNG file (Solution
                6-8), 169
        toDataURL(), 170
ports attribute, 216
Position object
        properties, list of, 270
        using (Solution 10-3), 270
PositionError object, 268, 274
        error codes, list of, 273
postMessage API
        Access-Control-Allow-Origin header, 220
        addEventListener(), 216, 221
        avoiding the use of innerHTML or
                outerHTML, 218
        browser's sandbox security, definition
                of, 216
        chatIframe.html, complete code
                listing, 225
        checking for browser support, code
                example, 219
        checking for postMessage API browser
                support (Solution 8-1), 218
        checking the origin property, 217
        contentWindow property, 223
        creating a channel message (Solution
                8-4), 231
        Cross-Origin Resource Sharing
                (CORS), 220
        cross-domain font usage, enabling, 220
        cross-origin communication, 216
        cross-site HTTP requests, enabling, 220
        EventSource(), 226
        exchanging messages between two web
                pages, code example, 221–226

init(), 222
message parameter, 216
MessageChannel(), 231–232
messageHandler event handler, 221
MessagePort objects, 231
origin property, 217, 221
ports attribute, 216
postMessage(), 216, 221–222, 232
preventing information leakage, 216
registering an event handler for a
        message event, 216
registering an event listener on the
        onmessage event, 227
restricting a message to same-origin
        targets only, 216
returning the WindowProxy of the
        source window, 217
sendBtn button, 222
sending a message to a target, 216
sending messages between windows
        and iframes (Solution 8-2), 221
Solution_8.2.html, complete code
        listing, 223
source property, 217
supported browsers, list of, 218
syntax of, 216
targetOrigin parameter, 216–217, 222
textContent property, 218
typeof operator, table of possible
        returned values, 218
user agents offloading connection
        management to a network
        proxy, 227
using Server-Sent Events to write
        real-time web applications
        (Solution 8-3), 226
using the postMessage API
        securely, 217
viewing the EventSource() constructor in
        action, code listing, 228–230
Web Fonts, 220
web server proxies, 216
postMessage(), 232
preload attribute, 116
properties
        defining a property of an item, 32
        itemprop attribute, 32
protocols parameter, 244
putImageData(), 196
pywebsocket, procedure for installing and
        using, 247

Q

quadraticCurveTo(), 143–144

R

radial gradient
  createRadialGradient(), 159
  creating, 159
range input type, 118–119
  adding a slider control using the range
    input type (Solution 4-4), 75
  code example, 77
  syntax of, 76
  table of valid attributes, 76
readyState attribute, 172, 234, 249
  table of values, 244
Recipe element
  complete code listing, 38
  creating (Solution 3-1), 34
  creating a new element, 35
  declaring its properties, 36
  specifying a custom vocabulary, 35
  valid properties, table of, 34
rect(), 150
regular expressions
  creating custom input types using regular
    expressions (Solution 4-8), 88
  validating an American Zip code, code
    example, 89
rel attribute
  link types, table of, 46
  table of values, 26
relative font size, 167
required attribute, code example, 84
responseText property, 234
responseXML property, 234
restore(), 177, 179–180, 191–192
rgb() property, 155
rgba() property, 155
Rich Snippets Testing Tool, 44
roles, definition of, 328
rotate(), 191–192

S

save(), 177, 179–180, 191
saveCanvas(), 171
saveImage.php, 172–173
saveImage(), 171
scale(), 190
screen readers, 308
  ARIA project support among browsers
    and screen readers, 324

specifying navigational content within a
    page, 310
seamless attribute, lack of browser support
    for, 22
Search Engine Optimization (SEO), 47
<section> tab, 3–4
<section> tag, 19
seek bar
  creating a custom seek bar for a video
    (Solution 5-5), 117
  creating a custom seek bar for a video,
    complete code listing, 121
  YouTube's seek bar, 117
<select> tag, 83
semantic web
  Berners-Lee, Tim, 31
  creating a semantic structure for a web
    page, 31
send(), 234, 244, 248–249, 256
sendBtn button, 222
sendForm(), 236
sendMsg(), 256
server.php, 255
Server-Sent Events
  EventSource(), 226
  registering an event listener on the
    onmessage event, 227
  writing real-time web applications
    (Solution 8-3), 226
sessionStorage, 286
setInterval(), 207
setRequestHeader(), 234
setTimeout(), 208–209
setTransform(), 191
shadowBlur property, 202
shadowColor property, 202
shadowOffsetX property, 202
shadowOffsetY property, 202
sidebars
  adding two aside elements, code
    listing, 56
  <aside> tag, 5–6, 56
  associating additional text (a tangent) to
    an article or page (Solution 3-6), 56
  creating (Solution 1-5), 5
Simple Tool for Error Prioritization
    (STEP), 321
skip links
  code examples, 309
  creating skip links with the <nav> tag
    (Solution 12-1), 308
  visible and hidden skip links, 309

slider control
    adding a slider control using the range
        input type (Solution 4-4), 75
    definition of, 75
    syntax of, 76
Solution_3_4.css, 51
Solution_8.2.html, complete code listing, 223
source attribute, 127, 134
<source> tag, 102
    using the <source> tag for exposing
        video formats to browsers, code
        example, 126
spinner control
    code example, 73
    definition of, 72
    using to insert numbers (Solution 4-3), 71
src attribute, 25, 100
SSID, 264
start(), 125
startTime property, 124–125
Status property, 234
stroke(), 143, 148, 151, 155–156, 161
strokeFill(), 160, 164
strokeRect(), 151
strokeStyle property, 155
strokeText(), 164
Studt, Jim, 166
submit(), 235
subtitles
    Lawson, Bruce, 322
    MAGpie Media Access Generator, 320
    options for adding subtitles to a
        video, 320
    subtitling software, using, 320
successGeo(), 267, 279
summary attribute, 313
SVG format, exporting a vector file in, 150
SWF files, 98
Synchronized Multimedia Integration
        Language (SMIL), 322

T

tabindex property, 325
targetOrigin parameter, 216–217, 222
text
    canvas text plug-in, 166
    drawing text in a canvas (Solution
        6-6), 163
    drawText(), 165
    em value, 167
    fillText(), 164

font sizes, absolute versus relative, 167
    setting relative font sizes (Solution
        6-7), 167
    setting the font property and its
        attributes, 163
    setting the text baseline attributes, 164
    strokeText(), 164
    Studt, Jim, 166
    textAlign property, 163
    textContent property, 218
Theora, 24
time control, example of, 94
timeout property, 269
timeupdate event, 114, 118
title attribute, 89, 92
toDataURL(), 170, 201
transform(), 191
translate(), 190
Transmission Control Protocol (TCP), 241
type attribute, 25
typeof operator, table of possible returned
        values, 218, 242

U

updateready event, 299
updateTime(), 114, 120, 125
URL input type
    adding to an HTML page, code listing, 70
    using (Solution 4-2), 69
url parameter, 244
url(), 133
usemap attribute, 29
User Agent Accessibility Guidelines
        (UAAG), 308
user agents, 306, 308, 310, 313
userData, 285
UTF-8, 3
UTF-16, 3

V

video
    addEventListener(), 110, 120, 129
    adding a reflection of a video, 134
    Adobe Flash Player, 98, 105
    alpha channel, 132
    Apple iOS and Android devices,
        problems with HTML5 video
        support, 102
    attributes and events for video-playback
        features, 107

autobuffer attribute, 117
autoplay attribute, 117
browser support for full-screen
    mode, 128
browser support for video containers
    and formats, 102, 125
browsers supporting the HTML5 video
    and audio elements, 98
<button> tag, 109
canPlayType property, testing, 103
change event, 120
controls attribute, 106
creating a custom seek bar for a video
    (Solution 5-5), 117
creating a custom seek bar for a video,
    complete code listing, 121
creating a custom video controller
    (Solution 5-3), 106
creating a custom video controller,
    complete code listing, 112
creating a full-screen video feature,
    complete code listing, 129
creating a simple video controller, code
    example, 108
creating and applying a mask to a video
    (Solution 5-8), 131
creating and applying a mask to a video,
    code listing, 133
creating the event handlers for the
    control buttons, code listing, 111
creating the volume control function,
    code listing, 110
currentTime property, 108, 118
delivering a video in progressive
    download, 116
detecting video support across browsers
    (Solution 5-2), 102
duration property, 118, 124
<embed> tag, 98
embedding a video in a web page
    (Solution 5-1), 99
end(), 125
Flash Video, definition of, 98
Flowplayer JavaScript library, 105
FLV files, 98
forceFullScreen(), 129
getElementById(), 110, 119
getElementsByTagName(), 110
H.264 codec, 99
HTML5media project, 105
importing and displaying a video in a
    web page, code example, 100

increasing the chance that users will
    load and play your video, 125
initSeekBar(), 120, 124
innerHTML, 114
loadedmetadata event, 129
lossy data compression, 97
Macromedia, 98
makeVisible(), 129
max property, 119
media attribute, 127
Modernizr JavaScript library, code
    example, 103–104
<object> tag, 98
Ogg Theora codec, 98
opening a video in full screen (Solution
    5-7), 127
pause(), 112
play(), 108, 112
preload attribute, 116
preloading a video (Solution 5-4), 115
properties supported by the <video>
    tag, 100
providing alternative content in case a
    video fails to load, 101
range input type, 118–119
source attribute, 127
<source> tag, 102, 126
specify the video codec in the type
    attribute, 126
specifying an image to use as a
    mask, 132
specifying the MIME type of each
    video, 126
src attribute, 100
start(), 125
startTime property, 124–125
SWF files, 98
third-party plug-ins for delivering video
    content, 97
timeupdate event, 114, 118
updateTime(), 114, 120, 125
url(), 133
using multiple source video elements
    (Solution 5-6), 125
using the <source> tag for exposing
    video formats to browsers, code
    example, 126
video codec, definition of, 97
video controls, as rendered by the major
    browsers, 107
video controls, displaying, 106
<video> tag, 100, 126

video (*continued*)
    Vodafone's Visual Bracelet, 131
    VP8/WebM codec, 99
    WebKit, definition of, 132
    -webkit-box-reflect property, 134
    webkitEnterFullscreen(), 128
    -webkit-mask-box-image property,
        132–133
    webkitSupportsFullscreen property,
        128–129
    YouTube's seek bar, 117
vocabulary
    creating a custom vocabulary for
        defining an element's valid
        properties, 32
    custom vocabularies defined by Google,
        list of, 34, 41
    custom vocabulary, creating (Solution
        3-2), 40
    defining a name-value pair group, 40
    specifying a custom vocabulary using
        the itemtype attribute, 35
Vodafone's Visual Bracelet, 131
VP8/WebM codec, 99

W

WAI-ARIA, 330
watchPosition(), 266, 275–276
Web Accessibility Initiative (WAI), 306
Web Applications 1.0, publication of, 1
Web Content Accessibility Guidelines
        (WCAG)
    Authoring Tool Accessibility Guidelines
        (ATAG), 308
    purpose of, 306
    three levels of, 307
    User Agent Accessibility Guidelines
        (UAAG), 308
    WCAG 2, 307
Web Fonts, 220
Web Forms 2 library, downloading and
        importing, 90
Web Hypertext Application Technology
        Working Group (WHATWG), 175
web resources
    caniuse.com, 16
    findmebyip.com, 15
    modernizr.com, 16, 189
web server proxies, 216
WebGL, support for 3D drawing, 137, 177
WebKit, definition of, 132

-webkit-box-reflect property, 134
webkitEnterFullscreen(), 128
-webkit-mask-box-image property, 132–133
webkitSupportsFullscreen property, 128–129
WebSocket
    capabilities of, 241
    checking for WebSocket browser
        support (Solution 9-1), 241
    checking if the browser supports
        postMessage, code example, 243
    checking if the browser supports the
        WebSocket API, code listing,
        245–246
    checking if your local web server is up
        and running, 253
    close(), 244, 256
    establishing an open connection
        between the client and server
        (Solution 9-2), 244
    establishSocket(), 245, 256
    init(), 245
    keycode property, 260
    managing WebSocket events (Solution
        9-3), 247–250
    onkey(), 260
    onkeypress event, 260
    phpwebsocket, downloading and
        installing, 254
    protocols parameter, 244
    pywebsocket, procedure for installing
        and using, 247
    readyState attribute, 244, 249
    send(), 244, 248–249, 256
    sendMsg(), 256
    server.php, 255
    setting up a WebSocket connection,
        code example, 244
    solving the low-latency issue with real-
        time web applications, 241
    testing a real socket connection with the
        WebSocket API, code listing,
        255–259
    Transmission Control Protocol
        (TCP), 241
    typeof operator, table of possible
        returned values, 242
    url parameter, 244
    using a WebSocket server with the
        WebSocket API (Solution 9-4), 250
    WebSocket events, table of, 248
    XAMPP, installing on Mac OS X, 252
    XAMPP, list of distributions, 251

week and month input types, 94
widget roles, 328
withCredentials property, 238
World Wide Web Consortium (W3C), 306
    HTML5, publication of, 1

X

XAMPP
    checking if your local web server is up
        and running, 253
    installing on Mac OS X, 252
    list of distributions, 251
XdomainRequest object, using when cross-
        site security is not an issue, 239
XMLHttpRequest, 215, 233
XMLHttpRequest Level 2
    abort(), 234
    addEventListener(), 238
    append(), 236
    browser support, table of, 237
    calling the XMLHttpRequest()
        constructor, 233

checking for cross-origin browser
        support (Solution 8-6), 237
creating a form using the post method to
        send data with one input file
        element, 235–236
formData object, 234, 236
getResponseHeaders(), 234
open(), 233–234
<output> tag, 236
readyState property, 234
responseText property, 234
responseXML property, 234
send(), 234
sendForm(), 236
setRequestHeader(), 234
Status property, 234
submit(), 235
support for CORS, 237
taking a file or a BLOB object as a
        parameter, 233
uploading files (Solution 8-5), 232
withCredentials property, 238
XdomainRequest object, 239

CPSIA information can be obtained at www.ICGtesting.com
Printed in the USA
236873LV00013B/4/P